THE
TRAITOR
OF
COLDITZ

THE
TRAITOR
OF
COLDITZ

ROBERT VERKAIK

WELBECK

Published by Welbeck
An imprint of Welbeck Non-Fiction Limited,
part of Welbeck Publishing Group.
Based in London and Sydney
www.welbeckpublishing.com

First published by Welbeck in 2022

A CIP catalogue record for this book is available from the British Library

ISBN
Hardback – 9781802790764
Trade Paperback – 9781802790818
eBook – 9781802790771

Typeset by seagulls.net
Printed and bound in the UK

10 9 8 7 6 5 4 3 2 1

In the name of my father

Contents

Author's note

And what does anyone know about traitors,
or why Judas did what he did?

Jean Rhys, Wide Sargasso Sea

I first learned of Walter 'Roy' Purdy from fleeting and often inscrutable references found in the memoirs and interviews of some of the POWs held at Colditz. Such was the sensitivity surrounding the events that take place in this book that many of the contemporary accounts only refer to Purdy by an alias, if at all. Long after the war had finished, both Captain Reinhold Eggers, the head of security at the castle, and Captain Julius Green, the MI9 spy who was working against him, felt duty-bound to refer to him only as 'Lieutenant Grey'. Even Purdy's German girlfriend only ever knew him by a pseudonym.

The most candid accounts of Purdy's time in Colditz are those written by Lt Colonel Gris Davies-Scourfield, the only POW to speak freely about Purdy's treatment by the other inmates, and Lt Commander James 'Mike' Moran who refused MI5's request to give evidence against Purdy at his trial. Both these versions of events begged far more questions than they answered.

The more I dug, the more it became clear there was a conspiracy of silence about what really transpired between Lt Walter Purdy and the hardened POW escapers locked up together at Colditz in the final year of the war.

Equally intriguing was why so little is known about Battery Quartermaster Sergeant John Brown, the self-taught MI9 double agent whose extraordinary bravery helped save the lives of scores of British servicemen and uncovered the activities of at least 20 British traitors in Berlin.

When I discovered that the secret work of John 'Busty' Brown was also inextricably linked to Colditz and Walter Purdy, I knew I was on to a story that had never been told before.

All I had to do was chase it down.

My enquiries took me from the Imperial War Museum in London to the National Archives in Kew, where there are more than 1,500 recently declassified pages relating to the Purdy case and many more concerning the spies and traitors he came into contact with.

Then it was on to Germany and the German Federal Archives (Bundesarchiv) in Koblenz and Berlin before heading to Ludwigsburg which houses the former West German Nazi war crimes investigation centre. From Germany I sought access to the Red Cross files in Bern, Switzerland, and then finally to the world-famous Colditz castle itself where I spent five days and nights retracing the disturbing events of March 1944 that took place in the dark corridors and attics of the most secure prison camp of the Second World War.

The Hanging Party

High above the sleepy German town, the twilight gave way to darkness as a detachment of purposeful soldiers strode through the castle corridor. They stopped at a door and, after exchanging knowing glances with the men keeping guard, entered the room. Acting in military unison they placed their hands on the prisoner, pulled him to his feet and marched him up the spiral stone staircase, which wound its way to one of the attic rooms at the top of the most famous prisoner-of-war camp of the Second World War.[1]

On either side of the accused stood a soldier ready to hold him up if he collapsed. A dozen more men silently filed into the room and waited for the senior officer to give the order. The prisoner, a sub-lieutenant in the Royal Navy, was visibly shaking as he tried to come to terms with the desperate circumstances in which he now found himself.

This was not a Nazi court; the men gathered in that half-lit room at the top of Colditz Castle on 11 March 1944[2] were all British officers, bent on a rough kind of justice. Some of the British officers had been defendants in the German court martial system for infringements committed at Colditz and were well aware of the rights of an accused soldier.[3]

They knew there were strict rules for the discipline of servicemen accused of breaking British military and civil law.[4] The wartime protocols required a minimum of three officers to sit in judgement. In death penalty cases the verdict had to be unanimous.

The officer in charge of this British 'court martial' proceeding was Captain Richard Howe.[5] And it was Howe who had arranged for the defendant to be pulled from his bed and placed before the clandestine tribunal.

Howe, a captain in the 3rd Battalion Royal Tank Regiment, had gallantly served with the British Expeditionary Force during the French campaign. Captured in June 1940, along with many of the other long-standing Colditz POWs, he had fought a desperate rearguard action in the evacuation of British and French troops from the French port of Calais for which he had been awarded the Military Cross.

After his capture, Howe was sent to Laufen Castle, south eastern Bavaria, which the German Army had turned into an officers' prison camp, Oflag (short for Offizierslager) VII-C. Within two months, Howe and five other British officers, including the legendary WWII escapee Major Patrick Reid, had dug a 24-foot-long tunnel from the prison basement to a small shed adjoining a nearby house. The six British prisoners, dubbed the 'Laufen Six', escaped on 5 September 1940 – only to be recaptured five days later in Radstadt, Austria.

These were men for whom it was their duty, like every British officer, to try to escape. The determination of the Laufen Six to pursue freedom at almost any cost had earned them a transfer to Colditz Castle in eastern Germany, the first British officers to be sent there. One of their first acts upon arriving at the castle was to appoint Pat Reid to the position of escape officer. But Reid had no wish to spend the rest of the war helping other prisoners escape. He wanted his own chance at freedom. So when in the spring of 1942 a reluctant Howe agreed to replace him as the British man in charge of escapes, Reid and three other British POWS waited just four months before slipping through the Colditz kitchens into the castle yard, forced their way into a cellar, squeezed through a narrow slit window, dropped down a grass bank, scrambled up a steep earthen terraced wall and ran free out of the prison grounds.

All four made successful 'home runs' back to Britain, not forgetting to send a postcard to their comrades in Colditz once they had reached the safety of Switzerland. They would be the last British officers to escape from Colditz Castle. Many tried to follow them but were thwarted before leaving the castle grounds or were later captured and returned to the camp. Others made it no further than the perimeter walls. And one British officer was shot dead after clambering over the barbed-wire fence and running for the wood.

As escape officer it was Howe's job to personally approve all these plans, but by the spring of 1944 such a lamentable escape record weighed heavily on his shoulders, particularly as he had an agreement with the senior British officer in the camp that he would not escape himself until 10 British officers had made 'home runs'.

After more than two years of helpless watching as each of his meticulously organised escapes were foiled by the suspiciously well-informed Germans, Richard Howe was determined that nothing would upset his latest and most ambitious plan.

So now Howe found himself looking at a British naval officer who he believed intended to reveal to the Germans all the current crop of British escape plans, including the secret tunnel that had taken six months of back-breaking work to complete, which scores of men were now counting on as their best bet for rejoining the war.

Howe stood and gestured for silence before reading out the charge of treason and then reminding the assembled group that Lieutenant Walter Purdy was a spy sent by the Germans to betray his country. He added that when Purdy was confronted with these allegations Purdy had admitted to being 'a traitor and a rat'.[6]

But there was more at stake than just escaping. The Nazis had long suspected that the British POWs detained at Colditz had also established a secret communications system to transmit vital intelligence to London as they crossed occupied Europe trying to make it home.

The Colditz commandant and his head of security, working closely with German military intelligence, the Abwehr, and the feared secret police, the Gestapo, had invested substantial resources in cracking the British system. This included planting French and Polish spies and using clandestine listening devices, but the Germans had been unable to stop the flow of secret messages leaking out of Colditz.

A key reason for this was a new branch of British military intelligence called MI9, which had been given the task of aiding Allied escapers and evaders in occupied Europe.

MI9 began its life in 1939 in a small room of the Metropole Hotel in Northumberland Avenue, central London. At first the new agency received little financial support, was understaffed, and lacked influence due to power struggles and personality clashes with officers at MI6 and other wartime units such as the Special Operations Executive (SOE) and the Political Warfare Executive (PWE).[7]

But by 1944 MI9 had come into its own, strengthened by the influence of a growing number of escaped POWs who had made home runs to Britain.

The most famous and most useful agent to MI9 was Airey Neave, who on 5 January 1942 had become the first British prisoner to escape from Colditz.[8] Disguised as a German officer in a home-made uniform, Lieutenant Neave crawled through a hole in the floor of the camp theatre and, after reaching the guardhouse, confidently marched out of the castle unchallenged. Four days later he crossed the Swiss border and within the month was back in London where his value was immediately recognised by MI9.

Neave's expert knowledge of Colditz and the key figures among the POWs helped MI9 set up a cell of British coders operating from within the prison right under the nose of the camp commandant.

The man chosen by MI9 as their senior Colditz coder was Captain Rupert Barry, another member of the 'Laufen Six'. Before the war, Barry had run his own radio company and his expertise was now being put to vital use in the service of his country. Barry became the focal point in the communication chain between the prison camp and British intelligence in London. He had developed an ingenious and almost foolproof means of using encrypted codes hidden in letters written by the POWs to genuine as well as fictitious members of their families. It was of considerable satisfaction to Barry that the coded gibberish sent by the POWs to their loved ones back in Britain had completely fooled the German censors.

Through this valuable communication line the British prisoners fed intelligence to the War Office, identifying RAF bombing targets, German air defences, U-boat bases, troop movements, and the whereabouts and identities of a group of VIP prisoners whom the Nazis had secretly brought to Colditz to use as hostages.

But the stakes were high. If the Germans ever managed to break the codes, Rupert Barry knew there would be dire consequences for those involved. Their status as prisoners of war would no longer protect them and they ran the risk of being shot as spies.

MI9[9] also aided the POWs in their escape planning by ensuring the prisoners had the tools to survive in occupied Europe. MI9 boffins devised ingenious methods to conceal escape equipment using parcels, clothes and letters sent from Britain to the prisoners. The escape contraband smuggled into Colditz in this way included maps, compasses, blades and metal files, as well as intelligence to help the POWs with their clandestine work. These were all put to good and enthusiastic use.

From 1942 to 1943, the Colditz POWs had spent seven long months excavating two tunnels, one leading from the prison chapel and the other from the canteen. Despite the digging being carried out under the utmost secrecy, the Germans uncovered both tunnels as well as a cache of escape equipment. The British were convinced they had a 'stool pigeon' in their midst. Although both of the tunnels and much of the escape activity were discovered through obvious means – suspicious POW behaviour, dumped tunnel waste or spot searches – the diary[10] of one of the senior

German guards at Colditz confirms that the British were right to suspect one of their own. Martin Schädlich, nicknamed 'the ferret' by the British POWs because of his uncanny success in foiling escape plans, claimed it was intelligence from a British informer working for the Germans which led to the discovery of at least one of these early tunnels.

Captain Reinhold Eggers was the German officer in charge of security at Colditz. It was his job to make sure the camp lived up to his boast that Colditz was escape-proof. Eggers believed he understood the English because he had led school exchange trips to England just before the war and maintained correspondence with his English friends. His inflated confidence in his own appreciation of the English psyche had the unfortunate effect of making him come across as unctuous and sinister rather than ingratiating. The prisoners had learned long ago that they trusted him at their peril.

By the time of Walter Purdy's court martial, twelve French officers, seven Dutch officers, one Polish officer, one Belgian officer and five British officers had made home runs from Colditz or its jurisdiction – all on Eggers's watch.[11] The Colditz security officer had come to rue the day he made his Colditz boast. Any more runaway POWs and he feared he would be doing his next spell of duty on the Russian front. He was convinced that if he could break the Colditz codes he would not only end all the escapes but also deal a serious blow to British intelligence.

To this end he had already recruited three POWs[12] to spy on the inmates. One of them was the unnamed British soldier described by Schädlich as the informant who had led the Germans to one of the tunnels. But this prisoner was no longer playing ball with the Germans, and Eggers was blind to the secret escape planning and messaging being carried out by the British. In an effort to recruit other prison informants, Eggers tried bribing the small number of British non-commissioned orderlies who he surmised were fed up with fagging for their public-school officers. One had come to Eggers requesting a transfer from Colditz to a prison camp for NCOs, far away from his escape-obsessed officer masters. But when Eggers suggested he might like to improve his conditions of captivity by acting as an informer, the orderly flatly refused: 'Captain Eggers, I may not like it here but I'm still British.'[13]

Eggers had much better luck with the French and Polish prisoners. With the help of the Gestapo the Germans were able to make very real threats against the prisoners whose families were living in occupied Europe. They could and did force wives and children to write letters pleading with imprisoned husbands and fathers to cooperate with the Germans. If this failed then the threat of being sent to a concentration camp or the use of torture gave the Gestapo a terrifying edge. And the Gestapo made sure they sweetened the pill, since collaboration was always accompanied by a reward: transfer to a prison camp with a more lenient regime; a visit from a family member; or even the promise of freedom and the chance to go home. While Britain remained free and unconquered, these coercive techniques were not available to the Gestapo to use on the British prisoners. Nevertheless, the Germans had a special talent for identifying and playing on all of the prisoners' vulnerabilities. And Eggers was careful to learn from past mistakes.

Any offer or threat made by the Colditz security officer was made well outside the sight and hearing of the other prisoners. The only time the POWs could be sure that one of their own had turned informant was when he was suddenly whisked off in the dead of night to another camp, by which time the damage had already been done.

The German occupation of Europe had divided loyalties among the many nationalities held prisoner in the early years of Colditz.

Treachery and betrayal in the tense atmosphere of the prison had taken on complex sectarian and political dimensions which the British often had trouble understanding. When it came to the French this was particularly so. Some French officers remained loyal to Marshal Pétain, leader of Vichy France, out of respect for his contribution to the national cause during the First World War. Others swore allegiance to the Free French of General Charles de Gaulle, who continued to carry the fight to the Nazis. These two French groups despised each other almost as much as they hated the Germans. But on one thing they were united: the Jewish officers[14] held at Colditz should not be allowed to mix with either group. An official French request made to the commandant asking him to separate the Jewish officers and hold them in a different part of the castle cast the French prisoners in a very poor light among the other Allies.

And in Colditz there were a number of Jewish officers and orderlies among the British contingent so the French action rankled. When the War Office in London found out about the exclusion of the French Jewish officers, MI9 sent word to the senior British officer in Colditz instructing him to resist any apartheid policy involving known or suspected British Jewish POWs.[15]

The Dutch were also divided, but in their case it was between those officers who had signed a 1940 declaration of loyalty to the Wehrmacht, giving their word not to harm German interests, and those who had refused. The Polish schism was a more straightforward split between those who were born in Germany and those who were native Poles.

Predictably, the German security officers in Colditz exploited these divisions whenever the opportunity arose, playing one group or nation against another. This sometimes left the British in an invidious position, knowing that whomever they sided with would cause offence to one of the other groups of prisoners.

For the British escapers this was a live issue as they often needed the help of other nationalities. They were particularly reliant on the Dutch and Polish prisoners, who spoke good German and were familiar with the country's geography and transport systems. The first British home run involved Airey Neave pairing up with a Dutch officer. But there was always tension when it came to sharing escape intelligence with other POWs.

While Britain fought on alone, the Germans continued to find their recruitment of potential informants among Allied prisoners less successful than with those of the occupied nations. But there were other ways of getting men to talk. Homosexuality was still a criminal offence in Britain and was a source of scandal whenever it came to light, especially at Colditz. Some of these incidents were reported to the British padre who passed them on to a British senior officer.

Eggers knew only too well the shame that would follow an allegation of a homosexual act, and the prison guards were told to report to him any British officers who were caught *in flagrante delicto*. The subject was so sensitive that long after the war there were attempts to deny that any homosexual acts had ever taken place in Colditz. The subject came up in 1979 when the published diary of Colditz padre Ellison Platt set out allegations of sexual impropriety. Richard Howe wrote to the Colditz Society saying neither he nor any of his camp lookouts had ever witnessed such an act: 'It would have been easier to have had a homosexual relationship in a tube train.'[16]

The Germans' hunt for suitable collaborators among the POWs, and in turn the British efforts to smoke out the stool pigeons, consumed a great deal of time and energy on both sides. In this dangerous game of cat and mouse, thwarted escapes and the return of recaptured escapees contributed to an already febrile atmosphere of suspicion among the British.

In the first weeks of the admittance of the first British prisoners in the winter of 1940, the senior British officer in charge had decided that the only way to counter the German spies was to establish a security vetting team to make sure all new arrivals were properly scrutinised.[17] Two senior Allied officers were given the job of investigating and then interrogating suspected British POWs.

In 1944 the officers in charge of this process were Lieutenant Colonel Charles Cecil Merritt, a Canadian lawyer who had won a VC a year earlier for his outstanding bravery leading his troops against enemy positions in the doomed raid on Dieppe, and Lieutenant Colonel George Young of 52 Commando who had been captured on 1 June 1941. They were assisted by Lieutenant James Mike Moran, a paymaster in the Royal Navy, who had the job of keeping a detailed account of every British prisoner, which he recorded on a secret camp roll. Moran recalled years later: 'We had spies, stool pigeons in the foremost of our minds.'[18]

Each POW had his own personal theory about who might be a camp spy: the officer caught having a quiet word with a German guard in one of the dark castle corridors; the prisoner who had come into possession of a box of fresh eggs; the bolshie orderly who wouldn't take orders; or the officer who had no interest in escaping. A prisoner didn't have to do very much to raise the suspicions of his fellow officers, especially if his face didn't fit.

Yet in 1944 the German spy network hadn't delivered the key intelligence Reinhold Eggers and his Wehrmacht commanders were hoping for. The Colditz communication line with London remained intact and MI9 was continuing to smuggle vital equipment into the castle and intelligence out. Eggers knew this because every time the Germans carried out a successful search they would inevitably uncover another specially adapted escape implement which had been made to order in England. Some of the finds were embarrassing for the Germans, like board games sent from England which concealed metal compasses or playing cards with maps printed under the face of each card.

When Eggers was made chief of security at Colditz in January 1944, the promotion came with high expectations from his superiors at Oberkommando der Wehrmacht (High Command of the German Army). Berlin expected results.

If Eggers was going to crack the British system he needed a personal stool pigeon, someone he could plant in the camp over whom he had total authority and whom he could rely on to insinuate himself into the heart of the British security structure in the castle.

In February 1944 he received a phone call from the Gestapo headquarters in Berlin informing him they had found just the man Eggers had been looking for.

Before sending Walter Purdy into the castle, Eggers briefed the naval lieutenant on the critical importance of finding out how the British were transmitting messages and what escapes they were scheming. Eggers knew full well what might happen if Purdy's treacherous mission was discovered by the other British officers and so he warned him to prepare a good story because he was sure to be questioned by the POWs.

Purdy arrived with an incredible story of his attempted escape from Berlin. After several hours of questioning, Merritt and Young exposed glaring inconsistencies in his account. At last, Purdy decided to come clean and admit he had been working for the Germans, telling his inquisitors that he had indeed been a 'traitor and a rat'. He was sent for a second interview with the senior British officer Colonel William Tod to whom he repeated his confession. When Purdy refused to give assurances not to inform the Germans about the secret activities of the British POWs, Tod ordered Purdy's arrest.[19]

Several hours later, standing to forced attention in the prison attic, Purdy must have feared the worst. Yet he must have seen it coming. How could he possibly expect not to have been recognised by the other POWs from his days at Marlag? While he might have got away with his tale of sabotage in Berlin, there were officers from Marlag who knew of his fascist beliefs and that the reason he was in Berlin was because he had accepted a German invitation to be transferred to the so-called Nazi 'holiday camp' in the German capital. He told his British interrogators that he had made a terrible mistake, he had stupidly backed the wrong side, and now he pleaded for leniency and to be given a second chance. But as he surveyed the vengeful faces of the British officers standing in front of him, he must have realised there could be no reprieve, and the best he could wish for was a quick death.

Richard Howe had no trouble sourcing a suitable rope for the grisly task in hand – in a prison obsessed with escaping, rope-making was a common pastime. All that was left was to find a man willing to do the job of the hangman.

The British captain once again addressed his brother officers: 'We are all here because we agree that it is our very painful duty to carry out the hanging of the traitor Purdy. He came here as a stool pigeon and unless we put him away for good and all, he will be taken away by the Germans and sent to another camp, and discover more secrets. So it is quite clearly our duty to do it, is it not?'[20]

Then Howe called for two volunteers. A stool was brought forward and Purdy was forced to stand on it. Another man swung the rope over one of the attic beams, leaving the noose dangling next to Purdy's wretched head. Both men stepped backwards, rejoining the other POWs.

Among the gathered officers were Lieutenant Gris Davies-Scourfield and Lieutenant Mike Sinclair, both of the King's Royal Rifle Corps (KRRC).[21]

Davies-Scourfield and Sinclair were friends from Winchester College who answered their country's call just before the declaration of war. Young men in a hurry, they were excited to be given a chance to play their part in the illustrious histories of their school and regiment. But in May 1940 they found themselves serving as part of an ad hoc force sacrificed to defend Calais as the Germans advanced on the Channel coast. Both men were in the thick of the fighting as the German panzers closed in on the town. The British defenders, who also included Richard Howe and Airey Neave, suffered terribly as they were ceaselessly pounded by German artillery and Stuka dive-bombers. Their rations had run out and they were down to their last few rounds of ammunition. Sinclair was captured when his Bren-gun carrier was knocked out by German fire. Davies-Scourfield was badly wounded after being shot three times during a reconnaissance mission on the outskirts of the town. He had resigned himself to death only for the Germans to find him just before he bled out in a French barn.

The defence of Calais and other Channel seaports had bought the British vital time for the evacuation by the Royal Navy at Dunkirk. But the sacrifice had come at a military and personal cost. Davies-Scourfield and Sinclair's war had been cut short before it had got started. And although both men's bravery had been recognised by their senior commander's recommendation of medals, neither recommendation was acted upon.

The remnants of the British Calais defence force were loaded on to cattle wagons and sent to Fort VIII at Stalag XXI-D at Poznań, an eighteenth-century Polish fort. Here the two officers teamed up with another old Wykehamist, Ronnie Littledale, and led an escape by burying themselves at the bottom of a rubbish cart. They managed to evade the Germans for several months, hiding out in Warsaw until the Polish underground network who were looking after them was betrayed to the Gestapo. Davies-Scourfield later discovered he had met the Gestapo informant several times and could never forget or forgive his treachery, especially as it led to weeks of his own interrogation at the hands of the Gestapo.[22]

After capture, Davies-Scourfield and Sinclair were detained at a number of German camps before their spirited resistance earned them a transfer to Colditz.

Davies-Scourfield made three escape attempts from Colditz, one of which involved three days on the run before his recapture near the town of Hildesheim. This and other escapes won him admiration from his fellow POWs.

Nevertheless, Davies-Scourfield's daring escape record paled into insignificance when compared with that of Lieutenant Michael Sinclair.

Mike Sinclair, ginger-haired and a gifted Cambridge linguist who spoke perfect German, had taken part in a total of seven unsuccessful escapes from Colditz. This record had earned him the sobriquet 'Red Fox of Colditz', conferred on him by the German guards as a mark of their grudging respect for such a determined escaper. In his most audacious attempt, Sinclair impersonated a German sergeant major but was rumbled at the last moment, ending with Sinclair[23] being shot at close range by one of the guards. He recovered from the bullet wound, which had just missed his heart, and although he never made it back to England, Sinclair would spend more time on the run in enemy territory than any other British POW during WWII.

In March 1944 the two friends were approaching four long years of captivity and life on the run. During this time they had read and occasionally heard first-hand accounts of their comrades' military success in the North African desert or on the Italian landing beaches. The war was passing them by and unless they escaped soon all the glory would go to other men. Sinclair was born to a proud military family. His father was Colonel Thomas Charles Sinclair CBE, and his two older brothers were also serving in the British Army. He couldn't bear the thought of returning to England to face his family and regiment with nothing to show but a string of stirring stories about his failed escapes.

That January, Sinclair tried once again to make a home run. In the dead of night, after four months of meticulous planning, he slung a 90-foot home-made rope from his window and lowered himself down the outside wall onto the prison terrace. Knowing he only had a minute to cut the perimeter barbed wire before the sentry made his return pass, he got through just in time and was soon running free out of the castle park. It looked like Sinclair, after four years of trying, had finally made it. But a week later the Red Fox was marched back into the prison hof. He had been caught at Rheine on the Dutch border.

Davies-Scourfield had seen the growing strain on his friend's face. Three months later in March 1944, the tunnel on the first floor of the Kellerhaus was nearly ready.

It was the 15th tunnel excavated by the British POWs at Colditz[24] – all their previous efforts had been discovered by the Germans. This latest tunnel was the most technologically advanced of all the British efforts, constructed in such a way that it defied detection by the German 'tappers' whose job it was to locate suspicious voids in the castle building fabric.

At the time of Walter Purdy's arrival, the diggers were within touching distance of the boundary wall. Howe, Davies-Scourfield and Sinclair had all committed hundreds of hours of strenuous and dangerous labour to get it to such an advanced stage. It represented their very last chance of rejoining the war and restoring their military honour.

But how long before the Germans discovered it? In the days before the officers began keeping him under a close watch, while on a tour of the camp Purdy had passed the window seat on the first floor which was the site of the tunnel's secret entrance. As he walked by, Purdy saw one of the tunnellers popping his head out of the wooden flap which covered the entrance.

Davies-Scourfield, Sinclair and the other escapers had everything to lose if Purdy left the castle attic alive. But these two serial escapers weren't the only Calais veterans sitting out the war in Colditz who had reason to want Walter Purdy dead.

Lieutenant Anthony Rolt, an old Etonian and famous racing driver before the war, was pinning his hopes of freedom on a very different means of escape.

Rolt and two RAF officers, Lieutenant Bill Goldfinch and Flight Lieutenant Jack Best, had recently persuaded the escape committee to give the nod to the most audacious POW escape plan of the Second World War. When they first approached Richard Howe, he thought it so fantastical that he dismissed it out of hand. But then the idea started to grow in his mind and the more it did, the more Howe could see its potential brilliance. Rolt's plan was to build a life-scale model glider in the castle attic space above the living quarters where the men were now all gathered to put an end to Purdy. With the help of expert craftsmen like Flight Lt Jack Best, a skilled engineer, the POWs believed they could construct and then launch a model aeroplane from the castle roof using an ingenious pulley lift-off system and the weight of a metal bathtub. The castle was 200 feet above the top of the nearest houses and if they got 7th aerodynamic design right, and the glider had sufficient lift, the aircraft would carry two men to the other side of the River Mulde below.

The officers taking part in the project had already built a false wall to hide the secret gap in the attic and begun the construction of the glider from bed boards and any other wood they could source. Since the Germans were accustomed to looking down for tunnels, not up for secret workshops, the officers felt quite safe from detection. Nevertheless, they placed many lookouts and created an electric alarm system to warn the secret glider builders of approaching guards.

Ever since Purdy had been exposed as a spy, members of the escape committee had become nervous about what the traitor had learned about the glider project. In those few days when Purdy had been allowed to roam free among the POWs, no one could be sure he hadn't been told or discovered for himself the secret glider plan.

It is difficult to believe that Richard Howe had not discussed the disposal of Purdy with his commanding officer, Lieutenant Colonel William 'Willie' Tod. The Colditz senior British officer, who had taken charge of the POWs on November 18 1943, had supported Howe in all his escape plans. Recently Howe had detected a hard-hearted indifference from Tod which he had put down to the news two months earlier that Tod's only son had died from wounds suffered in action.

Perhaps Tod now contrasted his own dead son's bravery against Purdy's treachery.

Richard Howe, Rupert Barry, Gris Davies-Scourfield, Michael Sinclair, Tony Rolt, even their commanding officer, Willie Tod, all had reasons to want Purdy dead.

But for Captain Julius Green the stakes were higher still. He was a Jew who for four years had been pretending to the Nazis he was Scottish Presbyterian.[25] Green, an army dentist, had thrown away his identity tags upon capture but the Nazis were on to him and he had only recently survived a medical examination of his genitalia. During his conversations with Purdy, the Colditz dentist appeared to have made a dangerous misjudgement, confiding in Purdy that he was a Jew. Should Purdy choose to talk, the Germans would immediately see through Green's Presbyterian pretence. More importantly, Green was at the heart of an even deeper MI9 plot with connections to double agents operating with seeming impunity at the very heart of the Nazi establishment in wartime Berlin. His sources had already warned him that Walter Purdy was a Nazi spy and a traitor.

But were any of these British officers prepared to play the part of executioner? Who was willing to place a noose around the traitor's neck and kick the stool away?

As they gathered in the attic room at the top of the castle, Howe repeated his request: 'I need two volunteers.'

Gris Davies-Scourfield, the only Colditz prisoner who spoke about these events after the war, recalled: 'There were no offers. Dick [Howe] pressed us, and we suggested that perhaps he should be the hangman. "No," he said; he was too well known to the Germans – they would suspect him immediately.'

Howe continued to scour the faces, searching for an expression of interest, but none was forthcoming.

'It turned into a very British situation,' said Davies-Scourfield, 'because nobody was prepared to kill in cold blood one of our compatriots, no matter what he had done. On reflection, I think we were entirely wrong and should have gone on to do it because he [Purdy] undoubtedly went on to do more harm. We had failed in our duties.'[26]

Chapter 1

Fascist Sailor

Oswald Mosley stood at the back of the packed civic hall in Olympia, west London, contemptuously surveying the audience. The lights in the hall dimmed and the band struck up a slow German march.[1] Then the arc lamps swung round from the front of the stage, illuminating an aisle lined by men dressed in black uniforms. Thirty-five minutes after he was scheduled to speak, the leader of the Oswald Mosley British Union of Fascists, flanked by supporters waving black and gold Union Jack flags, marched towards the podium. It was 1934, and the 10,000 assembled Londoners could barely contain themselves. 'This shall be the epic generation which scales again the heights of time and history to see once more the immortal lights,' declaimed Mosley, 'the lights of sacrifice and high endeavour summoning through ordeal the soul of humanity to the sublime and the eternal. The alternatives of our age are heroism or oblivion. There are no lesser paths in the history of great nations. Can we, therefore, doubt which path to choose?'

Mosley stood back, his left hand resting on his waist and his right raised in an open fascist salute.

Then all hell broke loose. Communists who had infiltrated the hall started shouting abuse at Mosley. The intruders were ruthlessly hunted down by packs of patrolling Blackshirts who silenced them with punches and kicks before ejecting them from the building. Amid the brawling chaos, women and children began screaming, triggering a stampede for the exits. One of the protesters had managed to climb up to the hall roof's rafters so he could hurl more insults at Mosley. Out of reach of the Blackshirt thugs, he suddenly lost his balance and fell 150 feet to the floor. The strutting Mosley pretended not to notice the commotion and took two steps back from the stage, one finger stroking his Errol Flynn moustache. Once order had been restored, the Blackshirts led a cry of 'We want Mosley.'

Among those caught up in the excitement cheering on their fascist leader was the son of a London docklands worker. Walter Purdy was one of hundreds of young, working-class men who had rallied to the fascist cause on the evening of 7 June 1934. Mosley had promised them a start in life among a male fraternity led by a charismatic politician who valued them, rather than condemned them, for their youth.

For the first time in his life, the young, restless East Ender felt at home.

Roy Walter Purdy was born on 16 May 1918 in Barking. His father Edward was a 'hammerman', a blacksmith, employed by the Port of London Authority.[2]

Walter was a late arrival to the Purdy household, the last of 11 children of Edward and Alice Purdy, although four of the Purdy children died before they were two years old.

When Walter arrived on the scene, his eldest sibling Rose was 22 years old and his youngest, Millicent, was ten. His elder brother was already working as an apprentice car mechanic. The Purdys may have been cash-strapped but Alice Purdy doted on her youngest child and spoiled him rotten.

Walter did well at Barking Abbey School and left just before his 16th birthday with a smattering of exam passes.[3] But his qualifications didn't alter the fact he was entering the workplace when Britain was in the grip of a recession, where unemployment had reached three million, up to 70 per cent of the workforce in some parts of the country.

The 1930s saw the dawning of a new European political movement which blended policies of the far right with those of the far left. It was called fascism and gave rise to populist parties of National Socialism led by Italy's Benito Mussolini and Germany's Adolf Hitler. Britain's fascists gathered around the divisive figure of Oswald Mosley, a distant relation of the Royal Family who had been a senior member of both the Conservative Party and the Labour Party.

In 1932 he founded the British Union of Fascists (BUF). Mosley's new party's jingoist blend of anti-communism and patriotism, bolstered by support from the *Daily Mail* and the *Daily Mirror*, helped swell its membership to over 50,000. Far-right politicians like Mosley exploited the economic situation by promising jobs and prosperity in return for radical, nationalist policies.

Purdy left school full of teenage angst. He was out of work and felt worthless in his own community. So when his father told him that the Jews seemed to be the only people doing well out of the recession, Walter believed him. Mosley made regular visits to the East End to make speeches and stir up trouble. Purdy had listened to him and liked what the fascist leader had to say. He also got a kick out of the inevitable punch-ups with the communists who followed the fascists wherever they went. When Purdy asked to join the new party he was immediately signed up to the Ilford branch,[4] provocatively located at the heart of one of the country's largest Jewish communities.

It was here that the impressionable Purdy became entranced by another of the movement's charismatic speakers: William Joyce.

Joyce had a different kind of menace from Mosley. His most distinguishing feature was a permanent scar running from his right earlobe to the corner of his mouth, which he claimed was the result of being knifed in the face by a member of a Jewish mob who attacked him during a Conservative Party meeting in 1924. In fact his assailant was an anti-fascist communist gentile who had slashed him with a razor because he didn't like what he had to say. Joyce was born in New York and brought up in Galway, Ireland, where his father's family had strong unionist roots. During the Irish War of Independence, Joyce was recruited by British Army intelligence to spy on the restive Catholic community. After Home Rule in 1921 he left Ireland and travelled to Britain to enlist as a soldier in the British Army, only to be discharged when it was discovered he had lied about his age. So Joyce channelled his energies into academia, studying English at Birkbeck College in London and graduating with a first-class degree and plenty of experience in the university's Officer Training Corps.

Twelve years later, Joyce joined the British Union of Fascists where he perfected his powerful oratory and rabid anti-Semitism, which won him a loyal following among the Blackshirts. Purdy was just one of the scores of young men who had fallen under his spell.

When Joyce spoke about a new youth who could make Britain great again, Purdy believed he was talking directly to him. The young Blackshirt sought out Joyce wherever he was speaking, and eventually he met Joyce at an East End rally. According to MI5 files[5] the men became acquaintances, although it is not clear how close they were. It is unlikely that Joyce, the rising star among the BUF, would have had much time for the callow young man from the docklands. But in Purdy's short life, even this fleeting relationship made for one of his proudest moments.

By 1936, two years after the rally in Olympia, support for the BUF started to ebb away. The turning point had been the Battle of Cable Street, in which hundreds of people were injured when they turned out to block a Blackshirt march through the East End. There were also tensions within the BUF between Joyce and Mosley who battled over the political direction of the movement.

Then, in 1937, Mosley sacked Joyce as director of propaganda, ostensibly as part of a political restructuring, cutting his firebrand orator adrift to form his own party.

At the same time, Walter Purdy's employment fortunes had changed for the better and he found work as an apprentice engineer with the Concrete Piling Company at 10 Westminster Palace Gardens,[6] southwest London. This was a steady job which put money in his pocket, and the young Purdy was soon drawn to the bright lights of the West End – and its sleazy Soho underbelly. Here he mixed with the conmen, pimps, society gentlemen, louche-living rich and ordinary good-time punters. Purdy's handsome looks and unsophisticated arrogance made him attractive to women. Nevertheless, Purdy found he preferred paying for female company.

A Metropolitan Police report says he was 'fond of drinking and by his own admission… frequently in the company of prostitutes.' It appears that his bingeing made him 'offensive and quarrelsome',[7] especially with the local madams and the pimps who ran the brothels. When they kicked him out of their premises, he found trouble on the streets.

By the spring of 1939 Walter Purdy had grown tired of his carousing, desultory life and went in search of more expansive adventures. Just after his 21st birthday he used his engineer training to apply for a post as a junior mechanic with the Blue Star Line,[8] which ran luxury cruise liners sailing between Britain and America. These were the routes that promised excitement and adventure on the ocean-going voyages of a lifetime.

When war was declared in September 1939, Purdy was transferred to a bigger steamer of the Blue Star Line fleet.[9]

The *Vandyck*, a former ocean-going passenger liner, was fitted out with a solitary WWI gun and two Lewis machine guns, designated an armed merchantman and all the crew issued with naval uniforms. Purdy was suddenly a sub-lieutenant in the Royal Navy and about to go into battle against the German fleet. But he hadn't asked to join the Royal Navy and he certainly hadn't expected to find himself so quickly bearing arms against the German fascists.

Chapter 2

Busty Brown

John Owen Henry Brown had already read the runes – the rise of Hitler and the inevitable conflict between Britain and Germany – and at the beginning of 1939 he enlisted in the Territorial Army.[1] If Britain was going to have a fight, John Brown reckoned a little military training would come in handy.

His six-foot, two inches physique made him a perfect fit for the Royal Artillery, which prided itself on recruiting big, tough men who were capable of putting a shoulder to the wheel of a gun carriage.

But there was much more to John Brown than brawn and patriotism.

The youngest of four siblings, Brown was born into a working family in Tooting, south London. James and Priscilla Brown had carefully planned for three children, three years apart. But in the spring of 1908 Priscilla, now 36, told her husband – six years after she gave birth to their last child – that there was going to be an unexpected addition to the family. James Brown, 40, a printer whose own family was from the Woolwich docks, took the news in stride. He had pulled himself out of poverty working his way up from general dogsbody in a London printers to compositor and now a proofreader[2] with responsibility for checking and correcting the typeset. For an uneducated man this was a considerable achievement – and the job title came with a small raise in his salary which allowed him to move his family out of the East End slums to the new homes being built further west down the river.

But with an unexpected fourth child to clothe and feed, money was going to be tight again.

By the time little John was two years old, his brother Henry, 14, had been sent out to work as a motor mechanic.[3] James Brown doted on his youngest son for whom he had high hopes. All those years working at the printers had taught him how important a good education was to a child's start in life and he was determined John would win a place at the local grammar school. His youngest son rose to the challenge, fortunate to benefit from new laws granting poor children greater access to education, and more directly to the expansion of Small Wood Road School, a primary school built at the end of the street where the Browns lived in their two-up, two-down newly built terraced home. The school's Edwardian spires still dominate the area today. Spurred on by his father's ambition, John won a place at Battersea Grammar School where he excelled and later took the Cambridge University entrance exams. The sense of pride in the Brown household when the postman delivered the letter telling Mr and Mrs Brown that their son had won a scholarship to Cambridge was joyously shared with the rest of the street.

At Cambridge, the gulf between John Brown's working-class background and the privileged lives led by the other scholars was all too obvious, although that wasn't going to hold him back. James Brown had impressed upon his son that a place at Cambridge was a golden ticket to the rest of his life, and he must make the most of the wealthy and well-connected families with whom he was now mixing.

So he set about ingratiating himself with the British aristocracy. Brown, a rare representative of the genuine working classes at Cambridge, was something of a curiosity and attracted much interest from his fellow, better-off undergraduates. Very soon the very ordinary John Brown was keeping company with an illustrious array of champagne socialists of the day, among whose number included Maclean, Burgess, Philby and Blunt, who would later become known as the Cambridge spy ring. Brown was determined to turn all these contacts to his advantage.

The Great Depression, largely caused by the Wall Street Crash of 1929, meant paying jobs, never mind glittering careers, were hard to come by, even for a Cambridge graduate.

But Brown, 22, managed to secure a position as a junior clerk at the Truman Brewery[4] in Brick Lane, east London, where he met another young office worker, Dorothy Oakley, 21, an orphan who had been brought up by a factory chargehand and his family. The two became close and on 24 October 1931[5] they married at St Bartholomew's Church in Battersea with both families in attendance. Using their joint incomes, John and Dorothy were able to move into a house in nearby 106 Wycliffe Road. John settled down and appeared to have the rest of his life mapped out in front of him, but he was ambitious and wanted more than the humdrum domesticity of south London.

After leaving Cambridge he had made great efforts to stay in touch with his rich socialist friends, and in the months after his marriage he became drawn into the political movements they were championing.

Some of John Brown's old university friends were among Oswald Mosley's new converts and it wasn't long before Brown had been invited along to the 'Black House' in Chelsea, the former teacher training college which was now the BUF headquarters. Brown wasn't sure what to make of Mosley and his thuggish Blackshirts.[6] He only made the occasional visit and by 1938 Brown had cut any ties he had had with Mosley, Joyce and the BUF.

The married Brown, now approaching his thirties, had fallen in love.

The woman in question was Nancy Mason, the daughter of a well-known wallpaper designer. Nancy's middle-class background had turned Brown's head and he was besotted with a woman who promised to lift him into south London's middle classes. The couple began an affair and in the summer of 1938 Nancy became pregnant. Brown agreed to leave Dorothy and move in with the more upwardly mobile Nancy. The following year she gave birth to a daughter whom they named Marion, and John divorced Dorothy to marry Nancy.[7]

Life was good for John Brown and he was doing well in the brewery accounts department, partly thanks to his newly acquired membership with the Freemasons.[8] Brown relished the secret lodge meetings, the dressing-up rituals and the invaluable business contacts. Soon the Browns were able to afford a small house in the leafy suburbs of Sunbury-on-Thames, just across the road from Kempton racecourse. They named their new home 'The Wee Hoose' and prepared to settle down to family life.

John spent the weekends on manoeuvres with the Territorial Army, the 57th (East Surrey) Anti-Tank Regiment (226th Battery), which had been hastily formed in 1938 from men who lived in Surrey and southwest London.

His fellow gunners nicknamed him 'Busty' because of his size and likeness to the well-built American musician 'Busty Brown'.

On 3 September 1939 the Browns's hopes of domestic peace were shattered when Hitler invaded Poland, and Britain and France declared war on Germany. The government ordered a general mobilisation and the 57th was told to report to regimental headquarters in Wimbledon and then muster at Epsom racecourse.

Brown took to army life like a duck to water. A few months in, his natural leadership qualities were recognised by battalion command who promoted him from Gunner to Battery Quartermaster Sergeant (BQMS),[9] responsible for all supplies and equipment to his unit. His Cambridge background meant he was potential officer material, but Brown had mixed with enough British toffs to realise he was more at home in the barrack room where 'Busty' won the loyalty of the men in his battery by smuggling into camp little luxuries he had acquired trading army supplies on civvy street.

In early 1940 Brown followed the regiment to Chard in Somerset to prepare for deployment to France. For the next three months, the 57th, in common with the rest of the British Army, impatiently waited for the fighting to start.

Across the channel, the German Army was preoccupied with consolidating its conquests in Poland and Czechoslovakia. Britain, hoping to take the initiative, sent a British Expeditionary Force to France to bolster the French and Belgium defences, but through-out the winter of 1939/40 Germany remained stuck behind its Siegfried Line and the Allies behind the Maginot Line.

While the British waited for the Phoney War to end, new intelligence units led by MI9 began preparing the soldiers for all possible combat eventualities – including capture. A select group of officers and NCOs were separately sent to training camps where they were taught how to carry on supporting the war effort should they be unfortunate enough to be taken prisoner.[10] Cambridge graduate Brown, who had already demonstrated his ingenuity in administration and supply, was chosen as a suitable candidate to receive instructions in clandestine activities after capture. These included disruption of the enemy war machine, passing on mili-tary intelligence and, of course, escape. It was training that was to prove invaluable.

At these courses MI9 officers sought out the most discreet members of their audience for the important task of sending coded messages back to London should they fall into enemy hands. A calm temperament and fastidious attention to detail were the most suitable personality traits for doing this important and dangerous work. Yet by the spring of 1940 just 1 per cent[11] of the Army had been given training on surviving in hostile territory and carrying on the fight as a prisoner of war. A much smaller number, perhaps only a handful, had been entrusted with the top-secret codes, and Busty, with his outgoing personality, was not one of them. The British officers had underestimated the working class battery quartermaster sergeant. To a much greater cost the Germans would later make the same mistake.

In March 1940, the 57th arrived in Southampton ready to sail across the Channel to join the BEF in northern France. As the gunners marched through the city centre, Brown and his men were greeted with good luck messages hanging on the washing lines saying: ''ere's 'ow we'll string 'em up.'

Brown was contemptuous of whatever German Army laid in wait and he looked forward to what he was sure was going to be an emphatic victory.[12]

The battery disembarked in Normandy and drove their gun trucks to Outtersteene near the France–Belgium border where they were quartered. Brown made it his business to ferret out as many French luxuries as he could and fairly distribute them among the men. While the gunners busied themselves digging tank traps by day, Brown took charge of organising the evening entertainment, including the procurement of liquid refreshment and 'friendly mademoiselles'.[13]

Brown, like most of the British Army, believed the Germans would be on their economic knees before the end of the year. He might still make it home in time for Christmas, regaling Nancy about all his brave, military adventures on the continent: 'How could they win when all they had were cardboard tanks and no fuel to get their planes airborne? I sat in luxury billets sipping champagne thinking all those hours spent on the secret NCO course were totally useless,'[14] he later wrote.

Chapter 3

The Dentist and the Codes

At 9 p.m. on 9 May 1940, the fragility of mainland Europe's Phoney War was broken by the rumble of German armour on the streets of Luxembourg.

The Luxembourg defences, such as they were, offered little resistance, and Hitler's Army Group B rolled into Holland, supported by paratrooper landings at The Hague and on the road to Rotterdam.

Waves of Stukas launched ceaseless dive-bombing attacks on the lightly armed Dutch forces opposing the German tanks while medium bombers were used to terrorise the civilian population. Under the Nazis' Manstein Plan, a second daring thrust by German armoured columns bypassed the 'impregnable' Maginot Line and advanced into France through the cover of the forests of the Ardennes. The Allies, caught by surprise, found themselves defending the weakest point in the line against the might of the German army and air force.

Seventy miles northwest of John Brown's battery's position, the British were making a gallant stand outside the small port of Saint-Valery-en-Caux. The Glaswegian 51st (Highland) Infantry Division had been given the job of diverting German attention away from Dunkirk so the rest of the British and French forces could escape. Once the bulk of the Allied forces at Dunkirk had been evacuated off the beaches, the Germans turned their attention to mopping up the remnants of the British and French armies at Saint-Valery.

· Among the Saint-Valery defenders was Captain Julius Maurice Green, who found himself on the front-line defences administering general medical help to the British wounded.

The 51st were heavily outnumbered, had no heavy guns and were running very low on food and ammunition. German howitzers sent shells crashing into the town buildings, Stukas pummelled the British strongholds and enemy snipers seemed to lie in wait around every corner.

When it became apparent that the Battle of France was lost, the British planned the evacuation of this rearguard force. But bad weather and the vulnerability of the Royal Navy ships to air attack made a rescue operation impossible. The 51st would have to fight it out. One by one, clusters of British soldiers fell into German hands. Julius Green, who had been tending the wounded, left his position to look for medical supplies. He gingerly picked his way through the bombed-out town, passing abandoned equipment, burned out vehicles, piles of rubble, and dead bodies.

As he turned the next corner, he came face to face with an enemy tank. Green stood still, paralysed on the spot. The tank hatch slowly opened: 'A character in black dungarees emerged holding an automatic machine gun which he aimed at me...'[1]

The German tank commander must have been surprised to discover that the British officer he had captured was not a battle-hardened fighter but a dentist serving with the 152 (Highland) Field Ambulance.

At the onset of the war, the patriotic Green, a Glasgow dentist, had enlisted with the Edinburgh University Officer Training Corps, part of the Army Reserve. Born to a Jewish family in Carlisle in 1912, Julius spent his early childhood in Killarney in Ireland where his family ran a dental practice. When the Greens moved to Scotland, Julius followed in his father Jacob's footsteps and took up a career in dentistry, studying at the Dental School of the Royal College of Surgeons in Edinburgh before joining a practice in Parkhead, Glasgow.

In 1940 he was sent to France with the British Expeditionary Force to tend to the soldiers' toothaches and fillings. Julius Green was a gregarious character who liked to be in the thick of the action, whether it was sparring at one of the Parkhead boxing gyms, teeing off on a windswept Scottish golf course or, now, on the front line with the rest of the men taking on Hitler's panzers.

On the same day Green was captured, Major General Victor Fortune, the commanding officer of the 51st, met Major General Irwin Rommel, commander of the 7th Panzer Division, to negotiate the formal surrender of the British forces. German photographers were on hand to capture the historic moment, and in the famous photograph of the two opposing generals standing side by side is army dentist Julius Green.

For his work in retrieving casualties from open ground under enemy fire, Green was mentioned in dispatches. Once the fighting was over, the Germans put Green to work helping in the desperate care of the many hundreds of British and French wounded during the battle.

Captain Green and the other British officers from the 51st Highlanders were taken to Tittmoning POW camp, a medieval castle near Munich. Green was already planning his escape when the German commandant received orders to transfer the Army dentist to another POW camp deeper inside Nazi Germany where his dental skills were greatly needed.

The senior British officer at Tittmoning, Colonel Gamble[2] of the Sherwood Foresters, found out about Green's imminent departure and paid him a personal visit in his medical quarters. Gamble was in contact with MI9 in London via the POW letter system using the new code developed by British Intelligence.

He led Green to the bedside of a young British officer.

Six weeks after Dunkirk and the Saint-Valery-en-Caux surrender, MI9 had managed to send an agent from London on a secret mission to Tittmoning to help set up a spy network in the POW camps. The young officer chosen for the mission was gravely ill after contracting TB and had just a few months to live. Rather than ending his life waiting to die in a British hospital, he volunteered to sail to Jersey on a fake reconnaissance mission where he was to fall into enemy hands. He had memorised the up-to-date versions of the codes, the ones the British felt were most secure and the ones they had most confidence in using to carry secret intelligence between London and the POW camps.[3]

As intended, the Germans had no trouble capturing the British officer, and after interrogating him they sent him off to Tittmoning where he set about the job of passing on the codes among as many trusted officers and men as possible.

Time was precious as the Germans intended to move Green the following morning. Gamble realised how important it would be to have Green, a dentist who could travel between camps, trained in the art of secret communications.

For the next three hours, Green sat at the young officer's bedside while the dying man coached him in a secret method of writing coded messages in his letters home.

The British code taught to Green was called the '560' and worked like this: Only posted correspondence with the date written in the top right-hand corner and the signature underlined included a coded message. The precise number of words contained in the message was determined by multiplying the number of letters in the first two words of the second line. For example:

Dear Dad,

How are you? gives 3 (how) x 3 (are) = 9 words. This indicated that the person deciphering the code should draw a grid with nine squares and then every fifth and then sixth word (hence the 560 code) of the text were added to the grid until a message was spelled out.

The integrity of the codes was afforded the highest priority. In extreme circumstances, when London received intelligence giving rise to concerns that the system had been compromised, MI9 was prepared to arrange for one of their own agents to be captured so they could pass on operational changes or even issue updated codes directly to the POW camps.[4] The letters took on average five weeks to reach MI9 from Germany.

Major Norman Crockatt, head of MI9, was obsessive about security. Those brought into the MI9 network were warned never to discuss the codes with anyone, including close friends and even senior officers, unless there was an emergency operational reason.

Green's move to another camp fell under this category and so Gamble cleared Green to receive the codes.

Green was escorted from Tittmoning to his new destination by two German soldiers on a long train journey which took him from the far south to the far north of Germany. POWs weren't permitted to travel on the express trains, so the prisoner detail was restricted to the much slower local services. During his ride through Bavaria, Green passed flat rail trucks laden with tanks heading east – the start of Operation Barbarossa, Hitler's invasion of Russia. He made sure he put his photographic memory to good use by keeping mental notes of all the military hardware heading for the new front line.

Green discovered his next home was to be Sandbostel in Lower Saxony, northeast Germany, a newly built camp for 30,000 POWs from all over Europe.

As soon as he had been allocated his quarters he sought out the British postal orderly and told him that it was urgent that he send a letter to his family in Scotland. The coded letter contained details of the German armour and troops being sent eastwards in preparation for Barbarossa. Major Crockatt was delighted with the intelligence from his new agent.

Chapter 4

Hände Hoch!

Quartermaster Sergeant John Brown and the 226th Battery were ordered to join the bulk of the regiment which had been rapidly deployed in late May 1940 to the front line on the River Schelde (Escaut) near Oudenaarde in Belgium. Most of Brown's men were still taking advantage of the French hospitality and were widely dispersed across the bordellos and *estaminets*, many of them too drunk to take any notice of their new orders. Brown had his work cut out just getting them to the muster points.

A few miles away, Hitler's panzers had already crossed the Albert Canal and were threatening to overrun the British line. This was the moment of reckoning, the battle Brown and his men had been waiting for.

The 57th took up positions just behind the Oudenaarde Canal and used their heavy guns to break up the German attack.

Brown watched with pride and awe as the British guns laid a terrifying barrage across the German lines. After a 36-hour bombardment, Brown was convinced the guns had done the job. The next morning he made his way across the British camp to the mess hut for his breakfast. Suddenly there was a huge crash, forcing Brown to dive for cover. As he got up he could see that where the mess hut had once stood there was now a large crater.

The Germans continued to shell the British throughout the rest of the day and into the night. The next morning, it was the Luftwaffe's turn.

Brown somehow managed to get himself and his men out of the firing line. When the bombardment eased, he sought out the battery captain who ordered him to move all ammunition trucks to safety near regimental headquarters. Brown recalled later: 'Welcoming a break from the shelling we sped back to park the trucks in a forest near Roussell.'[1]

However, when Busty and the rest of his men had finally returned to their battery positions later that day, they discovered to their horror that the German infantry had already crossed the canal with reports of panzer units following on close behind. Brown was ordered to get back to Roussell and grab the ammo trucks as they would need everything they could lay their hands on to repel the assault. The artillery captain warned Brown they should be prepared to fight to the last man. When Brown reached RHQ to collect his vehicles, the colonel in command refused to believe the British position was so perilous – until a howitzer shell flattened the nearby living quarters. Brown and his men were issued with rifles and told to prepare to defend RHQ from the expected onslaught. But the Germans had paused for a final push, and the next morning the remnants of four more battery units from the 57th reached Brown and the rest of the regiment.

The situation was dire, and the regiment fell back from its defensive positions to the crossroads at Caestre, the roads now increasingly clogged with French and Belgian refugees. A BBC news report described it as a 'strategic withdrawal', but Brown called it a 'bloody fiasco'.

The 57th was ordered to head to the coast with instructions to try to get back to Britain as best they could.

Brown, who began marshalling his Matador trucks for a swift getaway, knew they would be travelling across open country with little cover. So he sent a dispatch rider in front to scout out for potential enemy ambushes.

The rider sped through the first village unmolested, allowing the British trucks to follow on. But the Germans had let the British motorcyclist pass their concealed positions. The first Brown knew about the ambush was when his windscreen shattered over his head as the German machine-gunners opened up.

Behind the trucks, the British Bren guns and rifles had started to return fire, catching Brown in the middle of a murderous cross-fire. His only hope was to drive on. Brown ducked down behind the metal dashboard, shouting at his driver to 'get me out of here' as fast as he could. But a German armoured truck rammed them and the two vehicles became locked fast. Immediately, figures in blue-grey ran around to Brown's cab door and one pointed an automatic machine gun at the quartermaster's head. Instinctively, Brown reached for his revolver, determined to get off at least one shot before they killed him. Fortunately, his driver intervened just in time: 'Don't do it, quarter. For the sake of us all put your ruddy hands up and surrender! We're hopelessly outnumbered.'[2]

Brown and his men were prisoners of the Germans. 'Put your hands above your heads and don't move from here until I tell you,' said the Nazi officer in a proficient English accent.

As Brown looked around he could see there were plenty of German casualties, but his battery had lost a lot of good men too, mostly in the trucks behind, unable to escape the enfilade of machine-gun fire which had raked the flimsy lorry skins.

Brown and the surviving men were lined up against a wall and six Germans pointed their Schmeisser MP40s at them.

The British prisoners had every reason to fear for their lives. Among the advancing German divisions were Waffen-SS units composed of fanatical Nazis. They had spearheaded many of the Blitzkrieg attacks and suffered the heaviest casualties. In revenge the SS commanders ordered the massacres of British and French POWs. Less than 40 miles west of Brown's position, 99 soldiers of the Royal Norfolk Regiment were captured by the 3rd SS 'Death's Head' Totenkopf Panzer Division on 27 May. The Norfolks were marched to a field, stripped of their equipment and personal effects and then machine-gunned. Those who survived the bullets were bludgeoned to death with rifle butts.

Brown, who spoke a little German, heard the German officers saying that they had sustained 67 dead and wounded.[3] He reasoned that the British, with 40 dead, wounded or captured, had come out on top. Although of course in his current predicament this did not feel like any sort of victory.

The Germans appeared angry. The English-speaking officer addressed Brown and his men: 'This morning you English swine have killed many men… you did not fight fairly and later you will pay the due penalty.'

The mood started to darken as the SS guards swore and bawled at the British whom they blamed for killing their comrades. Brown, who by now expected to be summarily executed, lit a cigarette in a show of defiant nonchalance which enraged the Germans, causing one officer to spew more vitriolic abuse at the British quartermaster.

A German staff car arrived on the scene and Brown, as the most senior soldier in the field, was bundled inside and driven a short distance to face questioning by a Nazi commander who had been in the thick of the fighting without rest for almost two weeks.

Brown was made to sit down on a chair in an empty farm building. The officer began to ask him questions about the location of the rest of his battery and the names of other British units in the area. Brown refused to answer, reminding the German officer that he was only permitted to give his name, rank and serial number. This infuriated the interrogator who lost his temper and struck Brown twice across the face. As Brown fell backwards the German once again demanded to know where the rest of his unit was located and where they might find the remainder of the BEF.

Brown told the German: 'I hope they are by now on their way home and out of your reach.'[4]

For this insolence the officer struck Brown once more across the face.

He then whispered into the ear of one of the guards and Brown was hauled back into the staff car. Brown now believed this must be his end: 'I felt utterly bereft, like a condemned man walking to the scaffold. As the car sped along, those last moments seemed very sweet to me. I closed my eyes, prayed for God's forgiveness and asked him to care for my wife and little daughter Marion.'[5]

But Brown was not executed. Instead he was reunited with the rest of his men who were still being guarded with their hands held high. They were relieved to see their battling 'quarter' alive, and their own fears were temporarily dissipated.

Chapter 5

Barbed-Wire Spy

At Sandbostel, the Germans established a clear hierarchy among the prisoners. Best off were the British POWs, who were generally treated according to the Geneva Conventions and in receipt of aid packages from the International Red Cross. Prisoners from western Europe (French, Dutch and Belgians) were also held under the terms of the conventions, but they received less outside contact and were not as well nourished. Serbian and Polish nationals were denied access to Red Cross observers. Worst off were the Russian POWs, at the mercy of the German guards who regularly shot them for minor breaches of military discipline and, when food became scarce, forced them to cannibalise the corpses of their fellow prisoners. Thousands of Russkies died from disease, starvation and the brutality of their guards.

Shortly after Green's arrival at Sandbostel, the British camp was divided into separate compounds for the Royal Navy (Marlag camp) and Merchant Navy (Milag camp).

Green, 28 years old in 1940, found that he had a very busy dental practice looking after patients at both camps. The Germans had supplied him with a selection of dental instruments, including forceps, dental cement, oxide and oil of cloves, but precious little anaesthetic. The scarcity of anaesthetic meant Green had to resort to some rudimentary dental procedures, and his tried and tested method for relieving toothache was extraction by a short, sharp yank on the troublesome tooth. He was also called upon to carry out general medical duties; on one day he vaccinated 600 men for TB and other diseases.

Green regarded himself as much as a soldier as he did a dentist and longed for an opportunity to get back at the enemy. He took out his frustrations in the boxing ring, offering to fight any German guard who thought he could take him on. These much anticipated German–British bouts were packed with spectators who on two occasions witnessed Green on the wrong end of some nasty beatings from the well-fed guards.

Green was based in the camp hospital where he enjoyed greater comforts than ordinary POWs, and his privileged prisoner status as a dentist allowed him more social access to the Germans, many of whom he was able to bribe for information with luxuries like chocolate and cigarettes. Together with a group of other British captives, Green established a network of trusted 'contacts'. One of Green's most valuable associates was a young man called Walter Skett, a skilled communications officer, of whom he had grown very fond and whom he looked upon as a younger brother.[1] Skett had also managed to establish a trading relationship with a German marine who patrolled the barbed-wire fence.

One evening Green heard shots ring out close to his quarters and he left his bunk to investigate. When he arrived at the scene, he found a group of Germans gathered around Skett's dead body dressed in pyjamas and slippers, and wrapped in an army greatcoat. The Germans claimed Skett had been shot trying to escape. But Green told[2] the commandant he had heard two shots. An examination of the body found one bullet had struck the British POW's left shoulder and while he lay face down on the ground another had been fired point blank into his back. The commandant tried to cover up the killing, which would later form the basis of a war crimes charge, by ordering Green to say only one shot was fired. But Green refused to change his testimony and promised himself to do all he could to avenge Skett's murder by holding the German guards to account after the war. He wrote a note of everything he knew about the events that led to Skett's murder, which he recorded on a tiny sheet of paper sewn into his lining of his army cap.

His friend's death encouraged Green to redouble his efforts, gathering more valuable intelligence on enemy operations and sending it back to London.

The British dentist discovered that he didn't have to go far to get what he needed.

With the war going so well for the Reich, his German patients became loose-tongued: 'All this time I was picking up bits of information about U-boats, merchant raiders, and the latitude and longitude at which these had refuelled and provisioned. I was getting replies [from London] to my signals and requests for specific items of information.'[3]

In one secret message, which was passed on to Air Intelligence, Green was able to describe how the Luftwaffe were making use of mobile airfields, where temporary hangars were dismantled and transported on the back of lorries to evade RAF reconnaissance. He found out that Nazi U-boats had been ordered to only cross the 100 fathom line in the Bay of Biscay at dawn, when Green realised they would be vulnerable to detection by British ships and aircraft. He also pinpointed a German training camp of 45,000 men at Seedorf, northern Germany.

Letters written to Green's family in Scotland show that MI9 was very pleased with their dentist agent and made good use of what he sent them.

On 2 January 1942, Green's father received this letter[4] from Room 653 in the War Office buildings at the Metropole in central London. It read: 'We have been informed by a British Prisoner of War in Germany that your son Captain J M Green, Army Dental Corps, Prisoner of War number 2601, possesses secret means of communicating with us through the medium of his letters home. This information, although only just received by us, was sent quite a long time ago, and we shall therefore be most grateful if you will kindly lend us all the letters which you have received from him since his capture... You will understand, of course, that both in your son's own interests as well as for the sake of national security, it is most important that this matter should be treated with the utmost discretion. Please do not refer to it to anyone and be sure to destroy this letter by burning it immediately after you have read it.'

MI9 were right to place their faith in their new starter agent. Green had managed to devise a form of invisible ink from a mixture of chemicals which the Germans had given him to carry out his dental procedures. It meant Green was now able to send secret messages to London on correspondence other than in letters home. This would greatly speed up the messaging system.

In March 1942, Green was disturbed from his dental ministrations by the arrival of German trucks carrying recently captured POWs. The soldiers were British commandos and so secret was their arrival that they were held in a separate compound and prevented from having any contact with other Allied POWs. Speculation quickly spread about where they had been captured and in what circumstances.

Green had access to a secret camp radio and heard a bulletin describing a military operation on the French coast that matched the timing of the soldiers' capture. These were the commandos who had carried out a daring British raid on the St Nazaire dry docks which the Germans U-boats were using to threaten Allied shipping.

Green used semaphore signals to secretly communicate with the commandos and was soon able to pass news to London of their safe arrival in Sandbostel. London wrote back to Green: 'TELL ST NAZAIRE CMDOS ALL VERY PROUD OF THEIR SUCCESSFUL EXPLOIT SEND FULLEST POSSIBLE DETAILS.'[5]

Chapter 6

Test of Loyalty

Captain Green soon discovered that not all the British POWs interned at Sandbostel were quite as battle-hardened or professionally trained as the St Nazaire commandos.

A few months before the commandos's arrival, prison camp numbers swelled by more than 100 naval officers and ratings. These were the surviving crew of Walter Purdy's ship, the *Vandyck*, which had been sunk off the coast of Norway. The survivors had been marched up from Norway, trucked through Denmark and then taken by boat to a transit camp near Cuxhaven before safely arriving at Spangenberg Castle Oflag IX-A in Hesse.[1] Three months later they were packed off to Sandbostel.

Green wasn't impressed by the calibre of the *Vandyck* crew, the Merchant Navy men who had been hastily pressed into the service of the King in time of war. When he heard the fate of the *Vandyck* and saw the survivors traipsing into the Sandbostel camp, Green wasn't entirely surprised to learn that few of them appeared interested in carrying on the war behind barbed-wire.

There were many sailors at Marlag who were resigned to captivity and quite happy to see out the war whingeing about the poor leadership of the British government. But Walter Purdy stood out.[2] Purdy found prison life and most of his fellow captives were not to his taste. He freely spoke about his desire for a fascist regime to replace the British government and told everyone who cared to listen that Britain was weak and heading for a calamitous defeat.[3]

To inject a little bit of excitement into his captivity, he laced his defeatism with fabricated stories about his own connections to the British establishment, bragging to one naval officer[4] that his sister Millicent was married to a 'Lord Horder' and that she had been presented to the Court of St James (in fact his sister was unmarried). These tales were designed to impress and give the impression that he was someone more interesting and important than he really was. As the months ticked by and Britain did indeed look to be heading for defeat, Purdy became increasingly outspoken and quarrelsome with his fellow prisoners. In the spring of 1941[5] the Germans made a general appeal for British POWs to come forward for special work programmes in Berlin. Purdy's ears pricked up and he approached the senior British officer in the camp, Captain Wilson, the *Vandyck* captain, seeking permission to be allowed to go to Berlin. Wilson was by now familiar with Purdy and his pro-German attitude. He had been with the young officer since leaving Liverpool for Norway in June 1940 and had been his commanding officer during the many prison camp transfers across Germany. He refused Purdy's request and reproached him for making it, warning him no officer on his watch should be collaborating with the enemy.[6]

Green respected Wilson, a former Royal Navy Lieutenant Commander in the First World War who had answered his country's call to take command of an undergunned merchantman pitched against the might of the German air force and navy. His opinion of Purdy, whom he considered to be a jumped-up rabble-rouser, could not have been more different. And he made his views known.

But Green now had much more pressing matters to attend to. New orders from London instructed the soldier dentist to concentrate his efforts on helping the St Nazaire commandos[7] who were in the advanced stage of an escape but desperately needed local maps and money. The resourceful Green duly obliged. A few days later the commandos had completed their tunnel and were ready to make their getaway. But the Germans had been tipped off, and a Nazi search party found the tunnel and all the contraband. Green, who had stored the maps and German currency in his room, was implicated in the escape plot and sentenced to 14 days' solitary confinement. More significantly, a report on the dentist and his activities was passed to the Gestapo. The commandos, who were quickly moved out of Sandbostel, never did discover who betrayed them.

Green lost his privileges and was also transferred to another camp, one in Nazi-occupied Poland where 300 British soldiers were being held.

Green's new home was the main labour camp at Blechhammer in Poland. The Nazis had designated Blechhammer as a sub-camp of Auschwitz, which would later be used as a site for the extermination of Polish Jews. Green, who had to disguise his own Jewish identity, was all too aware of what it meant to be a Jew in a Nazi-occupied territory; one of his medical staff, a Czech Jew, had been marched off to Auschwitz. Green had protested but he was powerless to help his colleague and friend.

Just a few metres beyond the camp wire, Green saw for himself the perilous and pitiful existence of the Polish and Jewish prisoners:

'Parties from the concentration camp,' observed Green, 'were worked from dawn to dusk with little food. Anyone who stopped work or fell down with exhaustion was flogged to their feet... the dead or dying were carried back to camp by the others who had to dig graves for them and fling them in.'[8]

The Nazis called this practice *vernichtung durch Arbeit* – extermination through labour. Green found the Nazi barbarism deeply troubling: 'One of the significant and terrible things about being in daily sight and contact with such horrors was that one became inured to it. I had to keep reminding myself it was not normal, that those fellow wretches were human beings, very often fellow Jews.'

His dental trips between camps meant Green had more exposure to the workings of the Nazi death machine.

On a visit to Lamsdorf POW camp, Green and his guard had to change trains. In a siding he saw a train of closed trucks from which he smelt an 'intolerable stench'. SS guards armed with machine guns were on both sides of the track and waved away Green and his guard. Although not before Green had heard the 'moaning and whimpering'.[9]

The trucks were packed with Hungarian Jews, part of what the Nazis classified as an inferior race, or *Untermenschen*, who were being transferred to an extermination camp for 'processing'. Green said after the war the pitiful, groaning hum from the trucks never left him.

During his travels between camps in Germany and occupied Poland, the circumcised Green must have known he was only one slip away – an enforced medical examination or a betrayal – from being 'processed' himself. He was constantly fearful that his claim to be a Scottish Presbyterian would be exposed.

Very soon Green had much more personal reasons for hating the Nazis. A number of Germans came to him for help with their teeth problems. One grateful officer presented him with a pet dachshund, whom Green named Sandy, and whom he let sleep on his bunk: 'I like dogs a hell of a lot more than I like people… he became a great pet and was thoroughly spoiled.'[10]

As the months drew on, Green found it harder to hide his hostility towards the Germans.

On one occasion, the camp second-in-command, a particularly arrogant Nazi, complained that Green had failed to salute him. When Green replied that he was withholding his salute because the German officer did not 'behave like a gentleman', the Nazi took out his Luger pistol and shot Green's dog dead, saying prisoners of war were not permitted pets.

Green, now isolated and suspected by the Gestapo, trusted no one. Each day he feared the Germans would discover his own Jewish ancestry and send him on the same journey as his Czech friend. If he was going to carry on his secret work serving Military Intelligence, he urgently needed an ally.

Chapter 7

Camp Racketeer

John Brown stood in line with the rest of the men, exhausted and almost beyond caring what might happen to him next.

'You are all going on a very long walk – all the way to Germany,' a German officer informed the British prisoners. 'You'll be guests of the Führer until we win the war.'[1]

It was 600 miles to the prison camps in occupied Poland where the Germans had decided to send the British POWs.

Brown, despite his exhaustion, had no intention of ending his war this way.

On the long march to captivity, he tried to remember everything the Military Intelligence officers had told him during the counter-capture course he had attended in southern England before embarkation. One of the lessons was guarding against spies planted by the Germans among the ranks of the captured British soldiers. He already knew of one rat who had shopped a spirited corporal for taking to a makeshift stage and urging his fellow prisoners to rise up against Hitler. The corporal was arrested, beaten on the spot and never seen again. A few days into the march, three British soldiers tried to make a run for it, but they were caught and brought back to the POW column. Brown watched helplessly as they were lined up alongside the road and shot.

On another occasion,[2] a young infantryman had stopped in the road and bent down to tie up his bootlaces. A guard strode towards him and without any warning bayoneted him from behind. The soldier, who Brown thought could be no more than eighteen years old, was left to die an agonising death on the road, and his tortured expression, a warning to all the other prisoners, left an indelible impression on Brown.

The Germans carried out their war crimes with impunity. Brown would have to be careful and much more devious if he was going to take revenge on the enemy. The surviving British POWs finally reached Lamsdorf prison camp in Upper Silesia near the border with Poland. Here, Brown was presented with the choice of staying behind the wires on starvation rations or given 'as much food as you can eat' by joining one of the outside working parties sent to German factories, coal mines and farms.

Brown couldn't stand the thought of being cooped up behind barbed wire for the duration of the war. He needed to get out of the cramped and morale-sapping Lamsdorf. So early one morning, the British quartermaster joined a group of volunteers who were loaded onto a cattle truck headed for Blechhammer, Kommando E3, a camp 50 miles further east. On the journey he took solace remembering what the intelligence instructors had told him: 'You'll be dealing with a lot of halfwits; you have absolutely nothing to fear.'

As Brown dismounted from the truck and gathered together his bag of belongings, he took in the spread and dimensions of the new camp; the barbed-wire security fences and watchtowers looked formidable.

Blechhammer had been a Hitler Youth Camp before the war. The lights which once showed off the camp to the local community were now switched backwards to make the perfect searchlights, illuminating the five large huts used to house the camp's POW occupants. The Adolf Hitler Canal ran along the northern side of the perimeter fence so the sentries only had to patrol the remaining three sides. All four fences were screened by machine-gun-armed guards posted in four corner watchtowers. The whole structure was concealed behind a screen of pine trees.

Brown was led to his room in one of the huts where the Germans had crammed 12 double-decker beds and a stove with enough coal for just two hours of heat a day. Busty flung his bag on the only empty bed before asking one of the POWs who had been at the camp for several weeks what conditions were like: 'There's more food than Lamsdorf but there's a lot of back-breaking work.'[3]

The main function of the camps around Blechhammer was to supply workers to help in the construction of a series of synthetic oil plants – a vital part of the Nazi programme to fuel its war economy which had little natural coal. British POWs were members of combined working parties which included Jewish and Polish labourers who were digging up the ground in preparation for the factory foundations. The days were long and the Germans were cruel taskmasters. Prisoners who stopped for a breather were given a bash in the ribs from a rifle butt to remind them they were working for the Führer now. The Jews and Poles, who were on meagre rations, were treated more brutally. Those who were too weak to lift up their shovels or axes received savage beatings.

Brown's natural leadership qualities were as recognisable to the Germans as they had been to the British, and they put him to work as a party foreman: 'That suited me of course as it gave me freedom to move around and keep my eyes open.'[4]

It was obvious to Brown and the other POWs just how important the synthetic oil plants were to the Germans. Brown was also picking up intelligence from the other foreign workers outside the camp about munitions factories and troop movements. It was during these early days as a foreman at Blechhammer that Brown resolved that the most effective use he could make to the war effort was to pass information back to England.

If he was to succeed as an effective spy, Brown decided he would have to cosy up to the Germans. He might have to grit his teeth and bite his tongue but he knew he would be more effective as a trusted prisoner rather than a hostile soldier. He began to soften his anti-German stance, speaking to the guards in his pigeon German. It didn't take long for the guards to respond favourably to the congenial British sergeant who was always ready to barter Red Cross luxuries. In return, Brown started to be allowed on unescorted visits to the nearby foreign labour camps where he found useful contacts with whom he could conduct his business.

Busty Brown and a few carefully chosen associates traded in Red Cross parcels and ran an illicit still (reliant on Brown's brewing knowledge from his time at Truman's).

But the key part of Brown's black-market operation[5] was the colour-coded soup tokens that the Germans issued every day to the labourers. Brown, who also ran the camp canteen, had discovered where the Germans dumped the surplus coupons each day. He arranged for these coupons to be recovered and then sold them on to the foreign workforce for valuable Deutschmarks.

Although the Germans changed the colour codes every day, Brown found out the colour designation for each day, matching it with his own stash of salvaged coupons. The camp bursar, who considered the coupon system to be foolproof, could never understand why the kitchen supplies never matched the demand for soup.

With the support of the commandant, Brown volunteered himself to be the camp impresario, laying on entertainment that ranged from musical shows to sporting events for the British soldiers to compete against each other.

One of the camp favourites was a Hawaiian dance night when the men dressed up in home-made grass skirts. The pre-war comedy *Mary's Black Eye* by F. A. Carter was another one of Brown's staged events that proved popular with the prisoners.

As in any prison camp, nerves were frayed and tempers sometimes boiled over. The entertainment helped the men keep a lid on things but if they didn't, Brown was always on hand. His big brown eyes, thick neck and large balding head supported a jocular, matey demeanour which he deployed to defuse many difficult situations.

Once Brown had committed to fraternising with the enemy, there was no turning back. 'My own roommates and workers became more and more suspicious of me, especially when I started asking for help to translate messages to the commandant. And so the feeling that I was anti-British spread though the camp. It was important that it should, for it would be a waste of time kidding the Germans unless my own men were deceived too.'[6]

Brown now turned his attention to escape planning. He used his freedom privileges to make contact with the foreign workers and establish a list of safe house addresses spread all over Europe which would form the basis of a secret escape line for Allied POWs. He even managed to persuade some of his foreign contacts to switch places with the British POWs so that the Germans wouldn't discover they were missing a prisoner. The thought of his own escape had, of course, occurred to Brown, but he decided he was of much more use inside the German camps picking up intelligence and assisting with helping others escape.

He also began forming in his mind a plan to hold individual Nazis to account for their crimes. Like Green, Brown found the persecution and mistreatment of the foreign and Jewish workers particularly troubling.

During one of his outside visits, Brown managed to smuggle a camera into the camp. He intended to use it to take pictures of victims of the Nazi torture which could be presented as evidence against the Germans after the war.[7]

There was, however, one particularly cruel Nazi guard, loathed by all the prisoners, for whom justice could not wait. Brown doesn't name the German who he says took sadistic pleasure baiting the POWs with the promise that he would personally rape their wives once the Germans were in England.

During one coal-shovelling work party outing, Brown was suddenly presented with an opportunity to take his revenge. He noticed that a coal lorry was operating close to where the unsuspecting

German was standing guard. Brown, knowing that the driver couldn't see the German, started directing the lorry towards an area suitable for offloading the coal. The German guard didn't stand a chance as the lorry tipped 10 tons of coals out of its side, crushing him to death. It was the perfect murder; the camp authorities suspected nothing, concluding that it was a terrible accident. For Brown it showed him that even behind barbed wire he could fight back against the enemy: 'Life had taught us to be ruthless and the more brutal the Germans became, the more intense our desire for revenge.'[8]

But the POWs found it was the effects of the war on the British home front that affected them the most. The German propaganda ministry flooded the camps with press cuttings of British cities being destroyed by Luftwaffe bombs. The helpless POWs could only hope and pray their own families and loved ones had survived the bombings.

Brown's desire for revenge was further heightened when he read a German report of a bombing raid on Sunbury-on-Thames in Surrey[9] where his wife and daughter were living. Despite his pleas to the commandant and the Red Cross for information about the raid, no one could tell him whether his family was safe. Brown could see how important it was to have a line of secret communication with London – even if it was only for his own peace of mind. Not knowing whether 'my family had died in the raid', Brown vowed to find a way to get in contact with England.

Until he had a reliable courier or means of sending messages home, his efforts to pass on intelligence about the German war machine would also come to nothing.

The Germans had recently stepped up work on Blechhammer's vital synthetic oil plants, which would soon be pumping thousands of tons of oil to the Nazi factories.

Brown first sought out a Dutch worker who he thought he could trust to send letters to England via a Dutch sea captain who was able to cross the Channel.

In letters addressed to relatives and written in his home-made code, Brown sent back information giving the location and characteristics of the Blechhammer plants. He hoped, but could not be sure, that his secret reports would find their way to British Intelligence.

He waited weeks for a sign that London was reading them, but all he got in return were Nancy's letters telling him to keep his chin up. He reread every word and checked every apostrophe for secret clues that London may be trying to make contact.

Towards the end of 1941, Brown's influence in the camp received a significant boost when the Oberkommando der Wehrmacht (OKW) appointed a new commandant to Blechhammer; the German aristocrat Waldemar, Prince of Hohenlohe-Oehringen, a relative of both Queen Victoria and Queen Elizabeth II's consort, Prince Philip. Hohenlohe, who spoke perfect English, was immediately impressed by the industrious and friendly British quartermaster. He told Brown he intended to run the camp in compliance with the Geneva Conventions and was prepared to settle any of the prisoners' grievances. Brown didn't need asking twice and rattled off a list of requests, including a proper sick bay, a well-stocked library and a concert hall. With the Prince's arrival, Brown decided to go for an 'all-out' fraternising operation to bolster his credibility with the Germans. Hohenlohe wanted to be sure he could trust Brown so he asked him to write an article for a Nazi quarterly magazine distributed among all the POW camps. Hohenlohe said this would help improve relations between the Germans and the POWs and ultimately improve conditions in the camps. Although Brown knew the intended article[10] would be seized upon as German propaganda, he decided to go ahead and wrote a glowing account of life as a British POW enjoying Saturday afternoon football matches and Friday night beers in the canteen. In it he thanked the Germans for their 'assistance' in smartening up the camps and said there is 'hardly a man who has not appreciated this and responded accordingly'. He even said the language barrier was being overcome and 'both sides are beginning to think a little of the other fellow's point of view... which will be all to the good when at last there is peace and friendship has been restored between the two nations.'[11]

The article was indeed used as Nazi propaganda and circulated all over Germany while at the same time advertising Brown's own collaboration to hundreds of thousands of British servicemen.

Brown hoped the article would convince the Germans of his loyalty, leaving him free to carry on his other black-market activities.

The tentacles of Brown's operations now reached deep into camp life.

He had bribed several key guards, accumulated hundreds of pounds worth of German currency and smuggled in a critically important camp radio to keep up with news from London. Busty had also gathered around him several trusted men whom he could rely on to help run his thriving black-market business.

One of them was Reg Beattie. Like Brown, Beattie, a soldier in the Sussex Yeomanry, had been captured in the retreat to Dunkirk in 1940. Beattie was fiercely patriotic and at first viewed Brown suspiciously, regarding the German-friendly quartermaster as a defeatist or even a collaborator. Brown realised Beattie's passionate hatred for the Germans could be put to good use in his own plans, although he also recognised that Beattie's antagonism towards him meant he had to tread carefully. How could he persuade Beattie to trust him? Beattie was from Brighton, a town Brown knew well from his frequent visits to the horse-racing tracks and his dealings with the black-market gangs that frequented 'the Lanes'. He convinced the young soldier, that far from being a traitor to his own country, he was secretly working to defeat the Germans. There was much at stake. Beattie knew if he joined up with Brown he too would be regarded as a traitor by his own side. But he told Brown he would do anything to get back at the Germans. Beattie soon became Brown's trusted 'lieutenant' who he used to ferret out genuine camp spies working for the

Germans. With Beattie watching his back, Brown could get on with the business of conning the Germans.

Brown may have installed himself as de facto camp leader, but in the eyes of most of the prisoners he was nothing more than a small-time racketeer who had a knack for playing the Germans. Unless he could make contact with London, he feared he would end up paying a high price for his fraternising and racketeering should the Allies win the war.

Chapter 8

Comrades in Codes

Julius Green had tried to keep Brown and his camp racketeers at arm's length. But in Blechhammer, Brown was a difficult character to avoid, and very soon the camp quartermaster realised he and the pugilist dentist might be able to do some business.

Green was the only British officer in the camp, which meant he had certain freedoms and licence with the Germans, privileges that Brown could make good use of. Busty decided to put his cards on the table and visited Green in his quarters, telling him how his operations were working against the Germans. As Green listened intently to what Brown had to say, he realised he had underestimated the larger-than-life quartermaster sergeant who he could see now was really the 'brains of the outfit'.[1] Green concluded there was 'a lot more to Busty than first met the eye' and decided that by joining forces with Brown's black-market gang he would be 'hurting the Germans' even more.

The two men had much in common – big personalities who recognised they would prosper better in partnership than in opposition – and they could see that the dentist's mobility between the POW camps meant the profits from the black-market business could be leveraged to obtain more bang for their Reichsmark.

In January 1942, Prince Hohenlohe summoned the trusted Busty Brown to his office informing him that his article about life in a German POW camp had been warmly received by Joseph Goebbels's office of propaganda. 'They have invited you on a special visit to Berlin which is a great honour for you and me,' said Hohenlohe, congratulating the British sergeant.[2]

It was the moment he had been waiting for – a real chance to strike back at the heart of the Nazi citadel. But before accepting, he paid a visit to his friend Julius Green who he knew was in direct contact with London and was in possession of the most up-to-date MI9 codes. He asked Green what he should do and whether Green would pass on the codes to him?

It was a telling moment for Green. He liked Brown and could see that he wanted to cause the Germans trouble, but could he trust him with the most valuable piece of military intelligence in the POW camps? Green reasoned that Brown was being offered something no other British agent had been offered. If Brown could work his way into the German spy machine he would be a unique asset for British intelligence. 'I figured that someone trustworthy in such a position would be useful and advised him to accept.'[3]

Green spent the next three hours teaching Brown the codes, 'impressing upon him the necessity for extreme caution and secrecy.'

That night Green wrote his own message[4] to London inform- ing MI9 to soon expect intelligence on the German operations in Berlin from a new agent.

Brown's journey to Berlin was by train, accompanied by two guards. All the carriages were crammed full of German soldiers called up to the Eastern Front. The wily quartermaster wasted no time making the most out of the situation. He told his guards to tell the stationmaster at Breslau that he was a very import- ant prisoner and that the red and blue colours on his artillery hat denoted the rank of a British general. Very soon the prisoner escort was moved to an officers' carriage where Brown found himself the object of intense German curiosity. Brown amused himself imagining the officers telling their wives and girlfriends about how they had met a 'British general on his way to Berlin on a secret mission'.

Brown and his guards arrived in the city in the early hours of the morning and walked to Stalag III-D in the southwest Berlin district of Steglitz-Zehlendorf. On the way through the city, Brown noticed the only outward signs of any Allied bombing was a single, slightly damaged bridge. When he pointed this out to the guards they laughed, telling him that unlike London, Berlin was 'immune' from air attack.

Brown and his guards reached the headquarters of the Berlin-based POW camps, a Stalag that had been converted from an office block, which Brown later found out had been once owned by a Jewish industrialist who was awaiting his fate in an extermination camp.

As he entered the building, the first thing to arouse Brown's curiosity was a large stack of Red Cross parcels and a pile of British Army uniforms that had been intercepted by the Germans. It seemed odd, as the parcels were always delivered straight to the POWs. Brown was taken to an office on the ground floor and told to step inside. Behind a large desk sat a German officer in full Wehrmacht military uniform. The German introduced himself as Rittmeister Alexander Heimpel, an officer attached to an officer attached to the Abwehr, Germany military intelligence. His glass eye and scarred face were testimony to his First World War combat service, while his brushed back, dark hair – in the style of Adolf Hitler – marked out his allegiance to the Nazi Party.

Heimpel hated the 'weak' British, and in the summer of 1940 had taken a tour of the Blitzkrieg battle sites where the BEF had been so comprehensively defeated. The Nazi officer took particular pleasure in stealing the prisoners' Red Cross parcels, which he sold for cash on the black market.

Heimpel, originally from Frankfurt am Main, Hesse, had volunteered for the German Imperial army in 1913, serving with the 5th Chevalier (cavalry) Regiment. He had worked his way up through the ranks: an ensign, then a lieutenant. But in 1916 he was badly wounded when his trench on the Western Front was hit by a British shell.[5] For the last two years of the war he was given a desk job in regimental headquarters. After Germany's surrender, Heimpel, like thousands of other soldiers, found it difficult to find work. His wounded, withered arm meant he couldn't carry out manual labour. For a few years he tried to become a film actor but he ran out of money trying.[6] Then in 1921, his wife Hedwig Kappelhöfer divorced him.

Times were tough and Heimpel was forced to pawn his furniture. Desperate for money, he became embroiled in a legal battle with the government to recover a larger war pension. But his fortunes changed under the Nazis. He enrolled[7] in the Reichswehr, the German Army, and was later promoted to department head of the welfare division of the Nazi Party. Heimpel was later recruited to the Sturmabteilung, the feared SA Brown Shirts, where he worked as a spy.

Using his new Nazi contacts he got a job as an insurance manager with Gerling-Konzern, the firm that had profited by plundering the premiums of Jewish policyholders. Then in 1933,[8] his wife began legal proceedings[9] against him, claiming tens of thousands of Reichsmarks in unpaid maintenance. Heimpel refused to pay, so the case went to court which he lost, threatening him with bankruptcy. In 1936 he wrote to Dr Joseph Goebbels in desperation, asking the Nazis's chief propagandist to overturn the judgement, claiming he was the victim of a Jewish conspiracy. He accused his wife of *Rassenschande* for defiling the German race by having sexual relations with her Jewish boyfriend, and suggested she was being represented by 'money-grabbing' Jewish lawyers. Goebbels arranged for the case to be overturned and the judge was forced to rule against Hedwig. Her husband also made sure she was sent to a correctional facility to 'cure' her of her affection for Jews.[10] The Second World War couldn't have come sooner for Alexander Heimpel. It not only gave him a new and important role in the SA – it meant his money troubles were soon eased by the illicit trade in Red Cross parcels.

In 1942, Heimpel was working closely with the Gestapo as security officer at Stalag III-D.[11] The Nazis had given him the job of turning Allied collaborators into spies who could work inside the prison camps, infiltrate the escape networks and break the British secret communication codes. And he was prepared to use any form of inducement or torture to succeed.

Chapter 9

House of Spies

Rising from behind his desk, Alexander Heimpel introduced himself to Brown, extending his good left arm: 'You must be very tired and dirty after your most uncomfortable train journey.'

Brown replied that he could certainly do with a wash.

'Sure, right away,' said the obliging Heimpel, 'and when you're ready I'll have a meal for you.'[1]

Heimpel told Brown that he was going to be staying in a 'very nice apartment' in the city where he would be interviewed by a senior Nazi figure and meet another Allied POW: 'You'll find out much more about that after you've been interviewed. You have nothing to worry about, have you?'

The Allied prisoner Heimpel was referring to was an Australian officer Lieutenant Ralph Holroyd, born in Hamburg to an Australian father and a German mother just before the family moved to Sydney. In March 1941 he was taken prisoner in Greece after being shot in the heel during an Allied operation near the Albanian border. While recuperating in a Greek hospital, Holroyd managed to escape and was given refuge by a local family who let him rest up until his wound had healed. But by then, the Germans had placed a bounty of 100,000 drachmas on his head. It was not long before he was betrayed and back in German custody.

Holroyd's mother had been visiting family in Germany just before the start of the war. She now found herself unable to get back to Australia. When she discovered her son had been taken prisoner she made enquiries with the German authorities. Unfortunately that tipped off the Abwehr that their Australian prisoner was German-born, and very soon Ralph Holroyd found himself a special guest of the Nazis in Berlin. Heimpel set up Holroyd in a two-bedroom flat overlooking the River Spree where he spent several months in the German capital being entertained by Heimpel and other senior Nazis who tried to persuade him to work for them. He was treated well and given sightseeing tours of the city. Heimpel's heavy-handed overtures had left Holroyd in no doubt what the Germans expected of him. His German heritage may have made him an obvious target for German military intelligence, but he had no history of fascism and he had served in the Australian army with distinction. But Heimpel knew that Holroyd's family was his Achilles heel.

Heimpel introduced Holroyd to Brown at the Berlin apartment. After they were left alone, the two POWs viewed each other suspiciously. Holroyd told Brown he was very worried about what the Gestapo might do to his mother if he didn't cooperate, leaving Busty little alternative but to ask Holroyd what he was planning to do next:

'Get all I can out of them first, and then tell them to go to hell as far as I'm concerned. I'm quite sure my mother would want me to remain loyal to my country – and I'm afraid they may harm her when they realise I won't cooperate.'[2]

Brown wasn't sure what to make of the Australian officer. Could he be a spy planted by Heimpel to test Brown? Brown decided not to tell Holroyd that he was working for British intelligence.

Heimpel's orders came directly from the Reich Ministry of Public Enlightenment and Propaganda, headed by his old acquaintance Joseph Goebbels, who had personally identified Holroyd and Brown as potential collaborators. Goebbels had decided to send an established British traitor to interview the two men and told Heimpel to carefully prepare for the meeting.

Brown and Holroyd were held in separate rooms and it was the Australian who was to be interviewed first. From his own room, Brown could hear the conversation being conducted in laboured German with occasional interjections of English vocabulary. The interviewer set out his offer to Holroyd, promising the Australian a meeting with his mother if he agreed to Goebbels's terms.

Brown thought the man's voice sounded familiar but he couldn't quite place it. He went outside into the corridor so he could hear more clearly and noticed the stranger's coat hanging on a hook in the hallway. It was a London greatcoat bought in Regent Street, and when he opened it he saw the inner pocket bore the monogram 'WJ'. Brown went back to his room mystified about the clues to the man's identity.

Shortly, Brown heard a gentle knock on his own door, answering: 'Come in.' There was no mistaking the short man with a scar running down the right side of his face standing in the doorway. William Joyce, Lord Haw-Haw himself, the former leading light of the British Union of Fascists who, after fleeing Britain, had been baiting the British in a series of 'Germany calling' broadcasts.

William Joyce was at the height of his influence and importance to the Germans. For him to interview Holroyd and Brown showed just how much value Goebbels had invested in the two new 'recruits' to the Nazi cause.

Brown was surprised that Joyce, who was an Irish-American, liked to carry himself as an English gentleman, sporting a well-cut suit and coat bought in Regent Street.[3]

Joyce asked him if he had ever heard of Lord Haw-Haw, to which Brown replied 'lots of people listen [to him]' and 'find him very amusing'.

This answer antagonised Joyce, who took himself very seriously and did not enjoy being regarded as a figure of ridicule. He responded by pouring scorn on the British Empire, pointing out its defeats by the Germans at Dunkirk and the Japanese at Singapore. 'Well maybe you did laugh at Lord Haw-Haw's broadcasts before, but the British people are not laughing now that the British Empire is finished.'[4]

Brown nodded approvingly. The two men had much to discuss, and it didn't take Brown long to suggest to Joyce that they shared values and goals that could be put to use in the service of the Reich. Joyce agreed and told Brown that the Germans wanted the chance to show the British POWs that the Nazis meant them no harm and indeed 'shared all the values and goals' Brown had mentioned. He said after the 'stupid' war was over the two peoples would have to get used to living in peace with each other again.

Joyce told Brown that if he was willing to help in the Nazi peace programme, he was sure the Germans would offer the British quartermaster certain privileges – including some freedoms in Berlin. The two men shook hands and Joyce left the flat to report back to Heimpel.

Brown and Holroyd were finally able to compare notes. Holroyd told Brown that he was being sent to another camp: 'Don't worry, John; wherever they send me they won't break my spirit. Besides, I've had a note from my mother saying I'm doing the right thing in refusing their filthy offer.' Brown thought this sounded rather too convenient and wondered how he had received a message from his mother while they were being held under such tight security.

Brown told Holroyd that he was staying in Berlin as it seemed he had passed his interview with Joyce, although he wasn't sure exactly what plans the Germans had for him.

Heimpel, as Joyce had promised, granted Brown some restricted access to the German capital which, although always escorted by a guard, allowed him the chance to secretly note the coordinates of strategic military targets which he was able to send back to London using Green's code.

One Nazi site was of particular interest to Brown: not far from where he was staying was Tempelhof Aerodrome, a key Luftwaffe experimental and training airfield. Brown had found a map of Berlin and asked his guards whether one day he could visit Viktoriapark, the giant waterfall and gardens sited on a hill dedicated to the Prussian victory over Napoleon. He told Heimpel the visit would be a welcome break from being cooped up with Holroyd in the apartment. Heimpel agreed, but told the guards to keep a close eye on their British prisoner. Brown and his guards travelled by train, and during one of the station changes Brown managed to slip his minders and made his own way on foot to the nearby Tempelhof Aerodrome. He got as close as he could without arousing suspicion from inside the aerodrome but was spotted by local police officers.

The impetuous Brown had pushed his luck too far and was now under arrest by the city police. Back at Stalag III-D Brown pleaded his innocence to Heimpel who was prepared to give him the benefit of the doubt, but issued him with a warning to stay away from military installations.

A few days later, Brown was told to attend a meeting of Indian Army officers. The officers, who had gathered in the Berlin house where Brown was staying, were being addressed by a high-ranking Nazi who was imploring them to switch sides and take up arms against the British.

After their military successes in Europe, the Germans were eyeing the British Empire with proprietary interest. India was still considered the jewel in the British crown, and Hitler had given the go-ahead to establish a Legion of 5,000 Indian-born POWs to spearhead an uprising against the British Raj. After the Nazi's speech, Joyce, adopting his signature rhetoric, took up the case for an Indian/German axis.

There was a brief hiatus while the Germans waited for the Indians's response, which was given by Captain Birendra Nath Mazumdar, an Indian officer in the Royal Army Medical Corps. Born in Bangalore, Mazumdar supported India home rule. When war was declared he was in London training to be a doctor. Instead of returning to India and ending his chances of a medical qualification, he decided to enlist with the Royal Army Medical Corps as a non-combatant.

In June 1940, while attached to the British Expeditionary Force in France, he was called upon to lead a convoy of six ambulances out of Étaples towards Boulogne. But the British vehicles were cornered by German tanks and Mazumdar was forced to surrender.

The Indian officer was considered an ideal candidate for a leadership role with the Nazi-created Free Indian Legion. But instead of pledging allegiance to the Nazis, he stepped forward and told Joyce that he regarded him as 'a traitor not only to England but to your own dear land. We will have nothing to do with your foul schemes. England has promised us that as soon as the war is over we shall be free. I give you five minutes to leave the room. After that I will not be responsible for my fellow officers.'[5]

Brown, who had been listening with astonishment to the officer's brave rejection of the Nazi offer, couldn't help himself stepping forward and shaking Mazumdar's hand.

Three days later Heimpel summoned Brown to his office: 'I heard what you did at the meeting of Indian officers, and you are showing far too much interest in Tempelhof Aerodrome and other such places... I have decided to send you back.'[6]

Heimpel told Brown to pack his bags and be ready to leave within the hour. Brown, cursing his poor judgement, was escorted back to Blechhammer. But knowing what he now knew about the Nazis' traitor recruitment operations, he was determined to find a way back to Berlin.

At Blechhammer, he was able to tell Green what he had discovered. Green could see just how valuable an agent Brown could be to the British counter-intelligence operations, and the two men contrived a plan to have him returned to Berlin.

One night, Brown entered Green's room and began aggressively lecturing the Glaswegian dentist and two other men about how the Germans were going to win the war and they might as well get used to it. Green retaliated, accusing Brown of being a filthy collaborator. The two men came to blows and had to be separated by the guards. The next day Commandant Hohenlohe called Brown to his office and asked him to explain the bust-up with his fellow soldiers. Brown told the commandant that the other prisoners regarded him as a collaborator. He begged Hohenlohe to grant him a transfer back to Berlin as he was sure the British prisoners were planning to slit his throat while he slept in his bed. Hohenlohe, who now believed in Brown's hostility to his own side, agreed to the request. Agent Brown was back in business.

Chapter 10

Holiday in Berlin

Walter Purdy was sitting on his bunk bed reading. He had spent almost three years in captivity. The life-sapping monotony of Marlag camp routine and the Germans' stranglehold over Europe was playing on his mind. His belligerent attitude towards the British government and his sympathy for totalitarian states had alienated his fellow naval officers, leaving him with little social company.

In May 1943,[1] an Abwehr officer[2] entered Purdy's room and asked to speak to him about a private matter. He said that he had a message from William Joyce, who wanted to know if Purdy would be interested in receiving a signed copy of his latest book, *Twilight Over England*, a fascist text decrying the weakness of the British Empire and its government's failure to stand up to the tyranny of the Jews. Purdy, who had already told some of the POWs he had met Joyce when he was a Blackshirt in London, was flattered by the approach and agreed for Joyce to send him the book. When the book arrived, Purdy made no effort to hide it from the British officers and even read select passages aloud to try to impress them.

Captain Wilson,[3] who was informed of Purdy's indirect contact with Joyce and his fascist readings, was livid, and once again warned the naval officer about the dangers of collaborating with the enemy.

But it was too late, and on 10 May 1943 Purdy left Marlag at Joyce's invitation to join him in Berlin at a special camp. Wilson, who protested[4] to the camp commandant about the planned visit, made sure Purdy was accompanied by three British officers who had orders to keep a close eye on the Royal Navy fascist. Before he left the camp, Purdy wrote a letter to Wilson excusing his actions and justifying his disobedience: 'You have given instructions to me in the presence of the three other officers concerned that under no circumstances must I give information nor must I act contrary to Admiralty instructions and regulations. Should an opportunity or occasion arise whereby I am promised by the German authorities that they will repatriate me to England or a neutral country, I intend to disregard the above orders, regulations or instructions.'[5]

Purdy handed the letter to another officer[6] with explicit instructions not to let Wilson see it until the end of the war. This was Purdy's insurance policy, in case the Germans lost the war and he had to answer for his intended collaboration.

Purdy's destination in Berlin was Kommando 999,[7] a city villa[8] in Zehlendorf attached to Stalag III-D. It was the site of a new kind of Nazi propaganda experiment, a POW 'holiday camp' for British officers who the Germans said deserved a break after more than three years of captivity. The concept was the brainchild of Dr Fritz Hesse, chairman of the Englanddienst (the England Committee of the Foreign Information Service), and Dr Arnold Hillen-Ziegfeld of the German Foreign Office. Both men were considered experts on England and Englishness. Hesse was well known to MI5 as he had worked at the German embassy in London during the lead-up to the war and had been involved in appeasement negotiations between Chamberlain and Hitler.[9] Ziegfeld had written two well-received books on the character of the English. Both men answered to Joseph Goebbels, and Paul Schmidt, Hitler's personal interpreter, in charge of all policy relating to propaganda against the British.

Their intention was to set up camps across Germany that would foster better understanding between the British and the Germans. Even in 1943, some Nazis held a genuine belief that the two Anglo-Saxon nations should not be fighting each other and that the war could be resolved amicably. To create the convivial conditions for such rapprochement in relations between the two peoples, Kommando 999 offered British officers a genuine holiday.[10] The only outward sign that this ordinary-looking city villa was a prison camp at all was the barbed-wire fence around the building and the two sentry boxes.[11]

Inside, the British 'guests' were given regular hot meals, cigarettes and as much beer as they could drink on Fridays.

Orchestras, playing a mix of British and German compositions, were brought in to entertain the men while coaches were laid on for sightseeing tours of Berlin. The Germans even arranged river cruises at the weekend.[12]

Hesse and Ziegfeld at first resisted attempts by Goebbels and his ministry to turn the camps into overt propaganda camps.

Nevertheless, the British knew there was no such thing as a free Nazi lunch and were naturally suspicious and resistant. So Hesse and Ziegfeld sought help from the offices of the OKW and the most senior British officer held by the Germans, General Victor Fortune, the British commander of the 51st (Highland) Infantry Division, with whom Julius Green had served at Saint-Valery. To settle the military ethics of the German holiday camp, Fortune asked Brigadier Leonard Parrington to take charge at Kommando 999 and report on what the Germans were up to. Parrington, who had been captured in Greece in April 1941, concluded that while it was obvious that the camp was part of a German soft propaganda programme, he saw no reason why the British officers should be prevented from taking advantage of the German hospitality provided they did nothing to support the enemy.

On 10 May 1943, the camp doors opened to the first British POW arrivals. Among them were Walter Purdy and the three officers Captain Wilson had sent as his unofficial escort.

The true intention behind the holiday camp was of course much more sinister. Goebbels, the Abwehr and the Gestapo all had vested interests in the exploitation of the POW camps and the men they held. Their collective efforts to recruit valuable collaborators from other nations was proof positive that there must be rich pickings among the British officer corps.

There was also a pressing need to replace and supplement the complement of British broadcasters working for the Germans.

The man chosen by the Nazis to head the broadcast operation was William Joyce. Joyce and his wife Margaret, whose affection for fascism was now well known and who naturally became known as Lady Haw-Haw, suddenly found themselves honoured guests in their adopted country. From extravagantly decorated offices in the old press boxes at the Reichssportfeld, the famous site of the 1936 Olympic Games in central Berlin, William Joyce turned out his polished scripts and reworked versions of the material he had used when he was a leading light in the British fascist movement in London. The couple wallowed in their celebrity status, partying by day and broadcasting by night.

Gathered around the Joyces were a number of British civilian collaborators, including Norman Baillie-Stewart, a former officer in the British Army who had been imprisoned in the Tower of London for selling military secrets to the Germans in the early 1930s. After his release, he departed Britain for Germany, just in time for the start of the Second World War in which he volunteered his broadcasting skills to the Nazis. The Germans had also managed to engage the service of the quintessential English author P G Wodehouse. Wodehouse was living in France when the Germans launched their Blitzkrieg. Like many Britons caught out by the speed of the German advance, he found himself trapped in France unable to reach the last ships sailing for England in early June 1940.

Now he and his wife and their entourage of agents, fixers and hangers-on, who had been living royally in Le Touquet in northern France, found they were all liable to internment by the Nazis. Wodehouse, approaching his 60th birthday, was taken to a detention camp for enemy civilians in Lille before being moved to Germany to another camp in Tost, Upper Silesia. His wife was allowed to continue living in Le Touquet and Wodehouse was permitted to carry on writing his novels in captivity. Then in 1941 Goebbels made his move. Wodehouse and his wife were invited to Berlin to stay at the Hotel Adlon – his new freedom conditional on his willingness to make a contribution to German radio propaganda. Wodehouse agreed and made a total of six broadcasts from the Büro Concordia. The content of these broadcasts may not have been anything like the rabid anti-British, anti-Semitism of Joyce and the other traitors, but Wodehouse's cooperation with the Nazis represented a major PR coup. The Germans were winning both the war on the ground and on the airwaves.

By 1943 these civilian British collaborators were familiar names on the New British Broadcasting Service (NBBS), a title deliberately chosen to borrow from and challenge the authority of the BBC. They were paid up to 1,200 marks a month, much more than a German radio speaker could earn, and were set up in luxury apartments while being given the freedom of Berlin.

Three years into the war the propaganda value of the big names was wearing thin. Even Lord Haw-Haw, by now a far too familiar figure of fun in Britain, was unable to make the same kind of impact the Germans believed he had achieved in the first two years of the war. The same was true of Baillie-Stewart and Wodehouse. Norman Baillie-Stewart had become disillusioned with the Nazis and the political corruption that underpinned the regime. He first fell out with Joyce and then parted company with the Reichs-Rundfunk-Gesellschaft, opting instead to work as translator for the German Foreign Office and lecturing in English at Berlin University. Wodehouse had been chastened by the hostile reaction of his broadcasts back in Britain where some newspapers had openly called him a traitor. He refused to do any more but was allowed to return to Paris where he stayed for the rest of the war.

Goebbels remained convinced that the success of his radio output was sapping British morale, but he desperately needed replacement collaborators drawn from the British officer corps, who could act as credible Nazi mouthpieces.

Using the cover of the Foreign Office and the England Committee, the German head of propaganda looked to fill the 'holiday camp' with POWs whom he could pressurise to become broadcasters, translators and propagandists.

The Abwehr and the Gestapo wanted to go further and find men they could turn into double agents, who could infiltrate POW escape lines or be planted in prison camps as spies.

Chapter 11

Germany Calling

If Colditz was a prison to house the POWs who posed the greatest threat to the Reich, then Kommando 999 was the camp the Germans hoped would deliver collaborators who would best serve their interests.

But the British officers selected for the holiday programmes proved to be far less cooperative than those from other nations. Most did exactly what Brigadier Parrington had advised: took full advantage of the German hospitality and then after a few weeks returned to their camps with full stomachs and interesting stories to tell. Others played along just so they could string out their 'vacations'. Some even tried to escape.

Yet the Germans knew there was a small but obvious minority for whom loyalty had its price, and at Kommando 999 one British officer stood out. Lieutenant Walter Purdy had done everything possible to make himself agreeable to the Germans. His batman, Private John Hibberd, who had arrived at the camp five days after Purdy, recalled the naval officer clearly: 'He argued in favour of setting up a dictatorship in Britain although he was careful not to outwardly side with the Germans. He said he was a member of the British Union of Fascists. This was his general trend of conversation at all times. In addition he recommended to me to read Joyce's book *Twilight Over England*, copies of which were to be found in the camp.'

Hibberd took a group photograph of Purdy sitting at the centre of the British officers at Kommando 999, which he sent back to his family in Sheen in west London. Others remember Purdy as 'offensively arrogant, quarrelsome and outspoken', and that he spent all his spare time studying German.

Outside the command and control of his senior commanding officer, Walter Purdy began lecturing his fellow POWs about the advantages of Nazi rule and, returning to his favourite theme, how the Jews had brought the British Empire to its knees. By now, Purdy had made up his mind about what he intended to do next.

A few weeks after his arrival at Kommando 999, Alexander Heimpel requested Purdy pay him a personal visit. In the privacy of Heimpel's office the British lieutenant was offered the chance to leave Kommando 999 to join Joyce as an apprentice broadcaster. He would be given a generous wage and accommodation in Berlin, and be free to mix with the other Allied big-name speakers.

The British officer knew if he accepted the Germans' offer he would be crossing a line, a line he had hitherto just about stayed on the right side of. There would be no going back, and he could no longer expect to be given the benefit of doubt from the other British officers, who already regarded him with disdain but had not yet openly called him a traitor.

With Europe under the complete control of the Third Reich, Purdy reckoned he could afford to chance his arm. The most likely scenario was that the British would do a deal with the Germans and there would be some kind of settlement in Europe. If that turned out to be the case, he would be safe from British retribution and would have spared himself several years of life-sapping imprisonment.

Heimpel put Purdy back in touch with Joyce. Joyce was delighted with his new recruit[1] who he claimed he had wooed with the 'promise of cakes and ale'.

But Purdy was still concerned about revealing his treachery to the other men. Heimpel was equally keen for the British POWs not to suspect the real reason Purdy was about to disappear from the camp. So they hatched a plan. One morning two guards came to arrest Purdy in his room. He was told he was to be court-martialled and given an hour to collect his belongings. Purdy spent this time telling the other officers that he had been involved with an argument with the camp Sonderführer, Dr Faulkner, a senior German officer at Kommando 999 representing the German Foreign Office. They had disagreed about the war and the treatment of British POWs. Purdy said he had become so enraged by Faulkner's line of questioning that he had lost his temper and ended up striking the German across the face. For this assault he was to be imprisoned and then transferred to another camp.[2]

Except, of course, the altercation never happened.

The story about his fight with Dr Faulkner gave Purdy cover to leave the camp without any difficult questions being asked.

But Purdy and Heimpel had not completely covered their tracks. A few days later, one of the British officers enquired with the guards as to where Purdy's mail should be forwarded. He was told all correspondence relating to Walter Purdy was to be personally addressed to Captain Heimpel.

In return for his cooperation, Purdy was given a room at ParadePlatz 8, Tempelhof in south central Berlin. He was also assigned a new identity – Robert Wallace, a Buenos Aires businessman – and issued with a freedom pass signed by the chief of police of Berlin granting him unhindered travel across the capital.

Purdy was sent away for voice tests at the Büro Concordia, the radio station's new headquarters, in the Rundfunkhaus in the Reichssportfeld.

After a hesitant start where Purdy struggled to find his voice, the naval lieutenant was eventually passed for broadcasting. Getting a British officer behind a German microphone was a small coup for Goebbels and his radio propaganda department.

At the Reichssportfeld Purdy was introduced to Peter Adami, the German controller of a new station called Radio National, and was closely tutored by William Joyce. The two traitors met almost every day to discuss their work and soon became close colleagues. Joyce taught Purdy how to draft his own scripts and suggested he assume his own distinct broadcasting identity. They chose for his pseudonym Robert Pointer, the name of a prisoner Purdy had met at one of his previous camps. Purdy's broadcasting contract paid 450 Reichsmarks a month, more than the average wage of an ordinary German worker but a quarter of what Joyce was on.

Purdy later claimed there was a written agreement between him and the Germans that after he had completed 10 broadcasts he would be allowed to escape to England. Evidence of such an agreement has never been found.

Around the time Purdy joined Büro Concordia, Goebbels had been forced to recognise the morale of the British people was much more robust than the Nazis had expected. Also, the character of the war had changed. After the defeat at Stalingrad in February 1943, the Germans were not the all-conquering Herrenvolk that Hitler proclaimed them to be.

The function of Radio National was no longer to attack the people of Britain, but to spread hatred of Russians and Jews who the Nazis said were the real cause of the war.

The Nazi controllers of Büro Concordia made sure the speakers exploited real political events and real news coming out of Britain to sow discord among the working population with attacks on the British Jewry. Purdy had carefully studied Joyce's vituperative, sneering style. He also liked the way his own voice sounded in the recording studio, especially when he put on his own fake upper-class British accent. Very soon he would be broadcasting into the living rooms of millions of British families.

Chapter 12

Radio War

On 2 August 1943 Walter Purdy was sitting in front of a large radial microphone in a soundproof booth behind a glass window. On the other side of the window sat a radio engineer twiddling a desk of sound level buttons. This was Purdy's first broadcast for the Germans and understandably he had some pre-broadcast nerves. It was his big moment in front of his mentor William Joyce and the other radio stars. But more than that, Walter Purdy, albeit in the guise of Robert Pointer, was about to announce to the world he was working for the Nazis.

Then the 'live' light flashed red and on the engineer's cue Purdy introduced himself as Robert Pointer, a British patriot who was speaking from a secret location in England.

'Tonight the subject of this speech is the air racket and the Jews,' he told his audience. The target of Purdy's broadcast was the chemical giant ICI, which he said was a Jewish-dominated corporation that had monopolised the market of bombs, fuses and detonators, and whose chief executive, Lord Melchett, 'had fingers in every armament firm in the world'.

As he became accustomed and pleased with the sound of his own voice, Purdy felt empowered.

Purdy declared: 'These Jewish armament kings are sending the youth of the world to their deaths. They are prolonging a war so they can profit.'

Back in Britain, the BBC secret monitoring service at Caversham, Berkshire, which had the job of recording the German propaganda output, registered a new voice and name broadcasting from Germany.[1]

Six days later, Caversham picked up another talk by Pointer. Once again, corrupt Jewry was his theme: 'We are paying £14 million for this war in order that our brothers, sons and friends may be taken from us... Who is benefiting from this war? The arms racketeers: Lords Melchett, Reading and Samuel. They are Jews. It is to them that our taxes are going. If there are profits from this war, let us the people benefit. If the Jews don't like it, send them to Moscow or the Arabs and let them deal with them.'

On 8 August 1943 he continued in this same anti-Semitic vein, but this time tailored to his own experiences in the East End of London: 'National Radio feels it their duty to express yet another criminal sideline of Jewry... National Radio can expose the Jews who are committing the crimes... The Jewish crooks are using the good reputations of the dock workers who have been wrongly accused of crimes to carry on their nefarious activities. Those of you who are dock workers can stop the thieving by the Jewish gangs once and for all. It is up to you to defend the good name of the workers.'

On 28 August Purdy went even further: 'I must apologise if what I have to say offends you, but it has to be said. Next time you travel by train or bus and one of your companions is obviously a Jew, I want you to observe his actions. You can hardly mistake their dominant characteristics – their coarse, greasy hair, their greasy fore-heads, their Negroid lips – but their actions betray their race more than their appearance. They enter the carriage with a swagger and will stand in the centre of the compartment and gaze with sensuous eyes at the occupants. They will edge near to the young and obvi-ously unattached female. When they are seated their eyes normally roam in the direction of our womenfolk. When the train is full they will remain seated, jeering and laughing... There is only one way to rid ourselves of this ill-mannered race. We must escort them to the chosen land and give the Arabs a chance to educate them.'

The German broadcasts received relatively wide audiences in Britain (when the radio reception was good), mostly because they offered a rare window into what the enemy was thinking, even if it was only what the Germans wanted the British to think they were thinking. 'Germany Calling' made a welcome change to the rather staid news bulletins of the BBC, a contrast that was heightened when the German broadcasters began peppering their speeches with expletives. The first time British audiences heard the word 'fuck' being said on air was during a broadcast from one of Germany's propaganda radio stations.

Towards the end of 1943, Goebbels ordered Adami[2] to get his broadcasters to engage with Britain's fascists. In the first weeks of the war, the leadership of the British Union of Fascists, including Oswald Mosley, had been rounded up by the security services and interned on the Isle of Man. The same fate befell those who followed the National Socialist League, the organisation Joyce founded after his split from Mosley. But there were perhaps thousands more Britons who still harboured sympathies for the fascist cause. Just because their leaders were in internment camps didn't mean the people of Britain had stopped being interested in National Socialism.

It was this silent minority whom Goebbels wanted to reach.

Purdy felt he instinctively knew the British fascist better than Joyce. While Joyce had lectured and preached to them, Purdy had worked and socialised with them in their own communities. Joyce and Adami could see the force of this argument. So it was Purdy who fronted the call-to-arms speeches which were once again delivered as if the speaker were broadcasting from inside England. And Purdy began like this: 'Men of the BFL (British Fascist League), for the first time since the inception of the great movement we are able to speak to our members by radio. We have not been idle these past few years although the cream of our most active officers have been unlawfully detained by the government in prisons throughout the country and in the Isle of Man... Decentralised as we were, there were still sufficient men of courage among us to carry on the fight against the warmongers. In all parts of the country we maintained our information groups which untiringly named the enemy in our midst; we named and exposed the Jews as the power behind the government, as the real culprits and instigators of this futile war without end... We have no quarrel with the Germans. Our policy has always been to mind Britain's business. We have always held that Danzig was not worth a single drop of British blood. We do not think that the whole of international Jewry is worth the life of a single British soldier... Our fight is against the corrupt, Jew-suborned government which has betrayed the true interests of the people, who have hung around our necks the millstone of a seven years' war... Men of the BFL, this is a call to action. The Chiefs of Staff [of the BFL] call up all officers and men, wherever they are attached, to get in touch immediately with your appointed DC [District Commander] and section leaders and to prepare for action. That's all for now, men. You have been listening to an announcement from National Headquarters. This announcement will be repeated tomorrow at 9.50 p.m. and on the same wavelength. This is Radio National signing off.'

Whether these broadcasts had any impact is difficult to gauge, but Goebbels was convinced his messages were penetrating the British psyche.

Purdy, who had found his stride and rhythm, was enjoying his work. Herbert Krumbiegel, Purdy's German radio engineer, who recorded the speeches based at the Büro, described Purdy as the 'most willing and enthusiastic' of all the foreign broadcasters. Purdy was also rather pleased with his new-found minor celebrity, boasting to one British POW who was being taken on a visit to the Reichssportfeld: 'I have a golden voice.' The same British soldier later recalled: 'He was a most conceited and loud-mouthed individual. He told me he was a first-class broadcaster, much sought after by other German radio stations.'[3]

Chapter 13

Collaborati Cabaret

Purdy stood out from the other broadcasters, not only because he had no 'shame working for the Nazis' but also because he now appeared to be living a 'very prosperous' life.

Purdy's trusted status among the Nazi hierarchy meant he was allowed to live alone in a comfortable Berlin apartment where the other prisoners said he cultivated a reputation as a ladies' man.

Private Robert Burridge[1] met Purdy outside the Reichssportfeld when he joined a party of British POWs from the Berlin 'holiday camp' on a sightseeing tour of Berlin. Burridge remembered Purdy from Kommando 999, where he was working as an orderly. The British 'tourists' arrived at the radio station at the same time Purdy was turning up for work. Purdy tapped Burridge on the shoulder, proudly telling the private that this was where he now worked: 'Of course I'm no longer English and my name is no longer Purdy. I've got my papers, changed my name and I'm German. I am going to marry a German girl in about three days' time.'[2] Purdy flashed his identity card at the guards and slipped into the park. Half an hour later he reappeared with the girl in question on his arm. 'Cheerio, boys,' he blithely called out to the British soldiers.

The girl on his arm was a 29-year-old widowed pastry cook named Margarete Weitemeier. Her father held an influential position at the Reichssportfeld where she had been introduced to the rising star. Margarete was vulnerable – her husband and two younger brothers, Willi and Hermann, had been killed fighting in the east. She soon fell for Purdy's mix of supreme confidence, good looks and calculating charm. Within weeks of their meeting, Purdy had proposed and moved into the Weitemeiers's comfortable town house at Reichsstrasse 6, Berlin-Charlottenburg. But Purdy would need special permission from the German Foreign Office before he would be allowed to marry a German citizen. Heimpel assured him such authority for his proposed marriage would take a few weeks, while his own German citizenship would take much longer.

Margarete was not allowed to know the true identity of the British collaborator. Purdy told her his name was Robert Wallace and lied about his date of birth, making out he was six years older than he actually was. Purdy didn't trust anyone, even the woman he was planning to marry. Only his German spymasters had a record of his true identity.

In Berlin, Purdy and 'Gretel', the pet name Purdy shortened from Margarete, were part of a social scene which centred on the Joyces, the other British collaborators and their German girlfriends, who enjoyed a merry-go-round of hotel cocktail bars, burlesque cabarets and raucous house parties. Nazi domination of Europe meant they could enjoy the spoils of war whether it was Bulgarian caviar, French champagne or Belgian chocolates.

In the summer these British wartime hedonists picnicked in the Tiergarten and in the winter dined at the Press Club with its leather armchairs, well-stocked wine cellars and all-night restaurant. There were even loudspeakers built into the walls that 'called' the patrons should the Büro need to get hold of them.

At the opera and in the music halls, they rubbed shoulders with the Nazi hierarchy and celebrities of the Third Reich. One of them was a famous opera singer whose beauty and performance at the Berlin State Opera had won her the patronage of Adolf Hitler. Her name was a Margery Booth, born in Wigan and married to Egon Strohm, a Berlin radio reporter who came from a wealthy beer brewing family. The couple had been married in Stockport when

Margery was already an established singer at the Covent Garden Opera House. When the Strohms moved back to Germany before the war, the German people, including many leading Nazis, had taken her into their hearts.

Purdy and his fellow radio collaborators revelled in their own celebrity, writing and recording their speeches at the Büro Concordia in the day and socialising together at night. Most of them shared an unshakeable belief in the strength and righteousness of the fascist cause. If they had doubts about what they were doing they kept these to themselves. But the undisputed leader of the British group was William Joyce, who remained resolute throughout.

Joyce's professional working life may have been organised and uncompromising, but his private affairs were chaotic. After the Joyces arrived in Germany in 1939 they had clung to each other for support. But the diminutive Irishman with a scar across his face was unable to satisfy his wife, who had acquired her own notoriety among German society. By 1943 Margaret was, more or less openly, enjoying a series of extramarital relationships. Among her lovers were German aristocrats and soldiers. This enraged her jealous husband who, when he found out about each infidelity, beat her as hard as he could. It seemed to make no difference to Margaret, who accepted her punishment for each new lover she took. The warring couple divorced, made up and even remarried. Margaret maintained she loved William but could not stop her lust getting the better of her.

Mrs Joyce also enjoyed the sexual and social company of the British collaborators. The handsome Walter Purdy may have been one of those who made a play for her affections. He had her Berlin number scribbled in the back of his contacts book, and later she fondly described him as 'dotty' and someone whose 'head was in a whirl'.[3]

Purdy kept a leather-bound diary[4] of his time in Berlin in which he faithfully recorded the glitz, the glamour and the loves of his Berlin life. It was the story of how a low-born hard-up sailor from the East End had become a leading light among the British collaborati.

The entries offer a fascinating insight into the lives of Purdy and his new friends in Berlin at the height of the Second World War

New Year's Eve 1943, according to the diary, was a drunken affair starting in a Berlin restaurant and pitching up at Gretel's house to see in 1944. It was an evening which Purdy said 'cost too much' and left him with a sore head – but he still made it to work on New Year's Day.

Two days later it was an 'afternoon in the hotel/restaurant Gerold with wine and good company'.

But then it was back to the Reichssportfeld to 'type out news for tomorrow until 10.30 p.m., then home'.

On 16 January, Purdy spent an evening at the cinema with Gretel and her friend Elizabeth.

The diary shows how not everyone in the social group was to Purdy's taste. He calls one of Gretel's friends 'Vicky the whore'.

Swept up in his new life of drinking, dancing, homemaking and work, it must have been easy to forget he was a British officer freely walking the streets of Berlin. But he was soon reminded of who and where he was when on 4 February, Purdy was arrested by a 'young Hitler Jugend' during a night out with Gretel drinking in town. He had to send a telegram to Adami who was able to confirm his identity and authorise his release.

He also ran into trouble at work when his lascivious nature got the better of him.

On 17 February he took a call from a Miss Wahlke who invited him out for a drink and they proceeded to 'get sozzled' while Gretel was on night-watch duty during the Allied bombing raids.

Purdy's close working relations with Fräulein Wahlke soon developed into a full-blown affair, and when Margarete found one of Fräulein Wahlke's letters in the apartment, the couple had a volcanic row.

To patch things up, he bought her a present, although he could see that she would no longer tolerate his philandering. Later that week Gretel announced she was 'leaving Berlin for a while to visit a family member who was ill'.

While she was away, Purdy planned to win her back by paying for dancing lessons so that when she returned to Berlin he could surprise her by leading her around the bedroom to their favourite song *'Hörst du mein heimliches Rufen?'* – 'Do you hear my secret calling?' It worked: 'I astounded her,' and Gretel presumably forgave him.

Every aspect of the quotidian grind of wartime Berlin was worthy of recording: 'A very peaceful night, went to sleep at 2.30 after a jolly good read; 11.30 bought a pair of shoes and three pairs of socks.'

There are further entries detailing visits to the barber's and his favourite Berlin pastry shops.

Interlaced with the humdrum are the recorded lies about his true identity which must have been written for Gretel's eyes. On 6 March 1944 he wrote: '31 today'. His true age was 26 and his date of birth was 16 May 1918.

Purdy was a loyal worker and his diary entries betray, perhaps deliberately, a consistent belief in the Nazi project. Next to the telephone number for Margaret Joyce was the one for Alexander Heimpel.

There are further hints and glimpses of his close connection to the Abwehr security officer, who was now working closely with the Gestapo. Away from the Reichssportfeld and his broadcasting role, Purdy was a frequent visitor to Stalag III-D's administrative headquarters in Stiglitz where Heimpel was based and where Purdy was issued with his food parcels, cigarettes, pay and any new orders. It was during these meetings that Purdy was expected to pass on intelligence about his fellow collaborators – Heimpel trusted none of them.

The supervision and management of Purdy placed him at the centre of a Nazi matrix[5] of Gestapo minders, Abwehr handlers and Foreign Office sponsors, all with a vested interest in their new collaborator. They bombarded his home with phone calls, secretly followed him and brought him into peripheral meetings for bigger espionage operations in the pipeline. It is hard to avoid the conclusion that the organisation of British treachery supported a well-remunerated job-creation racket that far too many Nazis were exploiting to keep them in gainful service of the Reich and far away from the front line.

But from 1944 onwards, more and more of his diary was taken up charting the wartime events encroaching on his freedom. By the close of 1943 there were almost daily visits from the British and American bomber forces; the US Air Force by day and the RAF by night.

On 4 January 1944 the threat of war was from the east: 'Russians crossed the old Polish–Russian border.'

21 Jan: 'Another visit. Spandau district got it badly.'

27 Jan: 'This evening the RAF hit Charlottenburg; three dropped on the Kaiserdamm.'

30 Jan: 'Today being the eleventh year of Hitler's accession, the Yanks were responsible for a late lunch. At 8 p.m. the English terror bombs inflicted more terror on Reichhauptstelle [Reich Headquarters]… Everybody is tired in this town from getting up at nights. Particularly me.'

After the all-clear was sounded following one daylight raid, Purdy ventured outside and picked up a USAF dropped pamphlet from the street telling Berliners they had lost the war and resistance was futile which he dismissed as: 'Yank propaganda which is even worse than ours – and that is bad enough.'

The raids had become so incessant that an evening of no air raid alarms was worth recording: 'A whole day without warning, spent last night on watch 12 – 4. G was wonderful. Stalag has some letters for me and some parcels.'

Reflecting what many Berliners must have also been feeling about the raids he added: 'The RAF seem to have decided the death of the civilian population will win the war for Britain and the dreaded Jews.'

This was at least partly true. The Luftwaffe may have been inflicting considerable casualties on the Allied air forces, but the Nazi fighters alone could not stop the raids. That year the Luftwaffe developed a German jet fighter that could outperform the Allies' fighters and was capable of bringing down many Allied bombers. But there were far too few of them to turn the tide of the air war.

Such was the unrelenting destructive force of the bombing campaign that it was threatening to break the resolve of the German people.

Unless the German air defences secured a tactical advantage over the Allied bombers, the Nazi high command realised that very soon there would be nothing left of urban Germany worth fighting for. The Nazis desperately needed an intelligence breakthrough – something that might give them the edge in the air battles over Germany. Heimpel ordered his POW spies, including Purdy, to make this their highest priority.

Chapter 14

Camp Leader

John Brown, after his staged altercation with Julius Green at Blechhammer, found himself back on a train to Berlin.

It had been only a few months since his last visit, yet he could see for himself that the German capital was no longer the impregnable citadel which the Nazis had once claimed it to be. Göring's boast that you 'can call me Meyer' [an insult in German] if a single bomb fell on Berlin was being thrown back at him by angry Berliners who were reaping the horrors of a blitz much worse than anything the Luftwaffe had dealt out to Londoners.

Indeed Brown's train journey was interrupted by several air raids, causing him to remark: 'On arriving the first thing to strike me was the way the population were preparing for severe air attacks – there were now huge stone shelters and ARP (Air Raid Precautions) activity in evidence everywhere.'[1]

Even part of the Stalag III-D administrative headquarters had suffered damage from one of the raids. But once Brown had stepped foot inside the building, he found everything else just as he remembered it from his previous visit.

Heimpel was on hand to greet him and warmly shook his hand 'as if I were his long-lost friend'.

'I am very pleased to see you again, Herr Brown,' said Heimpel, 'and I must apologise for the error which caused me to send you away last year.'[2]

Brown had been warned by Prince Hohenlohe before he left Blechhammer that the Abwehr and the Gestapo would have gone to a lot of trouble to ensure he was not trying to double-cross them. If they suspected him of working for British intelligence he could expect no mercy.

The British quartermaster, who was still carrying all his kit under his arm, followed Heimpel into his office. Heimpel tucked himself in behind his desk and gestured for Brown to throw his kit on the floor and join him at the table. The German officer said he had big plans for 'Busty' and he hoped he would like them.

'German high command has decided that certain British prisoners have been working very hard for the Third Reich. They are to be invited to come to Berlin for a rest. In addition we hope to have a few prisoners who have found favour with the various camp commandants in Germany.'[3]

Under the Geneva Conventions, the British officers were excused from manual labour, but other ranks had no choice in joining gruelling work parties, mining minerals, digging up potatoes or building factories. A holiday camp for ordinary men would be a genuine rest from their tiring and monotonous POW labours. Heimpel assured Brown that the new camp was not a propaganda camp and that it would be just like the one that had already been warmly welcomed by the British officers who benefited from German hospitality at Zehlendorf (Kommando 999).

'We want to break down the feeling of prejudice against the German nation and especially against the Nazi party. We want you to run it.' said Heimpel.

Brown was immediately suspicious. What was Heimpel's game? 'God only knows,' Brown thought to himself, 'what political tricks will be tried in the camp, for it is obvious the Germans were not going to give hundreds of British prisoners a holiday unless the Führer stood to gain something from it.'[4]

Brown decided to give Heimpel's proposition proper consideration. That night, Busty was sent back to his Berlin apartment where he sat on his bed thinking the whole matter through: 'I realised that if all went well, Heimpel had played completely into our hands. Here was my golden opportunity to make this the POW espionage centre in Germany. The men would come in from camps all over the Reich, would eventually return to them, and a network could be forged. Perhaps I could get escape kits to camps when no such articles were available. If I could gain a certain amount of freedom, I could carry out my special tasks using the camp as cover.'[5]

Heimpel had learned from Kommando 999 that the British responded more agreeably to a camp where the man in charge was one of their own. Heimpel also needed someone pliable, someone he could trust. Leonard Parrington, the senior British officer at Kommando 999, may have turned a blind eye to the propaganda element of the camp, but he had also strongly resisted attempts to suborn his men into helping the Germans.

The man in charge of the new men's camp would have to command the trust of both the British POWs and Heimpel. Heimpel, after consultation with Joyce, decided that the best man for the job was the friendly, gullible and eager to please John Brown. The fact that Brown was not an officer helped convince the Germans that the jolly sergeant would be a much more malleable stooge, willing to do the Wehrmacht's bidding. This assessment was based on a prejudicial Teutonic assumption about the character of the English non-officer class. German military intelligence failed to appreciate that the NCOs were proving to be just as valuable as the British officers to MI9 and its sister agencies in the supply of secret information and the subversion of the German war effort. Agent ZigZag, Eddie Chapman, the British double agent who ran rings around the Abwehr, was a case in point. It was a misreading of the British classes that would cost the Abwehr dearly.

Responsibility for German propaganda operations was divided between Goebbels's ministry and the Foreign Office, while German military intelligence and the Gestapo took care of the counter-intelligence operations at the POW camps. But it was the German Foreign Office that had the final say over policy. Heimpel had tried to work without recourse to the more conservative-minded Foreign Office, but Dr Fritz Hesse was on Hitler's personal staff and so his views carried weight. The final say over Brown's appointment would rest with Hesse and Ziegfeld.

On a bright morning in June 1943, Brown was taken by underground to Potsdamer Platz where Dr Hesse and Dr Ziegfeld had arranged to interview Brown in the Chancellery building. The Germans greeted Brown with handshakes. Busty immediately recognised Ziegfeld's handshake to be Masonic, and responded in kind.[6] Neither man said anything. Under the Nazis, Freemasonry was deemed to be part of a Jewish conspiracy and many Masons had been executed.

Hesse and Ziegfeld had exacting demands about how the 'holiday camp' should run. 'Mr Brown,' Hesse began, 'we understand that you have been a most reasonable prisoner. You have been selected by us to run a special camp, the first of its kind in Germany. We feel the time has now come for a better English understanding of German policy, so that when we've won the war Englishmen will be more ready to cooperate with us in the struggle against communism.'[7]

Brown, who had heard the same pitch from Heimpel, repeated his concern about the camp being used as a Nazi propaganda tool.

Hesse reassured him that all they wanted him to do was run a 'genuine holiday camp' for British POWs and he hoped he would be 'honoured' they had chosen him from all the other British prisoners.

The two Germans promised that the camp would play host to the best performers and artists The Reich had to offer, with shows at least once a week. Brown would even be able to meet each artist personally and discuss his or her programme beforehand so he could assure himself it was not propaganda.

Brown said he would be happy to help improve relations between the two nations but he would like to offer more recreation at the camp including films and sporting and musical events involving other camps. To do this he would need his own hand-selected staff who already had experience of putting on big entertainment.

Hesse and Ziegfeld agreed, but they warned him should he change his mind or prove unsuitable for the role he would not be able to return to his old camp. The Germans did not want anyone else to know about their plans for a holiday camp. What would actually happen to Brown if things didn't work out was left menacingly hanging in the air.

Brown agreed to their terms. 'Excellent,' said a very pleased-looking Hesse, who also suggested that Brown should wear civilian clothes in his new role, which the Germans knew would further compromise the British soldier in the eyes of his compatriots.

'To cover yourself when you are all alone in Berlin we will give you an Ausweis (a police pass) which will be very useful to you,' Hesse promised. 'It will say that because you are friendly towards German politics you must be given every consideration and when shopping must have every priority. It will mean you will practically have the freedom of Berlin and be able to go where you will and meet whomever you wish, including women. We hope you will enjoy yourself; but of course, don't take liberties.'

Chapter 15

Genshagen, Special Camp 517

The next day, with Hesse's threat still ringing in his ears, two of Heimpel's men accompanied Brown by train to his new camp, 10 miles south of Berlin, near a village called Genshagen.

Brown and the guards left the station by car and headed into the pine forest that surrounded the village.

The car turned off the road through a clearing and then along an avenue of elm trees which led to the camp entrance. Brown picked up his bag, jumped out of the car and stood surveying his new home – Special Camp 517 attached to Stalag III-D. It was true – if it wasn't for the barbed-wire fence and a single guard casually strolling around the perimeter, it could have all been dreamed up by Billy Butlin himself. There were 18 dormitory rooms in wooden huts, first-class shower and toilet facilities and a specially built concert hall in a separate compound also enclosed by barbed wire. Unlike the typical Stalags, all the living accommodation was located close to the perimeter fences. In the centre of the camp were a dozen or so slit trenches to be used in case of air raids, although it was hard to imagine the RAF bothering with or locating such a tucked away location in the middle of the forest. Outside the barbed wire was a field which was being turned into football and rounders pitches. Brown had his own small office but had to share his living quarters with three other men. The previous camp leader was regimental sergeant major Joseph Seward[1] who had been in charge for nearly two years, but his open hostility to any of

Heimpel's plans for Special Camp 517 had brought his tenure to an abrupt end and he was shipped out east. Before Brown's arrival, the camp had been the subject of a number of very critical Red Cross reports concerning the latrines and standard of accommodation. After a visit in March 1943, the Swiss inspector Rudolph Denzler[2] said it was one of the worst camps he had seen. Heimpel, who had accompanied the Swiss diplomat on his inspection, decided that since the Wehrmacht was going to have to go to the expense of bringing Genshagen up to scratch, they might as well go the whole hog and use it for their planned 'holiday camp'.

Heimpel had placed Sonderführer Oskar Lange, a former New York docker who spoke perfect American English, in charge of the German side of things at Genshagen. He was joined by a small group of British/German soldiers, some of whom had been members of Mosley's party before the war and had strong fascist leanings. It was their job to turn the 'holiday campers' into collaborators. Their fluency in English and their British or Commonwealth backgrounds meant the unsuspecting POWs would, the Germans hoped, be more susceptible to the propaganda.

Brown had twigged that this might be why so many of them were on the camp staff and began lobbying Hesse and Ziegfeld to replace them with his old comrades at Blechhammer who, he reminded them, had the necessary experience of staging entertainment events. Amazingly, the Germans agreed. First pick on Brown's list was Reg Beattie, his trusted lieutenant and Nazi baiter-in-chief, followed by Jimmy Newcomb, his right-hand man running the camp rackets.

The first group of 200 British POWs arrived in June 1943 and stayed until August.

Brown put Beattie in charge of 'camp intelligence' because he had a 'flair for smelling out pro-German prisoners'. Once Beattie had identified a potential collaborator, Brown and his staff went to work: 'I kept in the background but should any of my men find it difficult to dissuade someone from the traitor's path, I would sow a grain of suspicion with the Germans, suggesting the man in question was trying to double-cross them; he was known to us as a communist and it was obvious he had come to the camp to wreck the good feelings the Germans were trying to foster.'[3] The grateful Heimpel and Lange soon moved the suspect POW out of Genshagen – several of them found themselves in punishment camps for the rest of the war.

For nearly three months Brown's men subverted the Nazi collaboration programme. Before Heimpel had a chance to work on a possible recruit, Brown had undermined the candidate's fascist credentials.

Now Brown started to turn the steady churn of POWs to his advantage. With so many British prisoners visiting Genshagen from all over Germany, Brown was able to pick up vital intelligence about the movement and whereabouts of German military units which he passed on to London using the secret coded letters.

He was also able to seek out trusted men whom he could include in his network of contacts across the camps and help build the escape lines.

Brown had to keep his wits about him, because all the time the Germans were looking for new methods of picking up useful intelligence from the holidaying POWs. Heimpel wanted Brown to arrange a weekly event where the POWs were encouraged to entertain the rest of the prisoners with interesting stories about their time before they were captured or their lives at home. In this way Heimpel hoped to harvest intelligence from drunken servicemen while their guard was down. Brown had an answer to this and arranged for the POW talks to contain fake stories that would 'lead the Germans up the garden path'.

It seemed whatever subterfuge Heimpel tried, Brown found a way of undermining it.

But the truth was Heimpel had become distracted from his professional duties by his complex personal life. His former wife had been released from the correctional camp for those accused of Rassenschande (race defilement) and had reinstated her legal claim for backdated maintenance payments which once again threatened to bankrupt the Nazi intelligence chief. At the same time his teenage nephew had been publicly accused of committing acts of homosexuality.[4] Heimpel had taken it upon himself to 'rescue' the boy, Hans Dietrich, from his mother, Heimpel's sister-in-law, and then forced the mother to confess she had criminally neglected her son. He later arranged for her to be sent to a re-education camp for un-German mothers, which allowed him to apply to the courts to take sole custody of the boy so that he could correct his homosexual urges.[5] With both matters taken care of (he used the Red Cross parcel slush fund to pay off his wife), he was finally able to give Genshagen his full attention.

One morning Heimpel, who spent most of his time at the Stalag III headquarters in Steglitz, asked his driver to get his car ready as he was planning a surprise visit to Genshagen. On a good day it took Heimpel half an hour to beetle across Berlin and reach the camp, but under military restrictions it could take a lot longer. Heimpel left early to beat the traffic and as soon as he arrived he went straight to Lange's office and asked him to bring Brown to see him. The British sergeant was accustomed to Heimpel's 'surprise' visits. The German officer may have perfected an air of menace but Brown reckoned he had the measure of him and believed the German officer lacked the imagination to really understand the character and devious ingenuity of the British soldier. Heimpel, however, was not so easily fooled. During the years he had survived and prospered in the service of the German military, a nest of vipers even before the rise of Nazism, and then the SA, Heimpel had acquired a sixth sense for suspicious incongruity, a nose for knowing when something wasn't quite right. And something didn't smell right about the smiling British sergeant who appeared to be so helpful to the German cause. There was nothing he could quite put his finger on but after rereading Lange's reports it seemed very odd that nearly all the POW holiday camp visitors who had shown any interest in helping the Germans turned out to be British loyalists who had all the time been faking their collaboration

Until he had settled his niggling doubts about Brown he decided to block his Berlin freedom pass. This represented a serious setback for Brown's intelligence work. Brown protested, but it was no use. Heimpel said he was to be camp-bound until further notice.

Busty knew that unless he was able to travel around Berlin, his spying operations for MI9 would be severely curtailed.

Brown decided to make an appeal to his more biddable friends at the German Foreign Office. Once again Brown was sitting in the Chancellery in front of Hesse and Ziegfeld, this time reminding them of their promise of a freedom pass which Heimpel had blocked. Hesse told him: 'We have received your request to go out in civilian clothing, but we must have good reason before granting such a request.'[6] Hesse explained that although they had previously promised him his freedom, there were now growing concerns about British spies who were identifying bombing targets for the RAF.

'Surely you are not suggesting I would associate with spies?' Brown indignantly replied.

'Of course not, we trust you, but you must also realise we have to be very careful.'

Then Brown played his trump card: 'I would suggest you don't want to issue me a pass because you are afraid of Captain Heimpel.'[7]

Hesse took the bait and angrily told Brown it was he who was directly accountable to Hitler, not Heimpel, whose sole role was to provide security guards for Stalag III-D.

A few days later Brown received his pass.

Brown was delighted with the small green card and the authorising letter accompanying it: 'Because of John Brown's political allegiance to the Wehrmacht he is to be granted the freedom of Berlin.'[8]

Brown wasted no time and arranged for the camp tailors to stitch him a civilian suit that would make him blend in with the Berlin crowds. Careful not to arouse suspicions in Genshagen among the British soldiers, he walked through the gates in his army uniform carrying a small suitcase and then changed into his new suit in the nearby wood before heading off to the railway station.

He could hardly believe it: a British prisoner in Germany freely mixing with the German public going about their daily business – and no one batted an eyelid. An exuberant Brown relished his new-found liberty: 'The breath of fresh air and the sight of so many charming women strutting about the streets of Berlin giving their Heil Hitler salute to passers-by caused the sap within me to rise.'[9]

With Berlin at his mercy, Brown began locating just the sort of key bombing targets Hesse and Ziegfeld were worried a British spy might be looking for. Close to the camp railway station at Grossburen, Brown noticed large numbers of disembarking workers were making their way to a building in the middle of a field which seemed far too small to accommodate so many people. His casual enquiries with a train guard revealed that the small building was in fact an entrance to an underground Daimler Benz Tiger Tank factory that the Germans had buried deep underground hidden from the prying eyes of Allied surveillance aircraft.

When Brown got back to the camp that night he told Lange that he required somewhere to change out of his British uniform into his Berlin civvies, explaining to the Sonderführer that if he was caught out in the open swapping British for German clothes he might be seen by a local farmer who would report him to the police or worse shoot him as a spy. Brown suggested one solution to the problem would be to allow him to change in the nearby caretaker's office at the Daimler Benz factory. To Brown's surprise, Lange agreed and made the necessary arrangements with the factory directors.

Before leaving for the factory the next day, Brown filled his suitcase with chocolate, a box of English cigarettes and some coffee. The caretaker and his wife and children were overjoyed with the gifts and after a few more visits they became very fond of 'Herr Busty'. Having gained the caretaker's confidence, Brown began praising the

German for keeping such a big factory so secure. The caretaker was sorry that he wasn't allowed to show him around the building but he was happy to let him see the floor plan. Brown had the caretaker in the palm of his hand and it wasn't long before he was telling Brown how the Tiger Tanks left the factory each day through two separated tunnels which led to exits on the other side of a hill.

Brown carefully relayed this information back to London. A few days later Allied bombers arrived over Genshagen and the factory took a direct hit which put it out of action for a few weeks. Unfortunately, Brown's temporary changing room was also destroyed in the raid, forcing him to resume his practice of changing clothes in the woods. There was worse to follow when stray bombs from another raid on the tank factory flattened part of the British camp quarters at Genshagen. Brown and his men were safe in the air raid shelter, although when they returned to their room it was missing a ceiling.

They soon got the place back in good order and ready for the camp entertainment, which brought in an array of singers, bands, famous sportspeople and Berlin artists to Genshagen. Not all of them were diehard Nazis.

Brown made sure that there were plenty of women performers on the Genshagen bill. One of the star turns was Margery Booth, the British-born opera singer who, with her German husband, had emigrated to Germany just before the start of the war. She had become a household name with a string of virtuoso performances in the starring role of *Carmen* at Bayreuth. Hitler was so taken by her that he sent her red roses wrapped in a Swastika flag.

When she arrived at Genshagen and sang 'Land of Hope and Glory', Brown, along with the rest of the men, was mesmerised. Her choice of song delighted the British soldiers as much as it irritated the Germans. What Brown didn't realise was that it was intended to. Booth and her German journalist husband were not what they seemed. Margery Booth had been recruited by MI9 in Berlin where she was risking her life sending messages back to London. It didn't take Brown long to check with his own handlers on the British songstress. When he got the all-clear, he took the calculated risk of revealing his own double agent credentials.

Booth gave him tickets to the Berlin State Opera and invited him back to her nearby flat. When he felt sure he could trust her, Brown told her about his secret operations at Genshagen. After that, Booth was a regular performer at the camp, which meant Brown could pass her secret documents whenever he needed something important smuggled past the guards. In Berlin she couriered fake travel documents and identification papers between escape line safe houses. Booth regularly concealed these documents in her underwear, once while singing in front of an audience which included Hitler, earning her the nickname the 'knicker spy' by her MI9 handlers in London. She also hid a number of Jewish women from the Gestapo.

Margery Booth was not the only woman Brown had brought into his fold. Margarete Langfelder held a personal hatred for the Nazis: her Jewish husband had been executed by the Gestapo in 1940. Despite her 'illegal marriage' to a Jew, the Nazis had allowed her to continue to own and run a music shop just off Potsdamer Platz.

Brown had been given permission to source violins and trumpets for the camp band and first met Frau Langfelder in July 1943 when he was shopping in Berlin for new musical instruments. During these transactions it became clear to Brown that the helpful shopkeeper reviled the Nazi Party. When he was sure he could trust her, Brown sought her help to hide escaped British POWs and captured spies who had been condemned to the concentration camps. Frau Langfelder agreed.

Several agents and prisoners were saved because Margarete Langfelder hid them in her Berlin villa until they could be safely smuggled out of the capital. One RAF flyer had been carried to Genshagen in the Blechhammer band's music box – a distance of 500 miles. He stayed in Frau Langfelder's house for four months before getting safely back to England.

A third German woman was to prove even more useful to the British agent. Gisela Maluche was a divorcee who owned a wine shop. Brown met her in Berlin when he and two of his men were enjoying an afternoon out at the Cafe Vaterland where they had exchanged Red Cross goodies for champagne. Brown had spotted a group of women in the cafe and persuaded the German guard accompanying them to invite the women over to their table. Busty had mistaken them for prostitutes and the group proceeded to get very drunk. When he found out Gisela Maluche was a respectable businesswoman, he decided to make a play for her.

At first Gisela refused to believe Brown was a British POW who had the run of Berlin. But she was sufficiently intrigued by his story and invited him back to her flat at Leinestrasse 6, Meinkoln. It wasn't long before Brown was sharing her bed.

Afterwards, the married Brown suffered an attack of guilt. 'God knows I was longing for the physical part of it. I felt, too, that Nan[cy] would understand, for it might help me dodge the barbed-wire mentality that had afflicted so many.'[10]

Brown knew that Gisela lived close to Dr Ziegfeld's house. He also remembered the busy Ziegfeld telling him that he was looking for someone to clean and look after his domestic affairs. Gisela's wine shop had been bombed out of business during an air raid. Now all Brown needed to do was to put them together and persuade Gisela to become Ziegfeld's housekeeper and be an unwitting spy in the home of one of the leading figures at the German Foreign Office. 'Gisela agreed and I found I was indeed able to combine a little tender lovemaking with hard research work… Gisela trusted me implicitly and she often told me things she'd overheard.'[11]

Chapter 16

Double Agent Brown

Back in London, British military intelligence had received several reports from Germany, including Brown's, implicating British POWs as collaborators.

To partly counter this growing threat, MI5 set up SLB3, the agency's Renegades Investigation and Prosecution Unit[1] which was headed by Lieutenant Colonel Vivian Home Seymer. Seymer was the son of Basil Thomson, the former Director of Intelligence at the Home Office, who during the First World War had interrogated the German spy and exotic dancer Mata Hari.[2] The Security Service had spent the interwar years mostly focused on communists, but had quickly adjusted to the threat posed by fascists on the home front.

Seymer's new unit came into being at the start of the war and was commissioned to work closely with MI9 to uncover the identities of the British traitors who were operating from inside enemy territory. William Joyce was well known, but the others had disguised their real names by using multiple aliases. MI9 instructed its agents to find out as much as they could about the British POWs who they suspected of collaborating with the Germans.[3] When MI9 revealed they were working with one agent, a Royal Artillery quartermaster sergeant, who had managed to immerse himself in the heart of the German counter-intelligence operations in Berlin, Seymer couldn't quite believe it.

Could he be trusted? MI9 assured their sister agency that Brown had already supplied valuable intelligence about German military targets as well as a number of key Nazi figures. MI5 now wanted more precise intelligence about the British traitors and asked MI9 to set Brown to work. A coded letter with exactly these instructions was sent to Brown at Genshagen. The British agent wasted no time getting to work.

Brown learned from Gisela that three British spies were living next door to Ziegfeld's house at ParadePlatz 8. One of them, she said, was a senior naval officer. Brown's interest was piqued and he decided to visit ParadePlatz for himself. He found out from Gisela when the house would be empty and knocked on the door. Gisela ushered him in and directed him to where the three British men were living. Brown began carefully searching through their belongings hoping for anything that might give away their true identities.

After discovering very little of intelligence value, he stumbled across a brown suitcase in one of the cupboards. Underneath the clothes, he found a letter written in German and addressed to the German Foreign Office. The author had set out his reasons for wanting to work for the Germans, which included his shared conviction that Hitler was right about the threat from communism, and that he feared it would conquer the world if Germany was defeated. It ended with Heil Hitler and was signed 'Lt Commander W Purdy'.

Brown had heard this name before.

'Soon after Julius Green had come to Blechhammer he told me about his former naval camp, Marlag/Milag. I remembered he had mentioned a naval engineer called Purdy; he had a reputation for being extremely pro-German so that when he eventually vanished from the camp he was suspected of having gone over to the German side.'[4]

Brown realised that Purdy, who had promoted himself to Lieutenant Commander,[5] was no longer a British prisoner of war and must be working for the Germans.

While he knew he had to inform London about the naval officer spy, he recognised that this intelligence was too important to risk using one of his own coded messages, which might be picked up by the suspicious Heimpel and his camp censors. Brown decided the best course of action was to make contact with Green, whom he could consult about Purdy, and whom he could try to persuade to write his own coded letter to warn London. But how was he going to convince the Germans to let him return to Blechhammer? He came up with an ingenious plan. Brown told Heimpel he needed to visit the YMCA headquarters at Stalag VIII-C in Sagan in Silesia to collect essential equipment for the camp. He said while he was there he could use the opportunity to persuade the YMCA that Genshagen really was a holiday camp and not, as they suspected, being run for propaganda or nefarious purposes. Since he would be close to Blechhammer, he suggested to Heimpel, he could drop in to see if he could recruit more German-friendly POWs for the holiday camp.

The German intelligence officer was immediately suspicious: 'But Mr Brown,' said Heimpel, 'don't you realise it would not be safe for you to go back to Blechhammer. They have threatened to kill you if you ever return!'[6]

'But why should they want to harm me, Captain Heimpel?'

'Because they are quite sure you are working for the enemy. Of course that's us, your friends, isn't it, Mr Brown,' the German officer added with a menacing sneer.

'I'm quite sure I've nothing to fear. They will welcome me back as soon as I tell them about the good work we are doing at Genshagen and how so many prisoners are benefiting from the Christian side of the camp.'

Heimpel couldn't quite believe Brown's naivety. But he was under pressure. Senior Nazis had begun to take an interest in Genshagen, including Himmler who had recently taken over responsibility for the Gestapo. If Genshagen was going to deliver the number of collaborators that Heimpel had promised, then he would need many more willing recruits from the POW camps.

So with Heimpel's guarded blessing, Brown set off for Sagan and then Blechhammer to warn Green about Purdy.

Arriving at Blechhammer, Brown discovered Heimpel had been right about one thing – most of the POWs believed Busty Brown had taken the German pfennig. As much as he wanted to share the truth with his old pals, Brown knew it would put in jeopardy all the work he had done. So he endured the cold shoulder and the barbed words. Brown would need a good reason to visit Green in his medical quarters on the German side of the camp; he could no longer rely on the friendly commandant for help. Shortly after Brown left Blechhammer for the second time, Prince Hohenlohe had been moved to another camp in Italy. The Nazis had found him to be too soft on the prisoners. Brown told the new commandant that he was suffering from a severe toothache and requested emergency dental attention. When Brown walked into Green's dental surgery, the two men were careful not to give themselves away. Green, pretending not to recognise Brown, quickly ushered his brother spy into his dentist chair.

Brown recalled: '... he kept his mouth shut and I opened mine. I told Julius exactly where Purdy was living and also what work he was doing for the Germans.'[7]

Green, immediately realising the significance of what Brown was telling him, sent a coded letter advising his MI9 handlers that the British naval officer had been turned and was now a dangerous Nazi spy. How he wished he had sent one sooner when he first got wind of Purdy's intended collaboration at Marlag.

The message to London about Walter Purdy was one of the last that Julius Green was able to send. A few weeks later, the Nazis decided to transfer the dentist to a more secure camp. It appeared the Germans had remembered Green's involvement in storing contraband for the St Nazaire commando escape plot at Marlag. Nor had the Nazis forgotten that Green was the only British witness to the murder of a British officer, the young radio officer Walter Skett.

His transfer was a blow for both Green and MI9. Green felt he had been 'a bit of a clot in becoming implicated in the St Nazaire boys' escape plans'. His sense of self-recrimination deepened when he received a letter from home in December which when he decoded it read 'HAD YOUR 10th May, 9th August & 4th September, 7th, 8th, 19th, CONGRATULATIONS ON REALLY EXCELLENT WORK KEEP IT UP STOP'.[8]

Green was first taken to Mährisch Trübau, a former Czech military academy now being used by the Germans as a POW camp, Oflag VIII-F.

The British officers put Green through a preliminary interrogation to 'establish my bona fides and make sure I wasn't a German stooge or a traitor being planted in the camp'.[9]

It was here that Green met one of the bravest soldiers of the Second World War: David Stirling, the father of the SAS, whose Long Range Desert Patrol Group had wreaked such havoc behind enemy lines in North Africa. Green believed his own usefulness as an undercover spy was blown and he asked Stirling for help in getting back to England. Stirling took one look at the unfit dentist and told him that his best chance of escape was to fake a mental illness and get repatriated by 'working your ticket'. Green reluctantly agreed and began researching symptoms for paranoia and manic depression. But before he could make his case to the commandant, the dentist was informed that he was to be on the move again to an unknown destination. Fearing the worst, Green bid farewell to Stirling and the rest of the men and headed out of the camp with his two-man guard. At Dresden railway station, the guard detail was joined by a group of emaciated Russian prisoners, most of whom were suffering from advanced stages of TB. Green handed out all his Red Cross food and chocolate to the dying Russians before being led away to another train.

This was a painfully slow local service that seemed to stop at every telegraph pole along the line meandering through the Saxony hills. After several hours, the train finally pulled into a rather unprepossessing station on the edge of town. The guards told Green this was their disembarkation stop and helped him lug his heavy bag, filled with three and half years's worth of dental gear, onto the platform. As he took stock of his new destination, he cast his eye around the station. It was late at night and the place looked deserted. Where was he being taken? What did the Germans have in store for him? Had they discovered his Jewish ancestry? Green pivoted his heavy bag on to his back and then followed the two guards along the narrow cobbled road that led down the hill to the Adolf Hitler Bridge spanning the River Mulde. At this point the guards stopped and pointed to a large building overlooking the town, which was illuminated with spotlights. One of them laughed and said this was to be Green's new home – a place from which there was no escape.

They continued over a small bridge, crossing an old moat and climbing up a passage between two very high walls until they reached the first sentry's post. There, they were checked and moved on to the guardhouse, which was built into the castle's steep outer curtain. The two enormous iron-studded gates were one of only two entrances. Here, the escort presented Green's papers and the dentist was formally transferred into the custody of his new guards. The British prisoner was now led 50 yards back down the passageway to a small postern gate, which opened onto a stairway and a wooden door with a narrow metal bar window. This was to be Green's cell for the night. Green took off his boots and climbed on to the pallet bed, dragging his army greatcoat over him. Before he fell to sleep, he remembered the rumours of special prisons, of Straflager punishment camps for prisoners who had made themselves more than usually obnoxious to the Germans. No one knew their whereabouts other than they were located in the east of the country, but rumour had it that the cells were small, the food minimal and the treatment harsh. Summary executions were carried out on the merest of pretexts. Green fell asleep wondering what the morning would bring. He was woken early by a guard who told him he was to meet the officer in charge. Waiting for him at the main entrance under the giant iron-studded gate was Captain Reinhold Eggers, who greeted him with a clipped good morning.

Green only had one question: 'What is this place?'

'Oflag IV-C Colditz,' Eggers replied.

'The Straflager?'

'No! No! Not Straflager – Sonderlager (special camp).'

All at once Green was besieged by feelings of fear, curiosity and pride. But by far the strongest was fear. 'Colditz may have carried a kind of distinction but as far I was concerned they could keep it. The less the Germans concerned themselves about me the better Mrs Green liked it.'[10]

Chapter 17

Suspicious Minds

Green arrived at Colditz in January 1944 during a difficult period for the British POWs. Several Allied tunnel escapes had been thwarted at the 11th hour by the German guards. The discoveries all seemed to follow the same pattern: the prisoners spent months digging a tunnel or perfecting an escape and then on the night or day of the break-out, a German search party would intervene, often catching the men in the act. It was as if the commandant and his security team were waiting for the best moment to foil the escape so they could catch the most escapees, recover all the contraband and strike the deepest blow to British morale. The French and the Poles had already identified informers from among their own ranks. One of them was a Polish POW called Lieutenant Ryszard Bednarski, who had been returned to Colditz after a failed escape and had been savagely tortured by the Gestapo. But on his reappearance at Colditz, Bednarski's behaviour raised suspicions, and after questioning by the Poles he confessed to collaborating with the Germans. The Polish officers court-martialled him and found him guilty of spying. They planned to throw him out of a castle window so that his death, looked like an accident, but before Bednarski could fall to his death a senior Polish officer halted the execution and requested that the commandant remove Bednarski from the prison for his own safety.

Was it possible that there were also traitors among the British POWs? The prisoners themselves certainly thought so. Rupert Barry says that some of the longest messages sent by MI9 concerned requests for more information about suspected traitors.[1] Green's appearance at Colditz, a camp reserved for hardened escapers and VIP prisoners, raised suspicions to begin with. Green had taken no direct part in escapes himself nor did he appear to hold any military or political value to the Germans. More significantly, Colditz already had a British dentist – Captain Eric Cooper.[2]

The senior British officer at Colditz was Lieutenant Colonel William Tod, 52, of the Royal Scots Fusiliers. He had been captured on 28 May 1940 after leading a desperate defence of the Dunkirk perimeter positions, a critical action in the naval miracle that saw 360,000 Allied troops escape to Britain.

Tod suggested that the camp security committee ask Green some tough questions. Charles Merritt VC, the most senior vetting officer, was put in charge of the interview. Merritt could find no evidence that Green was working for the Germans, but neither was he able to fathom why Green had been sent to Oflag IV-C.

The sense of mutual distrust in the prison was palpable. Green could feel the prisoners' eyes watching his every move. In those first few days he had never felt so alone.

It was a truth of life at Colditz that the prisoners who attracted the most scrutiny from their brother officers were those who turned up on their own. If none of the Colditz officers could vouch for them or they offered suspect accounts of their captivity, the new POW was placed under close watch. If the prisoner had any association at all with one of the propaganda camps in Berlin or even a tangential link to the Nazi regime, then he faced an uphill struggle to prove his loyalty. For Green, his predicament was made worse because even he himself didn't know why he had been sent to Colditz.

It was unfortunate that the one POW who was able to vouch for Green was Captain Michael Burn, a commando captured during the raid on St Nazaire in March 1942, and one of the group of prisoners whom Green had been in secret contact with when they were both detained at Marlag. Burn may have been a brave soldier, but he was also an unconventional character who enjoyed going against the grain.

Burn had grown up among the higher echelons of the British aristocracy. His father was secretary and solicitor to the Duchy of Cornwall and a trusted confidant of the King until his abdication. His mother's family were instrumental in developing the golf and gambling resort of Le Touquet, a fashionable seaside town south of Calais where P G Wodehouse and his wife were staying during the Nazi occupation. Burn had at one time formed a intimate relationship with Alice Keppel, the former mistress of Edward VII. He was also a close friend of Unity Mitford, one of the most prominent pre-war supporters of Adolf Hitler. Perhaps more scandalously to the sexually repressed public schoolboys at Colditz, Burn was openly bisexual. Among his lovers during his Cambridge University days in the 1930s was Guy Burgess, the spy and traitor who would defect to Russia after the war. Burn had been dabbling in politics in the 1930s, and during a number of long stays in Germany, often as a guest of one of the Mitford sisters, he became enthralled to National Socialism. He went back to England to try his hand as a journalist, but returned to Munich in 1935 where he was introduced to Hitler himself, on whom he made a lasting impression by vastly inflating the Führer's supposed popularity among the youth of Britain. Hitler was delighted and presented Burn with a personally signed copy of *Mein Kampf*. The following month Burn made sure he was photographed standing next to the Führer during a Nazi rally at Nuremberg, an event which he described as 'great lights in the sky, moving music, the rhetoric, the presentation, timing, performance, soundtrack, exultation and climax. It was almost aimed at the sexual parts of one's consciousness.'[3]

Once he was back in Britain, Burn's connections among both the British aristocracy and the Nazi Party leadership landed him a job as a journalist with *The Times*, but his admiration for Nazism had begun to wane. In 1937 he enlisted in a Territorial Army battalion of the King's Royal Rifle Corps, and after the declaration of war two years later, he volunteered for the special 'independent companies', forerunners of the commandos. His first taste of active service was guerrilla operations against the German forces in occupied Norway.

In March 1942, Burn took part in one of the most famous commando raids of the Second World War – the operation to destroy the huge dry dock at St Nazaire, the only naval base on the Atlantic coast of occupied Europe large enough to accommodate the battleship *Tirpitz*.

The extraordinarily dangerous mission called for 24 small groups of commandos to accompany the destroyer, HMS *Campbeltown*, loaded with explosives on delayed charges, into the French port. When the old destroyer struck the harbour walls, the commandos were to scatter ashore and blow up as many German gun towers and other installations as they could before escaping overland to Spain.

The approaching British force was detected sooner than they had hoped and caught in the beams of enemy searchlights. Burn, hearing the whistling of German tracer bullets, jumped from his motor launch and scrambled up on to a long jetty.

As he ran for cover, he was wounded by a burst of fire from a German gun emplacement and was later captured. His bravery in the face of enemy fire showed how far he had come since those days when he was intoxicated by Nazi ideology.

However, Hitler had taken a personal interest in the raid at St Nazaire, and when he became aware that one of the wounded prisoners was the young man who had flattered him so much few years earlier, the Führer sent a propaganda unit to film Burn as a German prisoner of war. He also dispatched his personal interpreter, Paul Schmidt, to interrogate him.

During the interrogation, *Campbeltown*'s payload detonated, causing a mighty explosion. Burn recorded the moment, as the windows in his interrogation room were blown in: 'Not only had she exploded,' he later wrote, 'but taken with her scores of German investigators, sightseers and souvenir hunters.' *Tirpitz* never ventured out into the Atlantic, and the dock remained out of action until after the war. Five men were eventually awarded the VC for their roles in the St Nazaire raid. Burn was the sole survivor of his unit and was decorated with the Military Cross.

None of this bothered German military intelligence, who couldn't wait to get their hands on the British 'Nazi sympathiser', and they sent Burn to Berlin for some special attention. Given his previous connections with the Third Reich and his personal link to Adolf Hitler, the Germans believed they had a spy in the making.

Little is known about what transpired between Burn and the Nazis in Berlin, and he was later packed off to Colditz as a recalcitrant POW. The arrival of the flamboyant minor aristocrat drew antagonism from almost every British serviceman in the camp. The haughty Burn didn't help his case by declaring he had absolutely no intention of trying to escape and so was immediately denounced as a German sympathiser and put under close watch. There were even mutterings among the British officers about having him tried as a traitor after the war. His participation in one of the most successful commando raids of the Second World War seemingly counted for nothing. The only thing Burn did have in his favour were his society ties and attendance at England's oldest public school, Winchester College, where a group of other Colditz officers and seasoned escapers, including Mike Sinclair and Gris Davies-Scourfield, had been educated.

Such establishment connections were not available to Captain Birendra Nath Mazumdar, who arrived at Colditz shortly after Burn. It was Mazumdar whose hand John Brown had shook in Berlin after hearing his brave speech against the Germans in the presence of William Joyce. Mazumdar had signed on with the British Army and he intended to remain loyal to his oath to the British Crown. However, he made no secret of his political views regarding Indian independence, which antagonised the British officers. In a previous

POW camp, anti-Indian feeling was so strong he was denied his fair share of rations. He later recalled: 'There was no spirit of camaraderie that I had read about in the books of World War I. They didn't want to share their food, and we lived on black coffee and bread. This was happening among so-called educated people. I couldn't believe my eyes.'[4]

In October 1942 Mazumdar was sent to Colditz, where the Gestapo calculated that the British would continue to treat him with hostility. And the British officers duly obliged, openly referring to him as the 'commandant's special spy'.

The Gestapo responded to his isolation with inducements and bribes in the hope that, if he wouldn't fight for them, he might help in the propaganda war against the Raj. Failing this, he could pass on intelligence about the secret activities of the 'hated' British officers at Colditz.[5] In 1943 the Gestapo arranged for Mazumdar to travel to Berlin. He was given a seat in a first-class train carriage and treated to a lavish lunch. When he arrived, he was whisked off to meet a man whom the Germans knew Mazumdar greatly admired. Subhas Chandra Bose was an Indian nationalist leader who had escaped British detention, fleeing to Germany just after the start of the war.

Bose told Hitler he would form a Free Indian Legion and had great success in recruiting more than 5,000 Indian soldiers to the cause.

When the two men met in Berlin, Mazumdar claims he explained to Bose that while he supported the overthrow of the Raj, he was a commissioned officer who had sworn an oath of loyalty to the King and as such he could not betray the British Army. Shortly afterwards he was sent to a Berlin house with a number of other Indian officers, the same meeting where he met William Joyce and John Brown. His rejection of the Nazis' overtures and his humiliation of Joyce was a huge disappointment to the Germans, who returned Mazumdar to Colditz in a third-class compartment. His reappearance at the castle just a few days after the British POWs had been chiding him about his trip to Berlin drew a great deal of suspicion. The British prisoners wondered why, if he had refused to work for the Germans, had they returned him to Colditz? After all, Mazumdar had already made it clear that he wished to leave Colditz and join a camp for Indian prisoners. The episode merely confirmed what most suspected – Mazumdar was a Gestapo plant who was passing on information to the Germans.

The job of trying to turn men like Burn and Mazumdar into Colditz informants fell to Captain Reinhold Eggers, the Abwehr officer at Colditz. Eggers was an old soldier who served with distinction in the First World War as an Unteroffizier with the First Regiment of Marine Infantry at Kiel. He was posted to the Western Front where in Mau, in 1915, he won the Iron Cross Second Class and then the Iron Cross First Class and the Hesse Medal for bravery on the Somme in December of the same year.

After the war he trained as a teacher but, like many Germans, fell on hard times during the hyperinflation of the Weimar Republic. Eggers was forced to leave teaching, selling all his furniture just to keep his family from starving. In the 1930s he again found work as a high-school teacher, and visited Britain and France with his students, promoting international relations. But he fell foul of the Nazi Party and was denounced by six of his colleagues as a left-winger and an internationalist. Despite Eggers's distinguished war record, the Party decided to punish him by restricting him to teaching at elementary school level.

He later made up with the Nazi Party and was called for military service at the outbreak of the next war. Because of his language skills, Eggers's first posting was Oflag IV-A Hohnstein, which housed French and Polish generals. In 1940 he was transferred to Colditz Castle.

The military discipline of the POW camps in Germany was the sole responsibility of the Wehrmacht, the German armed forces, not the Nazi Party. It was a critical distinction that had so far served to protect the Allied prisoners from abuses routinely carried out by the

SS and the Gestapo. The Colditz commandants had so far managed to keep the Gestapo at arm's length. But for how much longer?

In March 1944 another Allied officer pitched up at Colditz who had also been entertained by the Gestapo in Berlin. Lieutenant Ralph Holroyd dismounted from a German truck and was escorted through the Colditz cobblestone courtyard.

Captain Julius Green was among the POWs pressed against the iron window bars eager for a first glimpse of the new prisoner. As Green watched Holroyd being marched into the castle *hof*, he recalled that Brown had warned him about an Australian lieutenant he had met in Berlin.

Lt Walter Purdy. Photographed in Berlin in 1943 while working as a radio broadcaster for the Nazis' New British Broadcasting Service, a title deliberately chosen to borrow from and challenge the authority of the BBC. © The National Archives

John 'Busty' Brown. Battery Quartermaster Sergeant and MI9 agent who tracked down British collaborators in Berlin, including Walter Purdy, John Amery and Thomas Heller Cooper. His resourcefulness, courage and intelligence were underestimated by both the Germans and the British. © *In Durance Vile*. John Borrie

Army dentist Captain
Julius Green. Green is
wearing glasses on the
right of Major General
Irwin Rommel and Major
General Victor Fortune
after the surrender to
Rommel at Saint-Valery-
en-Caux on 12 June 1940.
© Topfoto

Green was later sent to
Colditz (Oflag IVC), from
where the Germans boasted
there was no escape.
© The Museum of Military Medicine

1671 Oflag IVC

Walter Purdy seated in the middle of a group of POWs at Kommando 999, the Nazi propaganda camp for British officers in Zehlendorf, Berlin. © The National Archives

John Brown seated in the middle of the cast of a show put on at Genshagen Special Camp 517, the Nazi 'holiday' camp for British NCOs and soldiers. © Trevor Beattie

John Brown meeting the spy Lydia Oswald at Genshagen in 1943. Oswald was posing as a Swiss journalist while working for the Gestapo. © *In Durance Vile*. John Borrie

Margery Booth, the British opera singer and femme fatale who married a German journalist. Booth was recruited by MI9 and worked with John Brown. She is pictured here performing at Genshagen at Brown's invitation.
© Trevor Beattie

Alexander Heimpel, the Abwher officer and Gestapo link man who recruited Walter Purdy and planted him in Colditz to break the British codes. Pictured while serving with the 5th Chevalier (calvary) Regiment during the First World War. © Bundesarchiv

At the end of the first war Heimpel enjoyed a burgeoning career as an actor before joining the Reichswehr, the army of the Wehrmacht, and then the Gestapo. © Bundesarchiv

In 1944 Major Alexander Heimpel, who had a glass eye, withered arm and scar on his cheek, was appointed head of counter-intelligence for all POW camps. © Bundesarchiv

Group photograph of British POWs taken at Colditz Castle. From left to right, first row – Captain Richard Howe, Captain Patrick R. Reid (Escape Officer), Lt Allan (in kilt). Second row – Captain Berry, Captain Elliott, Lt Col German, Padre Platt. © P. Storie-Pugh

Captain Reinhold Eggers, the German security chief at Colditz. Eggers worked with Heimpel to plant Purdy in the castle posing as an ordinary British officer recently arrested by the Gestapo.

Lt Col Willie Tod, (4th from left) the senior British officer at Colditz, seated with Group Captain Douglas Bader (2nd from left) and Lieutenant Colonel Charles Cecil Merritt (3rd from right), the Canadian officer who interrogated Purdy at Colditz. © The Museum of Military Medicine

The MI9 team who was in secret contact with Col Tod and the other Colditz POWs. Major Headley White, far left standing, investigated Walter Purdy and worked closely with Julius Green. The unit was led by Lt Col Leslie Winterbottom (centre) and based at the Hotel Victoria, Northumberland Avenue, London. © Imperial War Museum.

Chapter 18

London Calling

Major Headley White knocked on the door of 24 Westrow Drive, Faircross, New Barking, Essex, a three-bedroom stone-built house with an attractive sitting room bay window. To the side was an attached garage and behind it a neatly tended garden and potting shed, all standard features of this smart, new development for retired Docklanders.

The woman who answered the door was in her late fifties and recently widowed. The British officer, neatly turned out in his uniform, wanted to know whether she had received any news from her son who he understood was a prisoner of war in Germany. Yes, she said; her son had written to her regularly and the officer needn't worry about him because the Germans were looking after him very well. Why did the major want to know? Did he have any news?

Walter Purdy's family believed their naval officer son was being closely guarded in a POW camp somewhere in northern Germany. Major White put Mrs Purdy's mind at rest by telling her he had no news but was making routine enquiries about prisoners of war.

Alice Purdy was happy to say that, notwithstanding his predicament, her son's letters were remarkably upbeat, full of entertaining news and high hopes of a future life after the war. In one letter, Roy (to his family he was always known as Roy) had written to say he had fallen in love with a German girl whom he was planning to marry and he couldn't wait for everyone to meet her. Mrs Purdy said she did wonder whether it was normal behaviour in a prison camp for soldiers to have relationships with German girls.

Major White agreed this did seem unusual but suggested that her son was trying to give the best possible impression about his circumstances and didn't want to worry her.

He told Alice Purdy that the purpose of his visit was pastoral, and that it was his job to check up on the families of those men unfortunate enough to be taken prisoner by the Germans. He apologised for disturbing her and after reassuring her that there was nothing to worry about, he left Mrs Purdy to her housework.

But the truth was Major White knew quite a bit more about Walter Purdy than he had let on to his mother. White, who had started the war as a bright second lieutenant in the intelligence corps, was now a senior intelligence officer with MI9. He worked closely with Leslie Winterbottom's secret MI9 department based at the Hotel Victoria, Northumberland Avenue, in central London. Winterbottom, who during peacetime had been the personal assistant to Gordon Selfridge of Selfridges fame, was in charge of the counterintelligence team liaising with the families of POWs who were secretly communicating with British intelligence. One of the families he and White had kept in particularly close contact with was that of Captain Julius Green. MI9[1] had visited Green's mother and father, Jacob and Clara Green, in Dunfermline, Scotland, to explain how vital their son was to the war effort. White couldn't reveal exactly what their son was doing as this was top secret, but he emphasised to them that they shouldn't worry if Julius suddenly started writing to them in gibberish. They should simply redirect all his letters to Winterbottom and White. It would all make perfect sense at the end of the war.

In fact Headley White was already in secret correspondence with agent Green, pretending to be an old friend called Charles Outram, while a female MI9 officer was posing as his equally fictitious girlfriend, Philippa. This secret chain of communication had been running since May 1941, and it had helped the British know quite a bit about the camps visited by Green as well as gathering useful intelligence about the German military and the Nazi economy.

From very early on, MI9 had been alerted to the possibility of collaborators in prisoner of war camps, and on 22 November 1941 White asked Green to look out for 'any information about the Indian seaman being disloyal' at Marlag und Milag. Green hadn't had much to report on that matter.[2]

But in the early weeks of 1944, White received Green's coded letter about the possibility that Walter Purdy might be a German spy who was visiting POW camps posing as a genuine prisoner.[3] MI9 had actually been tipped off about the possibility that Purdy was collaborating with the Germans the year before.

A repatriated merchant seaman had told MI5 that he was sure Walter Purdy had been collaborating at Stalag III-D.[4] This combined intelligence prompted White to write to Naval Intelligence on 29 November 1943 but his enquiry had drawn a blank. Neither the Navy nor Scotland Yard had uncovered anything about Purdy's pre-war life that raised concerns.[5]

When White received Green's coded warning about Purdy, he decided to pay Mrs Purdy a personal visit. What she had told him immediately confirmed his suspicions. The unguarded tone of Purdy's letters to his mother and the details about meeting a German girl convinced White that wherever Purdy said he was writing from, it couldn't be a prisoner-of-war camp.

As a matter of urgency, he passed Green's secret per OED, communiqué to MI5, along with a detailed memo of what he had discovered about Purdy from his mother. A few weeks later MI5, who were keeping a record of all the British renegades, which they referred to as their 'black list', wrote back to White informing him that a closer cross-check with the membership records of the British Union of Fascists had come back positive, and that Purdy's membership card showed he was a member of the Ilford branch of the BUF which he joined in 1934.

Purdy's newly discovered fascist links, combined with what White had found out from his own enquiries, should have been enough to raise a red flag with MI5. But Purdy was one of many tip-offs about pro-German POWs.

MI5 had its hands full processing all the new information, separating good intelligence from all the baseless suspicions and accusations about suspected POWs who had got too close to the Germans. Purdy's name was added to the 'black list' but it was decided to take no further action against him until he was back in Britain.

Yet Purdy posed a much higher security threat than many of the other 'black-listed' prisoners. While snooping around the prison camps, Purdy had made it his business to seek out RAF officers. One of them had told him that the British had been working on a secret weapon to bring down German night bombers. The military technology was actually very simple – a fighter aircraft would attack enemy bomber formations by flying at them while towing a proximity fused bomb attached by a metal cable. The bomb was electronically detonated when it made 'contact' with the enemy bomber aircraft. Purdy took careful and detailed notes of everything that he had been told. What he couldn't have known was that his intelligence discovery was very real, and had once been given a high priority by the British government. It concerned an anti-aircraft device which the Air Ministry had been seriously considering during the height of the Blitz, but was later rejected as being too impractical.

Purdy could tell from the bombed-out buildings all around him that the Germans were taking a pasting from the British and American bombers. A revolutionary anti-aircraft weapon with the power to destroy several aircraft in one explosion in mid-air would surely bring the raids to an end.

But Purdy wasn't going to give away his secret weapon to the Germans cheaply. The Luftwaffe and Captain Heimpel would of course be interested, but Purdy doubted they would pay him for the intelligence. Instead he intended to write directly to Heinkel, the German aircraft manufacturer, to enquire whether the company would buy the plans from him. Purdy had made references in his diary to meetings with a mysterious man called 'Emil'. Could this have been Major Emil Kliemann, a senior Abwehr officer based in Paris who ran a number of agents including Ronald 'Ronnie' Seth and Nathalie 'Lily' Sergueiew?[6] Both were double agents actually working for the British. Sergueiew, known by her British handlers as Agent Treasure, played a vital role in the operation to deceive the Germans about the date and location of the D-Day landings. Kliemann was based in Paris, where he also had a senior role in Luftwaffe intelligence, but regularly visited Berlin to report to Abwehr headquarters. Was Kliemann the mysterious German that Purdy was meeting in order to cut a profitable deal for himself in return for the sale of his secret weapon?

Chapter 19

Traitors of St George

Busty Brown was too busy keeping track of all the British POWs being tapped up by the Germans at Genshagen to worry any more about Purdy. It seemed to Brown that he was surrounded by scores of British servicemen who, for the promise of better food and a walk around the Reichssportfeld, were prepared to throw their lot in with the Germans. His regular reports to MI9 meant the War Office and the Cabinet were now at least apprised of the threat posed to Britain by the Nazi collaboration operation.

Soon news of the existence of the 'holiday camps' reached Parliament where an MP had tabled a question in the House of Commons asking the government what it intended to do about 'the propaganda camp known as Genshagen'.

It was a question that ministers struggled to answer. Neither Brown nor his spymasters knew exactly why the Germans needed so many collaborators, most of whom seemed to be drawn from the rough and ready ranks of the British Army. Very few of them would make suitable broadcasters or spies.

A few weeks later, Brown stumbled across the answer – and what he discovered placed him at the centre of an operation that had serious ramifications for the next stage of the war.

Brown had recently become friendly with a young soldier from Bournemouth called Carl Britten,[1] who was being leant on by Heimpel and some of the British collaborators to work for the Germans. Brown, without giving away his own position, did his usual thing and tried to dissuade Britten from being tempted by the German inducements. Their discussions had run intermittently for a few weeks as Britten teetered on returning to the British fold.

During this time, Britten contracted a disease, possibly Crohn's,[2] and became gravely ill. The German doctors said he had just a few days to live.

Brown sat by his bedside for several nights comforting the young soldier, who was by now very weak. In this time the two men had grown very close. Brown had promised to take care of his affairs in camp and make sure his family received his final letters.

Then one night Britten sat up in his bunk and clutched Brown's arm: 'John, I believe I'm very ill and will probably die, so I want you to know what's going on here. I want you to listen because you have been decent while I have been ill.'[3]

Brown promised whatever he told him he would treat confidentially and Britten began opening up: 'Do you realise that most of us on the staff [of the German side of the camp] are either British fascists or violently anti-British?'

Brown nodded.

'Well, we've been going into Berlin to meet some high officials of the German Foreign Office, and it's their intention to start a British Free Corps for blokes like us with anti-British, anti-Bolshevik feelings… we'd become officers and get the plum jobs. It means I'd have freedom to go where I wanted and get any woman I want. We're going to have different badges to the ordinary Waffen-SS. Everybody will be able to see we are English. Our shoulder flashes will read "British Free Corps" and above a Union Jack, instead of the SS flashes on the lapels, they'll be lions from the Royal Standard.'[4]

Brown was stunned by what the dying Britten had confided in him. This was what Heimpel and his henchmen had been up to all along. The purpose of the holiday camps hadn't been to win over wavering soldiers to National Socialism but to establish an elite force of British fighting soldiers to form a British unit in the Waffen-SS.

The truth, however, was even more shocking than Brown could imagine. The original idea for the British Free Corps had come from the son of a member of Winston Churchill's cabinet, John Amery, whose father was the serving British Secretary of State for India. Leo Amery had struggled to control his tearaway son. Like his father, John was sent to Harrow but left after only one year, being described by his housemaster as 'without doubt, the most difficult boy I have ever tried to manage'. He later embarked on a desultory career in film production, each company he set up collapsing into financial disaster. Finally, his raucous living, heavy drinking and fraudulent dealings ended in bankruptcy. To escape his financial troubles and an impetuous marriage to a prostitute, he left Britain for France in 1936 where he fell under the spell of a leading French fascist called Jacques Doriot.

When war was declared, Amery was still in France, where he had hardened his interest in fascism and anti-Semitism, even though he was of Jewish heritage. (His father was Jewish on his mother's side.) In 1942, Amery was invited to Berlin by Dr Fritz Hesse of the German Foreign Office, who wanted to know whether they might share any mutual interests that would allow them to work together to help both their nations. Amery, who had been trying to get Berlin to take him seriously for nearly two years, told Hesse that he was sure they did. Amery immediately volunteered to broadcast for the Germans with the aim of fostering a closer understanding between the Anglo-Saxon peoples. Hesse agreed and arranged for Amery to perform a series of broadcasts and speeches at staged public events in France and Germany, which were filmed and exploited for their propaganda value.

Amery insisted on doing more, and asked permission to go into the POW camps so he could speak directly to the soldiers. Hesse made the arrangements. During these visits, Amery became convinced that he could make a much greater contribution to National Socialism by recruiting British soldiers for the German Army. Realising that this would be problematic, for the British Nazi sympathisers he told Hesse his idea was to establish a unit of British soldiers to fight the communists in the east – not their countrymen in the west. He even had a name for his new army – the Legion of St George[5] – and he volunteered himself to be its commander-in-chief. Hesse was delighted by the plan and congratulated Amery on his idea. News that the son of a British minister was going to command a detachment of British soldiers against the Russians was enthusiastically received in Berlin. It was an extraordinary plan which Hesse recognised would have huge military, political and propaganda value for the Wehrmacht.

Hitler gave it his personal blessing with a communiqué to Hesse:[6] 'The Führer is in agreement with the establishment of the English legion of former members of the English Fascist Party or those with similar ideology,' but added the unrealistic stipulation that the recruits must be of 'quality not quantity'.

Flattered by the Führer's imprimatur, Amery began planning his Legion of St George. Amery told Hesse he aimed to form a division of 5,000 men very quickly. But Hesse still required the cooperation of Heinrich Himmler, the head of the SS. Himmler had already successfully established Waffen-SS units fielding citizens from countries in occupied Europe. Hesse told Himmler that since there were combat divisions of Danish, French, Ukrainian and Dutch soldiers serving with the SS – why not the British?

Himmler, who quickly recognised the political value of such an enterprise, agreed and suggested calling the new force the British Legion, until he was advised that such an organisation, a long-established charity for old soldiers, already existed in England. Himmler delegated responsibility for the new British division to Brigadeführer Gottlob Berger, who had demonstrated to his SS boss to have both the cunning drive and bureaucratic skills to turn Himmler's orders into practical military success.

But first, the Germans would need to select and recruit suitable candidates. Hesse was dubious about letting Amery in the camps and after a number of failed ventures when he was booed off the stage, the Foreign Office decided to make use of the offices of Stalag III-D in Berlin which was already working with Irish, French and Russian collaboration camps.[7]

Hesse and Ziegfeld, from the Foreign Office's England Committee, with the support of Amery, would select the most suitable candidates from those that had been softened up at Genshagen. Instead of Amery's Legion of St George, Hesse favoured the name British Free Corps (BFC).

Britten may not have been able to tell Brown the full Nazi plan for the BFC, but Brown now knew enough to warn London of the BFC and some of its leaders. And in John Amery he had the name of a very dangerous high-profile collaborator.

When Brown's coded message reached MI9 a few weeks later, the news caused considerable consternation in Whitehall. Winterbottom marked the intelligence as the highest priority and made sure it crossed his boss Norman Crockatt's desk immediately.

A few days later, the British cabinet was told of the Nazi operation to recruit a division of British SS soldiers to fight alongside the Germans. Churchill recognised the potential damage it would do to British morale, especially among the forces serving on the front lines. MI5 estimated that a new SS unit of British and Commonwealth soldiers could number as many as 8,000 fighters, 3,000 more than Amery had actually promised.[8] British and American forces were already fighting their way through Italy. But with the D-Day Landings just a few months away, the British could not take the risk that the first hostile units encountered by the Allied assault troops would be made up of British soldiers in SS uniforms. It was only thanks to the intelligence supplied by MI9's agent in Berlin that the War Office planners were now forewarned.

MI9 messaged back to Brown, ordering him to do all he could to stop the BFC from becoming a fighting unit: 'Congratulations on your startling information. You must carry on. Get all the information, including names and numbers of suborned British POWs, and without fail you must sabotage the whole thing.'

Brown and his staff now knew they were in a race against time to thwart the Nazi BFC recruitment plan.

Crockatt and Winterbottom decided the best approach would be to sever the dragon's head and eliminate John Amery. But first they would have to find the aristocratic traitor, so they ordered Brown to locate Amery in Berlin and get incontrovertible proof that it was really him. Brown suddenly found himself promoted to MI9 spycatcher.

Amery had so far proved very illusive. Brown remembered Joyce had spoken of him in unflattering terms and been particularly critical of his speeches. But no one seemed to know where he was. During his speaking tours of occupied Europe, Amery had adopted a number of false names. His favourite alias was John Brown. So John Brown was looking for an Englishman also called John Brown in Berlin! Brown cursed the MI9 order as he thought it must have been obvious to British intelligence who John Amery was. But he said to himself 'orders were orders'. His only hope was that Amery would somehow advertise his presence in the city. The depravity that had coloured Amery's social life before the war had followed him to Germany. When Amery had first arrived in Berlin, he frequented the same drinking haunts as the Joyces and the rest of British collaborati – the Foreign Press Club and the Kaiserhof Hotel. Amery liked to be drunk (he liked to drink a bottle of gin a night) and his behaviour had become increasingly erratic and sometimes violent. One evening he took his excessive drinking too far.

After a day's carousing in the bars of Berlin in April 1942, Amery, already married twice, ended up in a blazing row with his French girlfriend, Jeanine Barde.

Barde, a high-class prostitute whom Amery had treated badly, was also the worse for wear for drink and, after shouting abuse at Amery, left the bar to return to their hotel room. That was the last time she was seen alive.

The following morning Amery claimed he found her dead beside him in bed, asphyxiated on her own vomit. Plenty thought he had had a direct hand in her death.

The Berlin police were called to the hotel and Amery was interviewed as the prime murder suspect. Amery's first thought was to call his friends at the Foreign Office to bail him out. Fritz Hesse managed to clear up the political mess and ensure his prize propaganda asset escaped any criminal culpability, but Amery was moved out of Berlin for a while. Hesse warned him that he had been lucky this time and if it happened again he may not be able to save him. The incident had heightened Amery's growing sense that his crimes and treachery would one day catch up with him. It had also made him more careful. He continued his drinking and womanising, but this time more discreetly and often in the confines of his hotel room.

Hesse and Heimpel could see that Amery was fast becoming a liability and judged he may have outlived his usefulness in terms of the formation of the BFC. They decided to step up efforts to recruit more British soldiers from the Genshagen POW complement.

The pretence that Genshagen was a holiday camp for British POWs who deserved a rest was dropped. Approaches to POWs were much more direct and forceful, and were accompanied by implied threats and inducements.

Chapter 20

To Trap a Traitor

All members of the BFC were required to carry and sign the following statement: 'I, (name), being a British subject, consider it my duty to offer my services in the common European struggle against communism, and hereby apply to enlist in the British Free Corps.' This signed statement permitted the signatory to receive pay books, military rations and all the other benefits conferred on soldiers of the Waffen-SS.[1] It was an offer that a growing number of POWs were finding hard to resist – especially those who had nothing much to look forward to back in Britain.

Heimpel and Lange also brought in a number of SS men to help turn the British recruits into a combat unit.

One morning Lange called Brown into his office for a meeting. Sitting on a wooden chair in the corner of the room was a Waffen-SS Oberscharführer introduced by Lange as Thomas Böttcher, who remained conspicuously silent while Brown and Lange conversed in English. The next day, Böttcher came to see Brown in his room to introduce himself more informally. Böttcher was a hardened soldier who had the SS tattoo, a small black ink SS insignia stamped on the underside of his left arm. He had trained as a member of the SS Totenkopf ('Death's Head') Division which had been assigned to guard the first Nazi concentration camps. Stationed in Poland, Böttcher took part in the rounding up of Jews, including women and children, who were sent to the death camps or murdered in street executions. Böttcher boasted he had once been in charge of a group of Ukrainian SS soldiers who had proudly told their commander that to save on ammunition 'we have found a new way of killing Jews'.[2] The soldiers systematically went through a block of flats in Warsaw throwing suspected Jews out of the windows. Most recently, Böttcher had served on the Eastern Front where he suffered a leg wound fighting the Russians. The Nazis decided to bring him back to Berlin so he could help lick the BFC into shape. There was something else about Böttcher which made him the perfect candidate for this job – he was British, and his real name was Thomas Cooper.

The British SS sergeant was born in 1919 in Chiswick to an English father, Ashley Cooper, and a German mother, Anna Maria (née Simon). The couple had met in Berlin. Cooper attended the public school Latymer Upper School, Hammersmith, and after leaving in 1936, attempted to find work with the police and the military. He was rejected by the Metropolitan Police, the Royal Navy and the Royal Air Force; on each occasion the reason given was that he had a German mother. Extremely resentful of his treatment, Cooper joined the British Union of Fascists in September 1938.[3]

A fluent German speaker, Cooper also contacted the German Academic Exchange Organisation in Russell Square, London.

In the summer of 1939, he was offered a place at the Reich Labour Service (RAD) office in Stuttgart. Finding himself in Germany when war was declared, Cooper was arrested as an enemy alien, but once he was able to prove his German heritage, he was released. Nevertheless, Cooper's papers found their way to SS-Hauptamt, SS headquarters, where they were read by Gottlob Berger, who as we have discovered was in charge of Waffen-SS recruitment. Because of Cooper's British nationality, he was barred from serving in the Wehrmacht military so Berger suggested he join one of the foreign divisions of the Waffen-SS, which had no such prohibition on non-Germans.

Brown listened intently to the story of the British fascist turned Nazi. To some degree, he could see that Cooper was a fellow traveller, and the two men eagerly swapped stories about Oswald Mosley and the British Nazis with Brown exaggerating his closeness to Joyce and the BUF. The loquacious Cooper told how he had been frustrated at earning 50 bob a week for 'some bloody Jewish timber merchants' with no sign of promotion, and so threw his lot in with Mosley: 'I took part in several meetings in the East End and had the satisfaction of helping smash up a few Jewish shops.'[4]

Brown was curious to know what Cooper intended to do at Genshagen. Cooper told him: 'I came here for a short holiday but I'm hoping to get a job on staff.'

'Doing what?' asked Brown.

'That I can't say at the moment. But when you do find out I hope you'll be willing to help.'

Brown was careful not to let on that he had already discovered the Germans were using Genshagen as a recruitment camp for the BFC. He now suspected that Heimpel and Lange wanted to replace him with Cooper. And he couldn't let that happen.

In return for helping to set up the BFC, Heimpel had promised Cooper the command of a German garrison based in London when the Germans won the war. But first he was told to enjoy a holiday snooping around Genshagen.

Cooper was going to be a problem – unless of course Brown could use the SS thug to his own advantage, and help with the mission to locate John Amery. Once Brown had told Cooper how much he had been enjoying listening again to some of Amery's speeches, it didn't take long before Cooper was bragging about how close he was to the self-appointed leader of the Legion of St George.

When Brown asked if he thought it was possible for him to meet Amery, the SS man said it would be no problem for him to arrange something in Berlin. A few days later Brown, Cooper and Amery were sitting in the lounge bar of the Hotel Adlon. Amery was accompanied by a new French girlfriend who Brown noted was heavily made up and wearing a dress that left little to the imagination.

The British fascist son of a Cabinet minister was short, smelt strongly of aftershave and had perfectly manicured fingernails. He immediately produced two bottles of French brandy, which he claimed to have purchased expensively on the black market.

Amery appeared pleased to be meeting Brown, who he imagined was helping with the discipline and enlisting of the new recruits. Brown was equally pleased to finally clap eyes on Amery, but how was he going to positively identify the British traitor to MI9?

'I was anxious to meet you,' began Amery, 'as I have heard so much about you from Tom Cooper, Dr Hesse and several others.'[5]

Amery was under the impression they were to discuss the formation of the BFC, and proceeded to tell Brown all about the new organisation, which he claimed already numbered 200 members. This was going to be easier than Brown had envisaged.

Amery said that that very morning he had had a meeting with Himmler where he told the leader of the SS that he was confident of reaching 'a minimum of five thousand ex-prisoners'.

Brown knew immediately that Amery was lying, as his own intelligence suggested that they had no more than 30 collaborators willing to fight for the Nazis.

Once Amery had confirmed his integral role with the BFC, Brown changed the subject of their conservation and began praising the new book Amery had just published, which was being distributed among the POW camps.

'By the way, Mr Amery, will you let me congratulate you on the excellent book you have written.'

'Do you like it?'

'Yes, very much indeed.'

'What do the other men think about it?'[6]

'They like it too, but there seems to be some doubt in their minds as to whether John Amery really did write it. Many of them say it must be written by a German.'

Amery, now fired up with brandy, reacted angrily to the suggestion that his great work might have been ghostwritten by one of Goebbels's men.

'That's a bloody silly thing to say – ask Tom [Cooper] whether I wrote it or not.'

Brown reassured Amery that he believed Amery to be the author; it was only the other POWs who needed convincing.

'How am I going to do that?' asked Amery.

'Well, you would have to give me some kind of proof of your identity.'

Almost immediately, Amery fished his passport out of his breast pocket and nonchalantly flung it onto the table, knocking over one of the brandy glasses. Brown picked it up, opened it and slid it back to Amery saying that he didn't think that would be necessary. Amery's word was good enough for him to report back to the other men. Shortly afterwards, the meeting broke up and Amery, Cooper and Amery's girlfriend headed off to another hotel and another bar. Brown, who had memorised the passport number, messaged London and confirmed Amery's identity.

The next time the three men would all be together, two of them would be on trial for their lives.

Chapter 21

An Officer but Not a Gentleman

The meeting with Amery had unsettled Brown. He knew that the number of BFC recruits Amery claimed to have recruited could not have come from Genshagen. Was it possible that the Germans had set up other 'holiday camps' he didn't know about? A few miles from Genshagen at Luckenwalde was a secret interrogation centre administered by Stalag III-D and overseen by Lange under Heimpel's authority. It too was in the business of turning POWs into members of the BFC. But unlike the holiday camps of Genshagen and Kommando 999 in Zehlendorf (the officers' camp), Luckenwalde used coercive methods to indoctrinate and subvert British POWs. Some of the experimental techniques were in breach of the Geneva Conventions. Several British soldiers had been forced into having sex with German women and then told this constituted a serious military offence. Lange offered them the choice of a court martial or joining the BFC. Others were brought to the camp shortly after capture and held in solitary confinement where the interrogators used threats to pressure them into signing on with the BFC.

Even if Brown had known what was going on at Luckenwalde there would have been little he could have done about it. The quartermaster sergeant was kept very busy at Genshagen fending off Cooper's close interest in his activities. Cooper was shortly joined by other British soldiers who were part of the BFC advance guard. They too needed to be closely watched. Brown told Bombardier

Blewitt and Gunner Beattie, two of his trusted staff, about the arrival of Cooper and the other British SS men, and warned them to be careful not to betray their real motives or put at risk any of their intelligence-gathering and counter-recruitment activities.

He suggested a policy of keeping their heads down until the heat was off. It was during this hiatus that another British soldier suddenly appeared at Genshagen – one who would prove to be even more troublesome than Cooper.

Lieutenant John Boucicault de Suffield Calthrop[1] was the son of the famous stage and screen actor Donald Calthrop. Before the war he occupied his time on the fringes of the London film industry, but like John Amery, he was more playboy than director or producer and had little filmic output to his name. Calthrop was much more interested in politics. In 1930 he became friendly with Oswald Mosley and in 1936 volunteered to join Franco's fascist forces fighting in Spain. When Britain declared war on Germany in 1939, he reluctantly followed his regiment, the Royal Sussex, into battle and was promptly captured in France in May 1940. He was held in a series of camps before persuading his senior British officer to let him volunteer for one of the German film units on the pretext he could dig out intelligence which might help the Allies. But his fascist background, especially his work with Mosley and Franco, made him a target for the German recruiters.

As soon as he was out of the camp and beyond the influence and discipline of the British officers, the Germans had him transferred to Berlin, where he was entertained by Hesse and Ziegfeld who in turn handed him over to Heimpel, who wanted to use him as a camp spy. Heimpel arranged for Calthrop to be issued with a countrywide freedom pass personally signed by Himmler so he could visit British POW camps unhindered. But when the British officers in one camp heard him speaking in support of the Nazis, they threatened to kill him. He was lucky to escape with his life and was returned to the Germans. He later claimed he was trying to find ways to bring the German and British peoples together.[2] But the truth was Calthrop had allowed himself to be passed up the German chain of military intelligence.

At Stalag III-D headquarters in Steglitz, Heimpel introduced him to his only other British officer collaborator, Walter Purdy. He suggested that the two men should get to know each other and booked a table at a hotel in the Kantstrasse district of Berlin.[3] As they sat downing brandies in the main bar, the two men eyed each other warily, neither sure of the other. Purdy liked to work alone and was suspicious of another officer being so feted by the Germans, and Calthrop didn't trust the jumped-up naval officer who was lording it in Berlin.

On 20 April 1944 Calthrop pitched up at Genshagen. Brown[4] was away on a shopping trip to Berlin and so the British officer was met by Bombardier Blewitt. All attempts by the inquisitive Calthrop to find out more about the camp from Blewitt were rebuffed with the response that he must wait for Brown's return from the city. Brown's men contained the British officer for most of the day before he left the camp for a meeting with Heimpel at Steglitz.

As soon as Brown returned, Blewitt and Beattie briefed him about all they knew of the inquisitive Calthrop. He had been asking a lot of questions and especially wanted to know about Brown whom Calthrop called the 'camp commandant'.

The following day Calthrop returned to Genshagen where he found Brown in his room working on a schedule for the weekend's entertainment. Calthrop said he was pleased to have at last made Brown's acquaintance. Then he came to the point. He was taking charge. Brown could carry on with his work as camp leader but Calthrop, as an officer, was to be the senior soldier at Genshagen.[5]

Brown immediately smelt a rat. What was a British officer doing at Genshagen holiday camp when there was a separate camp specially designated for British officers at Kommando 999? Brown challenged Calthrop about this, eliciting the explanation that he had been given express authority by another senior British officer to come to the camp to further his interest in a film project he was working on. He said he wanted to tighten up discipline at Genshagen, which he said was slack, even for a 'holiday camp'.

Brown, who regarded Calthrop pompous and conceited, had no choice but to defer to his rank, and decided to adopt a policy of non-cooperation with the interfering office.

Brown sensed Heimpel's hand in the new appointment; Calthrop spoke good German and was the only member of staff authorised to use the camp telephone. Whenever he spoke to Brown and the other men, he praised the German government and denigrated the Jews.

Brown later told MI5, 'At no time did I tell Calthrop I was in communication with England. I did not take him into my confidence because I did not trust him. Nor did I regard him as a credit to the rank of officer.'[6]

Brown's suspicions were soon justified. Intelligence reached Brown that Calthrop had been seen in Berlin at the Foreign Office wearing civilian clothes.

Calthrop further gave himself away during a visit to Genshagen by a number of Nazi VIPs, including a delegation of Wehrmacht officers led by Dr Ziegfeld.

Brown had arranged a musical and a short play to entertain the men and their German guests. After Margery Booth's regular visits to Genshagen, it had become customary at the end of each show for the camp band to strike up 'Land of Hope and Glory'. But this time, when the band leader rose to his feet to begin conducting the British anthem, Calthrop leapt from his seat and rushed over to the pit, motioning to the band to sit down.

Calthrop explained to Brown afterwards that it would be in 'bad taste' to play a national song in the presence of such high-ranking Germans. Brown was furious and demanded Calthrop put the order in writing. Brown kept the piece of paper, which had been deliberately signed Captain Calthrop, not Lieutenant, his true British rank, as evidence of his collaboration.

Shortly afterwards, Calthrop posted an announcement on the camp noticeboard offering to pay British POWs 1,000 Reichsmarks for their services if they agreed to take part in his propaganda films. For many men, this was a temptation hard to resist. But Brown warned them that the bribe was the slippery slope to collaboration.

Brown now had two very different German agents to worry about – the thuggish, guileless Cooper and the arrogant but dangerous Calthrop.

Cooper he could handle himself, but he would need help neutralising Calthrop. So Brown enlisted the services of Margery Booth.

Booth had remained in Berlin, where she continued to entertain the higher ranks of the Nazi Party with her operatic performances at the Berlin State Opera. Even after Goebbels ordered its closure in 1944, Booth was invited to make special appearances at various concert buildings in the city.

And despite living and working among the Nazis, she still managed to send important documents back to London. Now, Brown was in need of her help and arranged for Booth to sing at the next camp show. After her performance, Brown introduced her to Calthrop, who became instantly infatuated with the Wigan songstress, and very shortly the British officer was making a fool of himself kissing and cuddling Booth in front of the men. Brown gleefully recorded all Calthrop's inappropriate behaviour with Booth, as he felt sure he would be able to use it against him. Calthrop's involvement with Booth, who had kept him busy with invitations to the city, left the interfering officer with little time or inclination to bother Brown.

The British quartermaster permitted himself a rare moment of self-congratulation in the belief he had now neutralised both threats to his operations – Cooper and Calthrop.

But Brown had forgotten about the British officer who represented the most dangerous threat to MI9 operations in Berlin.

Lieutenant Walter Purdy was still Heimpel's eyes and ears among the POWs working for the Germans. He had licence to investigate and report on anyone he suspected of working against German interests in the camps.

Purdy had particular concerns about one officer: Squadron Leader George Carpenter, who reported directly to Stalag III-D. Carpenter had allowed the Germans to mistakenly believe he was a relative of Winston Churchill, and they had put pressure on him to broadcast for them. But the RAF officer resisted, holding out for the prospect of working with Goebbels at a later date. Heimpel, who overvalued the importance of British collaborators who were officers, showered Carpenter with privileges, allowing him to live in a Berlin hotel rather than with his other spies in a Wehrmacht house. Carpenter used this freedom to make contact with some of the pro-Nazi POWs and had uncovered the German plans for a BFC after snooping around one of the hotels used to entertain collaborators.

Carpenter's activities in Berlin had aroused Purdy's suspicion. The naval officer approached Carpenter, threatening to tell Heimpel that he believed he was a British spy.[7] Carpenter immediately denied the allegation and told Purdy he was being a bloody fool. Soon afterwards, the RAF officer was arrested and sent to a POW camp in Sagan, Stalag Luft III, the site of the Great Escape, in which 50 British officers were murdered by the Gestapo.

Chapter 22

Castle of No Escape

Colditz had been a thorn in the side of the Germans for more than four years. Two hundred Wehrmacht soldiers stationed in the castle, together with an SS battalion[1] quartered in the town, were tied up guarding around 220 prisoners, a greater guard/prisoner ratio than any other camp. Whenever one of the prisoners escaped, hundreds of desperately needed soldiers and Volkssturm, the national militia, were diverted from other vital wartime duties.

Throughout these years the Colditz coders had remained in uninterrupted contact with London, sending important information about potential Allied bombing targets and the movement and sighting of German military units.

The Colditz coders also passed on intelligence[2] about the locations of U-boat bases, anti-aircraft defences and Luftwaffe airfields – often reported by captured RAF officers who saw as much from the ground after capture as they had from the air.

It was a secret communication from Colditz sent by Captain Rupert Barry that uncovered the fate of six commandos captured after carrying out a secret mission to blow up a Nazi hydroelectricity plant in Norway. The commandos had been closely guarded in the Colditz town jail, and were later brought up to the castle to be photographed in the prison courtyard. They were prohibited from mixing with the other prisoners, but they managed to get a message to one of the British officers about their true identities and mission (Operation Musketoon). These details[3] were sent by Barry in a coded letter back to London. Three days later, a bus arrived and the commandos were driven away under escort for interrogation at the Reich Central Security Headquarters (Reichssicherheitshauptamt or RSHA) in Berlin and then taken to Sachsenhausen concentration camp where they were held in the medical block. The morning after they arrived, the commandos were told to assemble outside the building. They were lined up, and then each one was shot in the back of the head by an SS guard and their bodies burnt.

Barry's message was important because the Germans maintained that all six had died in an exchange of fire during the Norway operation. The Nazis committed atrocities to wage a total war against their enemies, but Britain continued to retain the upper hand in intelligence – even inside the Nazis' highest security prison.

This German military intelligence failure, coupled with a growing suspicion that the Abwehr was anti-Nazi and defeatist, moved Hitler to act. On 18 February 1944 the Führer signed a decree dissolving the Abwehr and handing its powers to The Reich Security Main Office headed by Heinrich Himmler in his dual capacity as Chef der Deutschen Polizei (Chief of German Police, including the Gestapo) and Reichsführer-SS (leader of the Nazi Party's Schutzstaffel [SS]).

Alexander Heimpel's position within the Abwehr was delicate, as he had been answering directly to both Wehrmacht generals and the Gestapo.[4] Some of his colleagues, including the head of the Abwehr, Wilhelm Canaris, had been removed from office and placed under house arrest, their roles handed to Gestapo men.

Heimpel may have been petty and vindictive, but above all else he was a survivor who had learned how to play the Wehrmacht generals off against the secret police. Moreover, he was an officer with a reputation for being a ruthless, uncomplicated Nazi whom the Gestapo could trust.

In Hitler's purge of the Abwehr, Heimpel emerged as one of the few winners.

And so, in 1944 the 52-year-old intelligence officer suddenly found himself head of counter-intelligence for all POW camps,[5] which meant his responsibilities now extended beyond the affairs of Genshagen and Stalag III-D. And his new role came with a promotion from Rittmeister to a full Wehrmacht major.

Heimpel was expected to justify the faith his Nazi bosses had placed in him by delivering results, and one mark of achievement would be to secure an intelligence breakthrough from inside Germany's most important POW camp.

A few days after Hitler had signed the order abolishing the Abwehr, Heimpel wrote to the Colditz security officer Reinhold Eggers briefing him about his new role as head of POW counter-intelligence and proposing a secret mission to crack the escape lines linking Colditz to the other POW camps and the underground networks.

Heimpel told Eggers that he intended to place informants inside the castle. Eggers, who had spent four years trying to break the British codes, resented Heimpel and the Gestapo muscling in on his work. He reminded Heimpel that the last time the Gestapo tried this, it ended badly: a French Nazi called Rudi Reichoffen[6] was planted in the camp in the summer of 1943, but was rumbled by his fellow officers and had to be spirited out of the castle by the Germans under threat of death. Reichoffen eventually joined a Waffen-SS unit. Then there was the Polish informant Bednarski, who had also only narrowly escaped being murdered by his own side. But Eggers was realistic enough to know this was not the time to resist a Nazi fanatic like Alexander Heimpel.

Towards the close of 1943, morale among the British POWs at Colditz had hit rock bottom.[7] The last successful escape had taken place the year before on 14 October 1942, when Pat Reid and three other British officers had got away through the camp kitchens. All hopes now hung on one of the most audacious escape attempts of the war. Lieutenant Michael Sinclair, a fluent German speaker, had spent months practising an impersonation of one of the camp guards,

Stabsfeldwebel (Sergeant Major) Franz Rothenberger, who was better known among the Germans and British as 'Franz Joseph' for his strong resemblance to Franz Joseph, the former Austrian emperor. On the evening of 19 May 1943, Sinclair and his two 'guards', John Hyde-Thomson and Lancelot Pope, both good German speakers, sneaked out of their rooms and crept into the main yard. Twenty British prisoners waited in the prison block for the signal that the German sentries had been 'relieved'. If Sinclair could succeed in opening the gates, dozens of POWs were ready to make their home runs. At the main gate, Sinclair successfully stood down one sentry and then another, their places taken by the British POWs dressed in German uniforms. But on the second post one of the guards became suspicious[8] and raised the alarm. Sinclair tried to bluff his way through but the Germans had rumbled him, and he was shot down in cold blood. Sinclair recovered from his wounds and at the cessation of hostilities, the War Office mounted a war crimes investigation into the incident, naming three German guards who were blamed for shooting Sinclair when his hands were raised in surrender.[9]

After 'Franz Joseph', the British attempted several other meticulously planned escapes, but each was foiled by the Colditz guards.

The small number of prisoners who had managed to breach the castle's security were usually returned to Colditz a few days later, dashing hopes of any more British 'home runs'.

Such failures continued to fuel rumours of an informant posing as one of the POWs. But the British could no longer blame Polish and French quislings for their failed escapes. The Wehrmacht High Command had ordered that by the end of July 1943, Colditz should house only Commonwealth and some American prisoners. In June, the Dutch were moved out, followed shortly afterwards by the Poles and Belgians. The final French group left on 12 July 1943. If there was a traitor, he had to be one of their own. There were plenty of suspects to choose from. Micky Burn's pre-war enthusiasm for the Nazi brand of National Socialism had been replaced by a passion for Bolshevism. At Colditz he hosted lectures extolling the virtues of a command economy and a radical redistribution of wealth. But rather than dampen suspicions of him working for the Germans, it merely stoked them, and a number of senior officers refused junior subalterns permission to attend his 'traitor' lectures.

Meanwhile, Birendra Mazumdar had ended all interactions with the British officers, preferring the company of the Dutch. He continued to lobby the commandant for a transfer to a camp with fellow Indian officers, his contempt for the British now out in the open. The commandant refused his request, still hoping Eggers might turn him into a valuable informant. But Mazumdar responded by going on hunger strike.

There were others who also fell under suspicion.

Alex 'Jock' Ross, a bandsman in the Seaforth Highlanders, was Douglas Bader's personal medical orderly in Colditz, who each morning uncomplainingly carried the legless squadron leader from the top of the castle to the bathroom at the bottom of the stairs.

As a non-combatant medical orderly, he was entitled to repatriation after three years of captivity, and the strain of being at Bader's constant beck and call was taking its toll.

In the autumn of 1943, Ross was approached by Hauptmann Pupcke, one of the Colditz staff, and handed a letter from the Red Cross telling him that his request had been granted. Delighted at the prospect, Ross went up to Douglas Bader, who was in the Colditz hof, and broke the news to the squadron leader: 'I'm going home!'

'No you're bloody not,' Bader replied. 'You came here as my skivvy and that's what you'll stay.'

Such fundamental bad faith between officer and orderly was ripe for an approach by Eggers and his men.

Burn, Mazumdar and Ross were now among a list of obvious suspects who might have reason to give away a tunnel, a secret hiding place or expose the secret codes.

There were also lingering doubts about the camp dentist Julius Green, who had made no effort to use his codes to send secret messages while at Colditz. It was true that he had arrived at the camp in January with excellent security credentials and could now call upon a number of Colditz inmates who were happy to vouch for him. Yet questions remained about the basis upon which he had gained entry to Colditz, a prison for hardened escapers or those POWs who the Germans considered had a higher worth as hostages. Green fell into neither of these categories. For some of the British officers, it was difficult to believe that the Germans had not already identified Green as a Jew.

Since his arrival at Colditz, Green had been engaged in a plan to work his ticket back to Britain by pretending to the Germans that his four years of captivity had turned him mad. Despite a rather half-hearted performance, the Germans appeared to have fallen for it, and he was placed on the repatriation list along with a seriously injured RAF pilot who had suffered severe facial burns when his aircraft was shot down. Other officers had tried to convince the Nazis they had gone mad had attempted suicide or acted out the part of a gibbering nervous wreck for months on end. One man had cut off his penis, declaring he had no use for it in Colditz. Green had simply written to the commandant explaining that he thought the other men were all talking about him behind his back.

But while the Nazis appeared to have been taken in by Green's claim of insanity, they were more suspicious about his Presbyterian faith.[10]

It was the 'mad' dentist's misfortune that one of his Jewish relatives from Scotland had misguidedly written[11] to Green in Colditz, referring to her visit to a synagogue and how much she was looking forward to a holiday she was planning during Passover. The camp censors picked up on these references and Green was summoned to a meeting with Eggers.

Green tried to play dumb but Eggers wasn't having any of it and he ordered the British officer to be subjected to a full medical inspection with a view to determining whether he was circumcised.

The dentist was taken to the Stabsarzt's (Staff Surgeon) room accompanied by the British medical officer Captain Dickie. He was told to stand next to a chair and take down his trousers. The Stabsarzt then moved the chair next to Green and with medical instrument in hand prodded Green's manhood. It was an utterly unnecessary procedure as it was plain to see that Green was circumcised. Green and Dickie had foreseen this and pretended to act unsurprised when the German doctor said he now had incontrovertible evidence that Green was indeed Jewish. Dickie calmly reassured the Stabsarzt that Green's medical procedure had been carried out in later life due to an embarrassing health issue. The Germans accepted this explanation, and Green returned to his quarters, minus another one of his nine lives.

Chapter 23

The Prominente

During the first months of 1944, the question as to who was the Colditz spy was no longer the local concern of a few hundred British POWs. The departure of the non-Commonwealth nationalities from Colditz made way for the arrival of a very select group of high-profile Allied prisoners. The detention of these VIP prisoners at Colditz had already attracted the personal attention of the British Prime Minister, Winston Churchill, who had been informed that one of them was his own nephew, the journalist Giles Romilly, captured in Norway in 1940. Churchill's wife, Clementine, Romilly's blood relation, was extremely agitated and asked her husband to find out more about her nephew's predicament. Churchill was told the Germans had named Romilly and the other high-value prisoners 'prominente', roughly translated as military and political celebrities. They included Lord Lascelles and John Elphinstone, nephews of King George VI and Queen Elizabeth; Captain The Lord Haig, son of World War I Field Marshal Douglas Haig; Lord Hopetoun, son of Lord Linlithgow, the Viceroy of India; Lieutenant John Winant Jr., son of John Gilbert Winant, US ambassador to Britain; Tadeusz Bór-Komorowski, commander of Armia Krajowa and the Warsaw Uprising; and five other Polish generals.

The Germans had gathered the 'prominente' together for one reason: to use them as hostages or bargaining chips in Hitler's end game as Germany faced the inevitability of defeat on the battlefield. Their identity, whereabouts, safety and eventual rescue was of paramount importance to the Allies, and could only be guaranteed if the system of secure and secret communication with the POWs was not compromised. If there was a Colditz spy working for the Germans, it was critical that British intelligence knew about him. Winston Churchill[1] asked the Secretary of State for War, James Grigg, to take a personal interest in the group. Churchill wrote to Grigg: 'Will you kindly interest yourself personally in this matter? The notes I enclose to you are written by Mrs Romilly, my sister-in-law, whose only surviving son, Giles Romilly, is in this plight. Let me know what can be done. I am far from thinking that a great outcry at this moment on the subject of these 'prominente' would necessarily be helpful. However, pray treat the matter with utmost consideration and let me know. The King also spoke to me on this subject some time ago.'

The Germans were twitchy about the prominente, keeping them locked up in their quarters for long periods of the day and all of the night. Himmler feared a British attempt to rescue them, and so stationed a rapid response unit of SS soldiers with armoured half-tracks and light tanks close to the town in case of Allied parachute landings.[2]

While both the British and the Germans were keeping a close watch on all developments in and around the castle, the significance of the arrival of a middle-aged Australian woman appeared to have gone unnoticed. Paula Holroyd had taken a room at the Colditz Hotel Goldenes Kreuz[3] in the centre of town. She had with her a letter signed by Adolf Hitler granting her permission to visit her son. The next day, 5 March 1944, she was escorted from her hotel quarters to the German officers' mess in the castle. Waiting for her was Reinhold Eggers and her son Ralph. On the table was a spread of home-made cakes and finely cut sandwiches that would have graced the Ritz Hotel in London. The official German record[4] shows that the conversation was taken up with news from Australia and family matters. But only the three participants know what was discussed while they were enjoying their afternoon tea at Colditz.

At the end of the meeting Ralph Holroyd was transferred from the quarters he had been sharing with the other prisoners and placed with the prominente.[5]

Had Heimpel finally planted his man with the group of prisoners that would prove to be the most important to Hitler in the last few months of the war?

Chapter 24

The Rat of Colditz

Three days later, on 7 March, a train pulled into Colditz town station. A British serviceman casually stepped on to the platform and waited for the German soldiers to join him. The escort party exchanged a few words with the station-master and then one of the guards pointed towards the direciton of the town. They all sauntered off along the cobbled track, making idle chatter as they went. When they reached the bridge over the River Mulde, they stopped to survey the imposing castle that loomed over the town. The group carried on through the town, across the main square and up the steep narrow passageway to the guardhouse at the castle entrance. Formalities with the sentry were perfunctory, and the prisoner was allowed to walk through the gates where he was ushered into one of the interrogation rooms in the German Kommandantur.

The next morning, the prison padre, Jock Ellison Platt, watched from his bedroom window as the new arrival was led through the prisoners' gate and solemnly marched into the Colditz hof. The guards returned to the main castle and their regular sentry duties, leaving the British officer alone, momentarily lost in the glaring spring sunlight, until he was rushed by a group of British prisoners, all at once firing questions at him.

'What was his name?' 'Where had he come from?' 'Did he have any news?'

They slapped him on the back and escorted him to see Lieutenant Colonel William Tod's adjutant.

'There was a new arrival this morning,' Platt wrote in his diary, 'which has caused quite a flutter in the naval dovecote. The story of his nine months in Berlin is something more than credible.'[1]

The naval officer whom Platt had spied entering the castle compound was Lieutenant Walter Purdy of the Royal Navy Reserve, and his story was indeed rather incredible.

Major Heimpel and Captain Eggers had come up with a cover story they felt sure would allay any suspicions and survive the kind of rigorous interrogation they expected Purdy would have to undergo.

In his final briefing with Captain Eggers, Purdy was put through his paces.

'I'll say I escaped from Oflag III-D,' Purdy told Eggers, 'and hid in Berlin for several months until I was caught in a razzia (police round-up) in the streets after an air raid.'[2]

'Well, be very careful inside the camp,' cautioned Eggers. 'You'll be a suspect until you are cleared. I think a Canadian officer, a lawyer, is in charge of POW security. Have your story ready.'

Purdy was led up the stairs into the Kellerhaus and allocated a bunk in a room with 11 other men. Dangling from the ceiling was a single light bulb under a grey metal lamp-shade illuminating a wooden table. Purdy slung his bag on the bed and prepared to unpack his carefully selected belongings which Heimpel and Eggers both agreed were typical of a British naval officer, even one who was supposed to have spent months on the run from the Gestapo.

It didn't take long for one or two of the other officers to recognise Purdy from Marlag and his first camp at Spangenberg Castle. Most had only vague recollections of Purdy. One of them was Lieutenant James Mike Moran[3] the security committee's record keeper, who remembered Purdy leaving Marlag for one of the German holiday camps but he didn't know what had happened to him after that. Lieutenant Jack Keats of the Royal Navy Volunteer Reserve also remembered him from Marlag. Father Cyril

Scarborough, who had spent two years as the Roman Catholic camp chaplain to Stalag III-D, could also recall Purdy. None of them knew Purdy well. And those who remembered anything at all were not prepared to vouch for him.

Yet one officer appeared to be very pleased to see the new arrival. Such was the enthusiasm with which Captain Julius Green welcomed Purdy to Colditz that the other prisoners thought the two men were long-lost comrades. Green immediately took the novice kriegie under his wing, showing him around the castle and insisting that he join his eating mess. Green said he would explain everything he needed to know about camp life. That evening some of the officers, including Green and Purdy, gathered in one of the rooms. An officer was sent out to stooge, or stand guard, so that he could warn the others of approaching German guards. The men all sat attentively on the bunks waiting for the stooge in the corridor to signal the all-clear. Once it had been given, an officer took out a piece of paper from his pocket and began reading out a transcription of that day's BBC news reports which had been secretly picked up from a radio smuggled into the castle. Afterwards, the group broke up for mess before retiring to their own bunk rooms for the rest of the night.

The next day, Green and Purdy remained together. Green, as promised, escorted Purdy on a guided tour of the camp. As the two men entered the first floor of the Kellerhaus, they encountered Lieutenant Ian Maclean emerging from a wooden flap opening above a stone lintel. This was the concealed entrance of a secret tunnel known as Crown Deep,[4] which had almost reached the outer walls of the castle's northern boundary. Maclean had finished his shift and was being relieved by another digger. Purdy, taken by surprise as Maclean's head popped out from the entrance, instinctively congratulated the British officer on his tunnel and how well it had been hidden from the Germans,[5] adding 'Ah, the Marlag boys are at it again.'[6] This was the tunnel upon which all the British had been pinning their escape hopes, the one that would deliver them their freedom before the end of the war.

Later that day, Lieutenant Keats told Green[7] that on another excursion, Purdy had discovered the whereabouts of the hide which contained a cache of escape equipment, the camp radio and a stash of German currency.

Purdy must have been feeling very pleased with himself. Just 36 hours into his mission and he had already uncovered enough intelligence to satisfy both Heimpel and Eggers. He would soon be back in Berlin and able to resume his life with Gretel.

Green continued to keep Purdy company and during the evening meal while they were sitting at their mess, the dentist started up a casual conversation with his old Marlag comrade.

'Where were you before you were sent to Colditz?'[8]

'I managed to escape from a holiday camp in Berlin and was recaptured after having lived in Berlin for some time,' replied Purdy, carefully sticking to his story.

At this point Green's curiosity seemed to desert him and he returned to his food.

So Purdy asked Green why he had been sent to Colditz.

'The Germans,' replied Green, 'have given me no reason but I think that it is because they suspect me of being a Jew and they may have rumbled that I was concerned in the code-letter business.'[9]

Green's openness greatly surprised Purdy but he wasn't going to look a gift horse in the mouth.

So he pressed Green further about what the dentist thought of the German holiday camps and the British POWs working in them.

Green knew plenty about Genshagen because of what Brown and the others had already told him.

Green asked: 'Did you meet a quartermaster called John Brown at the holiday camp?'

Purdy nodded.

Green then turned to Purdy and looked him straight in the eyes: 'If Brown appears to be working for the Germans, he's actually doing pretty good stuff for the British and is getting the names of people who are too friendly with or working for the Germans, back to England.'[10]

The blood drained from Purdy's face as he realised Green knew far more about the Berlin operation than he had first let on.[11] The menace in Green's expression suggested he also knew about Purdy. Suddenly Green got up and left the table. The next day Green approached Purdy at breakfast. This time there was no friendly greeting, instead, Green's tone was deliberately accusatory.

'I know exactly what you are up to in Berlin and even know where you are living. After the war you are going to be in serious trouble. I have already sent intelligence to London to warn them about you.'[12] Green then urged Purdy to come clean and tell the senior officer everything he knew about the British traitors in Berlin.

Purdy looked rattled. He tried to plead his innocence saying that he was just an ordinary POW like Green. But it was no use. Green had already passed on exactly what he knew about the traitor to Lieutenant Colonel William Tod, who arranged for Purdy to be interrogated by Colonel Merritt and Lieutenant Colonel Young that morning.

It didn't take long for the two officers to break down Purdy's story. Lieutenant Colonel Young of the Royal Engineers later told British intelligence officers: 'In accordance with our routine, I interrogated Purdy on 8 March 1944. Purdy told me that he was transferred from Marlag to the propaganda camp in Berlin. Whilst at this camp Purdy said he had escaped and had met a German woman with whom he had lived and he intended to marry as soon as possible. He claimed that whilst he was free in Berlin he had broadcast for the Allies.'

Young told Purdy he did not believe a single word of his story and that he was going to arrange for a second interview:

'Colonel Merritt and I covered the ground that Purdy had dealt with on the previous day. Purdy still maintained that he was an escapee in Berlin and that he had been arrested by the Gestapo and brought to Oflag IV-C. This was the position up to the lunch period.'[13]

After lunch, Purdy returned to the temporary interrogation room at the top of the castle, far away from prying German eyes and ears. It was during the second interview with both British interrogators that Purdy decided to make some partial admissions and told them that instead of joining an Allied underground network in Berlin he had been broadcasting propaganda for the Germans.

'After two hours' cross examination,' said Merritt, 'during which Purdy contradicted himself many times, he admitted that his whole story was a fabrication, that in fact he had left Marlag to go to a German propaganda camp from which place he had agreed to broadcast in English on behalf of the Germans and had been engaged in that work for eight months. The exact details of his duties he did not make clear and from his conversation I gathered he was a minor Lord Haw-Haw.'[14]

Merritt, who had only recently been put in charge of tunnel escape planning,[15] asked Purdy: 'Do you realise what a serious admission you have made?'

Purdy, who appeared resigned to his fate, said that he did.

The officers immediately placed Purdy under guard and passed on the findings of the interrogation to Lieutenant Colonel Tod.

The next day, Tod asked to see Purdy in his quarters.[16] Tod was extremely sensitive to the Germans' use of 'stool pigeons'. Just before the French left, he became aware of the Alsatian spy who had entered the prison and then disappeared very quickly once he had been rumbled.[17] He had always believed the Germans were trying to do the same with the British, suspicions that were confirmed when he read MI9's messages about suspected British traitors planted in the POW camps.

Purdy was led into Tod's quarters where Merritt and Young were also waiting for him.

'I understand you have admitted to have been working for the enemy,' began Tod. 'Is this true?'[18]

'Yes,' replied Purdy.

'You do realise you have been a traitor to your country?'

'Yes,' replied Purdy. 'I have behaved like a rat and a traitor… Sir, I am very sorry for everything, but you see I have this girl in Berlin who I have to get back to. I'm in love and we are going to get married. You do understand, sir, don't you?'

Tod listened to Purdy's pleadings and self-serving excuse-making for several minutes before he interrupted him.

'Will you tell the Germans about anything you see in this camp? Specifically I mean the escape tunnels and the wireless set.'

'No, I won't give away anything, you have my word.'

'But if the Germans send you back to Berlin and to the woman I understand you are living with, in return for telling them about anything you may have seen here, would you then tell them?'

Purdy remained silent.

'Well, Purdy,' urged Tod.

'I'm afraid I would.'

'In that case there is nothing I can do except look upon you as a traitor. You are to remain in your room under arrest. You will be under constant watch.'

Purdy was led out of the room.

According to Tod, a dozen officers took turns keeping watch on Purdy. Among the guard detail was Lord Hopetoun, a member of 51st (Highland) Division captured in 1940, and one of the Colditz Prominente.[19] Some of the other volunteers were naval officers like Keats who felt Purdy's treachery had sullied the reputation of the Royal Navy.

Purdy must have hoped that his confession had made his position in Colditz impossible and that it would only be a matter of time before Tod would hand him over to the Germans, who would be more than pleased with what he had to tell them. But Tod decided to wait before contacting the German commandant.

It didn't take long for the findings from Purdy's interrogation to spread through the prison. Once it emerged that a self-confessed traitor was being guarded inside Colditz, it was impossible to dampen the clamour for revenge. Keats reported back to Green that Purdy looked terrified. Green had done all he could to ensure Purdy would not leave the prison alive. Within hours of being placed under guard, Purdy had been removed from his room and taken to the top of the castle where a group of officers intended to hang him for high treason. If Purdy died, then the secrets he had uncovered would die with him.

Purdy had been given a fair chance to promise not to tell the Germans about what he had discovered, but he had point-blank refused. In the eyes of the prisoners that meant he had to die. The hanging party comprised a hard core of officers led by Captain Dick Howe, the escape officer, who had spent nearly four years in captivity and who seemed most prepared to carry out the hanging.

The hastily assembled court martial found Purdy guilty of treason and passed a death sentence on the naval officer.

Dick Howe[20] had convened the court martial, and he personally selected a group of men he felt were capable of backing him up, but when at the last minute he was unable to place the noose round Purdy's neck, suddenly none of the other officers had the stomach for a lynching either. The reality of it, in that stuffy attic room, was too much for them.

This left the British with a very serious problem. If they let Purdy live he would betray them all. Heated arguments ran into the night about how to keep their secrets while keeping Purdy alive. Green never said where he stood on the Purdy hanging, but after he told Tod what he knew about the Colditz traitor, he must have believed that the naval officer was as good as dead. He simply hadn't accounted for the British squeamishness in killing a fellow officer in cold blood.

In his statement to MI5, Tod told the intelligence officers: 'About 10 March 1944, I went to the German commandant, Lieutenant Colonel Prawitt, and told him that Purdy had admitted having worked for the Germans and that in consequence we no longer considered him a British officer and also it would be an insult to us if Purdy was allowed to remain.' He warned Prawitt: 'If you don't take Purdy into your custody, I won't be held responsible for his safety in the camp.'

After some argument, the German commandant agreed to have Purdy removed, and a few hours afterwards Purdy was taken away.

Later that night Tod sent a secret message to London alerting MI9 to Purdy's betrayal. It would take weeks to arrive.

Purdy's rough treatment at the hands of the British POWs meant the Germans had no doubts that their British 'stool pigeon' had done his job.

Meanwhile, Tod and Green had to think quickly. In Green's haste to rub Purdy's nose in his own treachery and confident that the traitor would soon be dead, Julius Green had given the game away about Brown and the Berlin operation. Purdy was sure to report all this to his German spymasters. As they couldn't kill Purdy then, they would have to come up with a plan that rendered useless everything Green had told Purdy and which Purdy would soon be telling Heimpel.

Green in particular must have been devastated. He had been living under intolerable pressure for years, as a spy, and as a Jew who had borne witness to the Nazi genocide. He had even had his dog shot in front of him. The opportunity to confront a fascist enemy and to get his own back had gone to his head. That indiscretion would not only jeopardise John Brown's life, but had tragic unforseen consequences which would, in a stunning irony, help to save Purdy from the hangman's noose a second time.

Chapter 25

Crown Deep

Two days later, a Colditz search party paid a surprise visit to the British quarters. Captain Eggers later claimed that in early March 1944, he had instructed his guards to start taking a close look at the foot of the castle clock tower. At the northwest part of the yard there were several neglected buildings and air shafts which had developed in a haphazard fashion over many years. On the ground floor of the cellar house, the Germans kept the parcel office. The above floors were occupied by the British. 'It was noticeable,' said Eggers, 'how smartly they raised the warning cry of 'goons up' when the riot squad or indeed any of us wandered in their direction.'[1]

A closer inspection of the cavity of the building led to the discovery of a number of suspicious items, including copper piping and discarded pieces of rope.

'Something was obviously going on around there but our microphones gave no sounds from the outside of the buildings of any work in progress.'[2]

Eggers decided to take no action and instead kept a watching brief on the cellar work, reasoning: 'At least it would keep them [the prisoners] occupied and so comparatively happy.'

But after the retrieval of Purdy, Eggers decided the time was right to get to the bottom of the POWs' activity in the Kellerhaus.

Eggers, a detachment of soldiers, a mason and a carpenter all filed into the entrance of the building.

'We found nothing on the ground floor or the first floor but when we came to the second floor, there in the bottom of a built-up cupboard, we did find a hide.'[3]

Three years earlier, the British had boasted to Eggers that they had over 2,000 Deutschmarks in their 'treasury', but the Germans had never come close to finding the money. In the hide the guards uncovered 2,250 Deutschmarks and 4,500 French francs plus two sacks full of fake ID cards, travel passes, escape tools and clothing. Sitting at the bottom of the hide was the most significant find of all – a miniature radio, the first radio of its kind to be uncovered in a German POW camp. Eggers now realised that such a piece of equipment could only have come into the camp by using a bribed guard or through a smuggled package from London. Which was it? Eggers reported the results of the searches to Heimpel and OKW in Dresden.

The next day Eggers led a second search party of the British quarters. German soldiers smashed their way into the base of the circular staircase in the Kellerhaus to reveal the entrance to the elusive tunnel the Germans had been searching for so long. Eggers was very pleased with the day's work, but was also careful to say he had been solely acting on a long-held hunch.

The British, however, knew exactly who had betrayed them and their precious tunnel, named Crown Deep. For Lieutenant Colonel Merritt the case against Purdy was open and shut: 'Two days after his removal from the camp a German search party entered and went straight to the site of a tunnel for which they had looked unsuccessfully for some time and discovered the entrance. They also went straight to the position of a "hide" which to my knowledge they had never suspected before. In view of the fact that in the two years I was in that camp, despite many thorough searches, the German authorities had not found any important "hide" and since this particular one had no suspicion cast upon it before, it is my opinion that Lieutenant Purdy had seen it in operation and had reported its position and that of the tunnel to the German security authorities.'

If Purdy had given away Crown Deep, he had perhaps inadvertently done the British escapers a favour.

A week later, the Gestapo murdered 50 of the RAF POWs who had taken part in the mass breakout from Stalag Luft III at Sagan, better known as the 'Great Escape'. And a few weeks afterwards, the Germans issued infamous Order K – the execution of any escaping POW.

However, one POW remained determined to escape whatever the cost. After four years of captivity, the mental strain on Lieutenant Michael Sinclair was beginning to tell. He had recently learned that his brother John had been killed in the bitter fighting on the Anzio beaches in Italy where the Allies had opened up a second front. Then in September 1944 Colonel Tod had the sombre duty of delivering the news of the death of Ronnie Littledale, who had escaped from Colditz in 1942. Sinclair's oldest and closest friend had rejoined his old regiment, the King's Royal Rifle Corps, and taken part in the Normandy landings. But three months later he was tragically killed commanding the 2nd Battalion in Airaines, France, when his Bren-gun carrier was ambushed by an SS anti-tank unit, which fired an artillery round into the vehicle killing all the occupants.[4]

Just a few days later, on 25 September 1944, Mike Sinclair made a final desperate escape bid running up and over the barbed wire in the exercise park. The young British officer had no chance of succeeding, and was gunned down before he could reach the safety of the woods. To his fellow officers it looked like suicide. A gifted academic and brave soldier, Sinclair made a total of nine escape attempts, including four from Colditz. In the end, the intolerable pressure of trying to best the Germans proved too much for him. It is hard not to feel that the failure of the hanging party to silence Purdy must have contributed in no small part to Sinclair's sense of hopelessness and his tragic death.

Eggers called the British officers into the courtyard so that he could properly explain to all of them how Sinclair had met his end.

It was an honourable[5] thing to do as he must have known feelings were running very high, and his action earned him the respect of many of the POWs. Sinclair and all the other prisoners knew the risks they were running when they climbed the wire in broad daylight and then refused to answer calls to halt. But Squadron Leader Peter Tunstall didn't see it like that and wasted no time in calling Eggers a 'bloody German schweinhund'. It was an accusation out of keeping with the mood of the sombre gathering in the prison yard. Tunstall's outburst angered Tod, who felt he had lost authority over the camp's goon-baiter-in-chief.

The discovery of the tunnel and the escape equipment were of secondary interest to Eggers and Heimpel. The Germans were confident that the precautions taken after the early escapes meant the castle's security was sufficiently secure to resist any further breaches. Order K and the brutality of the Gestapo in the wake of the Great Escape meant Eggers had other reasons to worry less about mass breakouts. As the war entered its final months, it was the British who were more concerned about escapes. With victory in sight, the War Cabinet could not countenance the needless loss of British lives, especially when Colditz housed so many VIP prisoners. MI9 sent a communication to Tod ordering him to stand down any further escape plans. For the British, as for the Germans, attention was now focused on the prominente and the MI9 codes.

None of this excused Purdy's betrayal of the British tunnel, radio, money and escape tools.

However, Heimpel was much more interested in what else his spy had to tell him. Purdy's intelligence about the existence of a British spy network operating out of Berlin, and the use of the communication codes which enabled London to communicate with such ease with the highest security prison in the Reich, was of much more value.

The information passed on to Purdy by Julius Green pointed the finger directly at John Brown. Heimpel had long suspected that the man he had put in charge of Genshagen was not the German patsy he appeared to be. If what Purdy said was true, Brown was a dangerous double agent who had been secretly corresponding with British intelligence in London while sabotaging the German collaborator recruitment programme. It explained why so few British soldiers had come forward to join the British Free Corps. Heimpel realised that Purdy's intelligence called into question the loyalty of both Brown's hand-selected Genshagen staff *and* the British Free Corps. It meant even collaborators like Thomas Cooper, who had a proven track record in the service of the Reich, may not be as loyal as they claimed.

Heimpel immediately informed Dr Ziegfeld about what Purdy had found out about Brown. At first Ziegfeld refused to believe it. The German diplomat felt he understood Brown better than Heimpel. He had formed a close relationship with the British quartermaster and the two wartime adversaries shared bonds of freemasonry and Christian brotherhood. They had spent many hours discussing the best way to bring the German and British peoples together under these ideologies. If what Heimpel was telling him was correct then he had been played for a fool. Ziegfeld told Heimpel that Brown simply didn't have the intelligence to be involved in such a devious and complex double game. But Heimpel was less convinced.

So the two Germans agreed that they should place Brown under close surveillance. If Purdy was right then Brown would lead them to the other members of the Berlin network.

Chapter 26

Honey Trap

Lydia Oswald, 38, arrived at Genshagen posing as a reporter for a Swiss magazine that had commissioned her to write an article about the holiday camp on the grounds that such a novel idea for prisoners of war had stirred up interest all over the world. John Brown, the camp leader, was on hand to welcome her and show her around. Her obvious beauty would not have escaped his attention.

British intelligence knew all about the Swiss-born Lydia Oswald.[1] She had been on Whitehall's radar since 1935, when she was arrested in northern France on espionage charges while working for German intelligence. Oswald had seduced two French naval officers, obtaining valuable intelligence about French plans. When her letters to her German handlers were decoded, they exposed her attempts to discover the secrets of two new French warships. The subsequent newspaper reports of her trial described Oswald as the 'blonde German beauty' who had tried to sink the French Navy. After her release, MI5 and the Secret Intelligence Service (MI6) kept her under close observation, and the following year caught her on a spying tour of British colonies, including India and Iraq, where she and another agent called Hans Leuenberger were posing as Swiss journalists on assignment. According to an MI5 report, they were actually engaged in arms trafficking and were subsequently denied entry to British territory. In 1941 Oswald once again came to the attention of the British when she was reported to be working for the Gestapo. Then she disappeared.

At Genshagen, Lydia Oswald told Brown she was 'anxious to find out the truth about the camp' because such a peaceful collaboration had 'excited interest' among her editors. She assured Brown that her report would be balanced and accurate, and that the Germans had made no restrictions on what she could write. Moreover, her article would be read by Dr Goebbels, who would be pleased that the 'holiday camps' were being seen as such a success in bringing the German and British peoples together.

Brown quickly succumbed to the charms of the glamorous blonde spy, accepting her invitation to participate in the reporting assignment, although he later claimed he knew he would have to 'keep his wits about him' as she might be trying 'to trap me'. The Swiss journalist and the British quartermaster soon became very close, arranging intimate meetings in central Berlin. During one of their liaisons, they found themselves caught in the middle of an RAF air raid and were forced to take refuge in a shelter beneath the Eden Hotel.

Recalled Brown: 'The raid went on for what seemed to be hours and after a time we adjourned to Lydia's room, and while we waited for the all-clear drank schnapps, raising our glasses to the gallant RAF and vilifying Hitler and his fellow maniacs.'[2]

After the air raid was over, it was too late to catch a train back to camp so Brown decided to make his way on foot: 'As I walked through the streets of Berlin I saw the desolation was complete. Buildings had fallen across the street and blocked the way. Others were in flames; it was nerve-shattering to hear the cries of the people trapped inside them. The heat from the flames was unbearable...'

Fearing that he might be stopped by the police and accused of sabotage, he decided to avoid the main roads and instead followed the railway line: 'It was quite dark when a second air raid warning came whining from the sirens. The bombs fell almost at once, and I appeared to be the target. The railway lines suddenly curled up in front and splinters began to fall around me.'

The desperate Brown tried to outrun the bombs, but deafening crashes all around him forced him to take cover in the sidings. 'I was frightened stiff. Both my nerves and wind had gone; I could go no further.'

Brown managed to crawl into a train carriage in a siding just outside a station and spent the night in one of the compartments. The following morning he carried on his journey to camp. But as he left the electric train at Lichterfelde Ost to board the steam train for Grossburen, he was stopped at gunpoint by a soldier in an SS uniform. It was Thomas Cooper.

'You're under arrest. You must come with me to Major Heimpel.'[3]

Brown asked Cooper why he was being arrested. Cooper said it was for spying but refused to elaborate. Brown's mind began to race. Who had informed on him? What did they know? He would have to think fast.

Cooper and another SS soldier escorted the British quartermaster to the headquarters of Stalag III-D in Steglitz.

Heimpel and two Gestapo officers were waiting for him in one of the interrogation rooms. Heimpel ordered him to strip naked. Brown[4] obliged and stood still in the middle of the floor while the Gestapo agents searched his clothes. When they found nothing incriminating, Brown was allowed to dress and then led to another room where Heimpel and the two Gestapo officers were joined by Dr Ziegfeld.

For two hours Heimpel and Ziegfeld fired questions at the British agent.

They repeated the questions over and over. Where had he been all night? Whom had he been with? Did he know any agents working for British intelligence?

Brown was unaware Oswald was a Nazi spy and he didn't want to betray her by letting Heimpel know he had been secretly meeting her in Berlin. So he told them he had stayed the night with Gisela Maluche after being caught in the middle of an air raid. Heimpel already knew from Lydia Oswald where Brown had been.

Heimpel raised himself from his chair: 'Brown, I'm accusing you of being a secret service agent. We have evidence to prove that you are sending messages home to England.'

Brown protested his innocence: 'How can I be, Major Heimpel? I am a prisoner of war, running a special camp for you.'

Then Brown played the card which had worked so well before, once again exploiting the disunity between the brutish Gestapo officer and the urbane diplomat Dr Ziegfeld: 'You have always disliked me, Major Heimpel, and I presume this is your method of getting me out of the way.'

Heimpel turned to Ziegfeld: 'Herr Ziegfeld, I would ask you to read the statement you have there.'

Ziegfeld gave Brown a long, sorrowful look and then picked up the document and read it out aloud:

As agreed with you I went to the camp and found that Green had been sent there as a suspected Jew. It was arranged by the German authorities for me to go in the same barrack room as Green and before long we were able to meet. Before I had the chance to question him as you wished, he turned on me and said, 'I know you are working for the German side so keep away from me.'[5]

'Don't be a silly fool; you know as well as I do that I'm a POW like yourself – weren't we in the same camp together?'

'Yes, but I know you are working for the Jerries in Berlin now, and I can even tell where you are living as a civilian.'

'Well, this is interesting. How did you find all this out?'

'Brown in Berlin told me. You think he is friendly with the Germans, but he is a good fellow really. He is a secret service agent and has already reported you to England for your Nazi actions!'[6]

Brown listened carefully to the damning evidence being laid against him. The situation was desperate, and if he didn't think fast an unmarked grave awaited him. His one hope lay in the fact that he was sure he knew who was responsible for the report. If he was right about the traitor's identity then he might still get out of this.

Brown told Ziegfeld that he suspected Walter Purdy was the author of the note he had just read out.

'Let me see it,' demanded Brown.

Ziegfeld grudgingly admitted that Purdy had written it but he refused to show him the statement in full. Brown now knew beyond any doubt Purdy was the British agent working directly for Heimpel and Ziegfeld. But how much did they really know about Brown's Berlin operations?

Ziegfeld turned to Brown: 'Well, what have you to say? It seems very black against you, and you know that the penalty for spying is death.'

During his conversation with Purdy in Colditz, Green had taken a huge risk by disclosing that he was a Jew. His status as a British prisoner of war offered him protection, in theory. Brown now realised that if he was going to save himself from torture and a gruesome death at the hands of the Gestapo, he had no choice but to use the Nazis' obsession with anti-Semitism to get himself off the hook.

Turning the tables on Ziegfeld and Heimpel, he asked: 'But surely you realise what is happening. I am surprised that you have been taken in by this fellow Green. You know he is a Jew and you know that the Jews hate the Genshagen camp for they don't want to see any friendship between the prisoners and the Germans. Can't you see they are trying to discredit me so as to break up the Genshagen holiday camp and ruin all the work I'm trying to do?'

Heimpel looked discomforted; this was an angle he had not considered.

Brown now gambled that the Germans had not broken the codes, and in any case he had taken great trouble to make sure it was Green who had sent the message back to London about Purdy, not him.

'If you think I have been sending messages to London then you only have to read my letters. But I can assure you I haven't.'

The two Gestapo officers who had remained in the room throughout Brown's interrogation said they thought the idea of a

Jewish conspiracy against Brown and the propaganda camp might be a plausible explanation. Ziegfeld was ready to agree with them. After all, it was in Ziegfeld's interests to believe Brown. And how could Heimpel be so sure that Purdy had not been turned by the British while he was in Colditz?

Ziegfeld told Heimpel he now thought Brown was the innocent victim of a Jewish conspiracy, and suggested he should check Green's evidence with Colditz one more time. When Heimpel spoke to Eggers by phone, the Colditz security officer said he had some bad news to pass on. Green had just passed a German medical board at Colditz, which had proved his insanity beyond doubt, and he was now cleared for repatriation to England. Eggers had in his possession a certificate signed by German and Swiss doctors declaring Green to be medically insane. Tod had successfully fast tracked Green's medical examination so that as soon as Purdy had been handed over to the Germans, the Swiss legation, who fortuitously were visiting the castle that week, were on hand to say that the dentist was not of sound mind. Green's allegations against Brown were now the ravings of an insane Jew. No Nazi could take them seriously. There was no way Brown could be regarded as the guilty party.

Heimpel was infuriated. He was still convinced Brown was a double agent, but he was outvoted three to one, and Ziegfeld outranked him. So effective were Brown's lies that the other Gestapo officers now even went so far as to become incensed by the idea that a Jew had tried to trick them, telling Brown: 'This is an attempt to discredit you, but we won't let them do it. This Jew will be punished for his lies.' Once again, Brown had demonstrated his extraordinary capacity to think on his feet, and what was perhaps his greatest skill: using people's underestimation of him to his advantage.

Ziegfeld told Brown he was free to go, but he should take great care not to go to Berlin without a minder.

As Brown put on his great coat, preparing to leave the building, Heimpel called him into his private office.[7]

'Well Brown, you can consider yourself lucky you've scraped through this time. I personally think you are a secret agent and I am going to do my utmost to trap you. You give me one chance to catch you and I will have you sent to Belsen – that is a slower death than shooting. I know how your people are sending their messages home so if you try to send any more you will be caught red-handed.'

Brown had escaped, just, but it must have been a desperate moment, and he knew that from now on his every move would be closely watched by the Gestapo. Furthermore, he had damaged his relationship with Ziegfeld, an ally whom he could no longer count on to protect him from Heimpel if anything else incriminating emerged. One upside was that Brown knew for certain Heimpel's claim that the Germans had broken the British codes was a bluff. If Heimpel had really cracked the code he would be already on the way to Belsen.

But he now also knew that if the Germans could plant Purdy in Colditz, then they could use the naval officer as a spy in any of the prison camps or set him up as a double agent in one of the Allied POW escape lines, putting hundreds of lives at risk. The question now was how was he going to warn London about the English traitor who was working for the Gestapo without condemning himself to a slow and terrifying death?

Chapter 27

The Mysterious Lieutenant Commander Beale

Purdy had not completed his spying mission at Colditz. Instead of sending him back to Berlin, Heimpel and Eggers arranged for their valued agent to be left in one of the cells, outside the POW compound, used to hold prisoners before introducing them to the main camp.

On 31 March 1944 two officers were placed in a cell next to Purdy's. Major Kenneth Wylie and his brother Captain Colin Wylie were captured during the Crete campaign and imprisoned in Spangenberg Castle, Oflag IX-A. Colin, the younger of the two brothers, had tried to escape from Spangenberg but was caught and sent to Colditz.[1] Major Wylie, who had not been involved in the escape, begged the commandant to transfer him with his younger brother. The Germans agreed and both brothers were taken to Colditz. Wylie was in contact with MI9 and had used the MI9 codes to send messages from Spangenberg back to London. The Germans were on to him, and suspected Kenneth Wylie of being involved in the Allied escape networks. By placing the brothers in the holding cell next to Purdy, the Abwehr hoped to get to the truth. Heimpel reasoned that because Purdy had spent a few months at Spangenberg before Marlag, he would be able to discuss the layout of the camp and some of the personnel without giving himself away.

Eggers had arranged for Purdy to communicate with the brothers' cell by removing a stove-pipe in the partition wall. Speaking

173

into the stove, Purdy introduced himself as Lieutenant Commander Beale. He explained he was the brother of another Spangenberg prisoner and that he was under a sentence of death for carrying out acts of sabotage against the Germans.

Purdy tried to win the brothers' trust by telling them how it was possible to pass secret messages to the main camp by underlining passages in books they were allowed to read while in the cells. The following morning the Germans released Colin Wylie, leaving the MI9 coder alone with Purdy.

For two weeks Purdy and Major Wylie were held in adjoining cells. During that time Purdy tirelessly worked on Wylie, trying to get him to give up his secrets. He told the British officer that he had spent weeks using the cover of the air raids in Berlin to carry out acts of sabotage against trains. And with another officer (Wing Commander Carpenter) he had used a secret radio set to send messages about the weather conditions over the German capital to assist the British bombers. But Wylie was suspicious of 'Beale', as he had already been warned that the Germans used stool pigeons to try to trick intelligence from vulnerable prisoners.[2] He also suspected the cell was miked and so said nothing of any value to Purdy.

On 15 April Wylie was reunited with his brother, who had by now been fully briefed by the other prisoners about the traitor Purdy and was able to confirm his brother's suspicions regarding the mysterious Commander Beale.

A week later, Purdy tried the same trick[3] on another British prisoner who was being held in the outside cells. Once again he claimed to be Lieutenant Commander Beale, who had escaped from a POW propaganda camp in Berlin where he said there were a lot of British 'rats' who were collaborating with the Germans. He repeated his claim to have been involved in the sabotage of the Berlin railway and that he had been sentenced to death, a sentence that had been commuted to imprisonment at Colditz. But this time, Purdy's cell neighbour was a Colditz veteran. Flight Lieutenant Dominic

Bruce was an inveterate escaper who had been placed in solitary confinement as punishment for cutting through the metal bars on his window and making a run for the barbed-wire fence, where his bid for freedom was prematurely ended when he was stopped by a vigilant guard. Bruce had been among the group of officers who had tried to hang Purdy, and so recognised the voice of the man in the next cell. He let Purdy reel off his spiel then spent the remainder of the time the two men were together verbally abusing the British traitor until the Germans were left with no choice but to return Bruce to the main camp.[4]

Purdy had not quite exhausted his usefulness at Colditz. Heimpel and Eggers thought of one more way to get the British officers to give up their secret codes. Purdy was instructed to begin writing a series of letters to his mother and sister in London in which he pretended to be trying to contact the Air Ministry with important information. By getting Purdy to use a fake code, Heimpel hoped to entice British intelligence into communicating with the naval officer as a genuine Colditz POW seeking to pass on intelligence to the British.

In one of his letters Purdy wrote:[5]

'Dear Mother. There is one important thing I would like you to do for me. Will you write to the firm of merchants for whom Eric works and ask them if my previous letters reached them and if they were able to follow my instructions? If they were, would you write straight back and tell me.

'I hope to be able to give them further help in that matter in the near future, but of course that depends on the trend of events this war will take. The instructions I gave were concerning weather they had been able to invest it in the securities I previously mentioned in my letters.'

Purdy's reference to Eric was a coded reference to his nephew who was serving in the RAF ('the firm of merchants') and the deliberate misspelling of *weather* was designed to alert the Air Ministry to the suggestion that he had been trying to pass on intelligence from inside the German capital.

Alice Purdy immediately recognised that her son was trying to tell her something important, and complied with his request to make contact with the Air Ministry. But the Air Ministry censors had no knowledge of Walter Purdy or his previous correspondence, so they sent Mrs Purdy's letters to MI9 where they ended up on the desk of Major Headley White. The British intelligence officer had been following Purdy's case from the year before, when he had visited Mrs Purdy at her home. These new letters with a Colditz postmark represented an important development in his investigation. Had British intelligence misunderstood Walter Purdy? Perhaps instead of working for the Germans he was really collecting intelligence for the British, and had been using messages that had been written in a home-made code passed on to him by an MI9 agent from one of the POW camps. White arranged to visit Mrs Purdy again to collect all of Purdy's letters, which he sent on to Intelligence School 9(Y) (IS9), MI9's decoding branch, for closer examination. But after careful and thorough analysis, the cyber experts could find no evidence that Purdy was using any recognised code. It was also pointed out by the IS9 coders that if he was trying to pass on intelligence about the weather it would be hopelessly out of date by the time the letter reached London and the information fed to the RAF.

White suspected that Purdy's letters were not what they appeared to be and he alerted MI5 accordingly. MI9 had not taken Heimpel's bait. Instead, White asked Diana Barnes[6] of MI5 to instruct Special Branch to step up its enquiries into Purdy and look at a POW claim, based on recently received MI9 intelligence, that the naval officer had been closely involved with William Joyce in London before the war.

Not long after these investigations were put in motion, Lieutenant Colonel Tod's coded message about Purdy's confession under interrogation at Colditz reached London. Barnes wrote an urgent report to her MI5 superiors about Purdy: 'I think you should see this file about a British prisoner who is reported to have admitted to working for the Germans in Berlin.'

Tom Shelford, who was running MI5's fascist investigation section,[7] replied noting Barnes's concern, but emphasised the 'necessity for caution' in case it leaked that MI5 were investigating Purdy's links to Joyce. The MI5 officer was also preparing the prosecution case against Joyce[8] and he did not want anything coming out in public that risked derailing his investigations into the two traitors. Meanwhile, the Colditz authorities had dropped any pretence that Purdy was a bona fide prisoner. A few days after the Bruce incident, he was seen by the other POWs walking freely around the castle grounds and strolling into town. One officer reported him marching up to a swastika flag and saluting it.

This was too much for some of the British prisoners.

Wing Commander Douglas Bader was so incensed by Purdy's treachery that he refused to let him have any of the British rations, telling the commandant, 'If he's working for you then you can feed him.'[9]

Padre Platt noted in his diary: 'I suppose Purdy has burned his boats with both Germany and England: with England for having betrayed his country and Germany for having revealed here that he has worked for the Germans.'

But Purdy had far from burned all his bridges with the Nazis.

Chapter 28

Breaking the Colditz Code

By the spring of 1944, the prospect of a German victory had vanished. The advent of D-Day and the inexorable Russian advance from the East meant Germany could not avoid defeat. The Nazi leadership and the Wehrmacht High Command now turned their thoughts to the hope of a negotiated settlement. The political spotlight once again was turned on the VIP prisoners held at Colditz, who would become crucial pawns in any peace negotiations with the Allies. It was a matter in which Hitler himself took a personal interest.

Eggers and Heimpel had long held suspicions that the Colditz POWs were not just corresponding with other POW camps but were also able to send letters to contacts outside Germany. If the Colditz coders were able to communicate with London, then the British would be able to jeopardise any plans the Germans had for the prominente. Winston Churchill and his war cabinet were acutely aware of the danger now facing them as potential hostages or victims of Nazi reprisals. The British Prime Minister ordered plans for a rescue operation. For such a mission to be successful, it was imperative that London remained in close touch with the situation on the ground in Colditz.

Coded letters sent from the prison to England took weeks to arrive. But if the POWs were able to send messages to British agents operating inside Germany, then the status and whereabouts of the prominente could be radioed to London within a few days.

Before sending Purdy into Colditz, Heimpel impressed upon him the importance of making the POWs's secret communications system his highest priority.

While his missions to elicit information from the officers in the outside cells and his letters home had ended in failure, other efforts were starting to bear fruit.

In the first days of his arrival at Colditz, before his interrogation by the British, Purdy had made one significant breakthrough. The naval officer had told the the British postal officer at Colditz that he desperately needed to contact a woman in Berlin. Innocently agreeing to help Purdy, the British officer let him know there was a secret way to do this and took his letter, assuring Purdy it would get to the correct address. Using a prearranged signal, Purdy secretly contacted one of the German guards, who pulled him out of the camp on the spurious grounds of having his photographs taken for his Colditz identity card. Once he was safely back with Eggers, he told the Colditz chief of security what he had discovered: 'I asked someone if I could get a letter out to a German addressee without going through the censorship. I was told to hand my letter to an officer I was shown. Don't know his name yet. I did so and later in the day I was told the letter had already been posted.'[1]

Purdy was returned to the camp, and by the time he had been exposed by the other POWs, the letter had already been dispatched via the secret messaging route. The British POWs were none the wiser.

In June, Purdy finally left Colditz and returned to Berlin at ParadePlatz 8, Tempelhof, the house next door to Dr Ziegfeld's, and discovered that the letter he had asked the British officer to post to an address in Berlin had safely arrived.

Purdy immediately wrote to Eggers telling him that he was pleased to report that he was in possession of the Colditz letter which had been sent using the POWs' secret communication:

'Sir, I have as promised by me two days ago before I left Oflag IV-C visited the person to whom I addressed a letter; unfortunately the envelope has been destroyed but I am assured that it was dispatched from Colditz. I cannot add any more suggestions to those I have already made concerning the posting of letters outside the camp. I can give you the assurance that never at any time while on walking exercise or on parole did I personally post a letter nor did I approach any citizen of the Reich to do so. All such actions were confined to the limits of the camp and I have already disclosed how that was done. Heil Hitler. RW [Roy Walter] Purdy 1674'[2]

Purdy's intelligence success confirmed Eggers's worst fears: 'Here to me,' Eggers later recalled, 'appeared proof of bribery among the guard company. Someone was acting as a carrier pigeon.' Eggers feared 'bribery and corruption' was now systemic at Colditz. 'It was going on the whole time and the dice were fully loaded on the side of the prisoners. They had more food and chocolate and coffee than they wanted and with this they used to bribe our men.'[3]

Purdy had made another more minor discovery. He told Eggers that the POWs and MI9 were using Colman's mustard pots as a means of secret communication. It explained why the British prisoners, who took great pleasure in disparaging French and German mustard, made such a fuss of only serving Colman's with their food. Unknown to the Germans, each pot that arrived from Britain contained a secret message. Eggers immediately cancelled the British mustard supply.

Purdy's snooping operations for the Germans had pleased Heimpel, and now that his spy was back in Berlin he decided to task him with one more assignment. The German intelligence chief long suspected Ziegfeld was being hoodwinked by Brown, who Heimpel still felt sure could not be trusted. So he told Purdy to keep a close watch on the British sergeant, who was still running the holiday camp at Genshagen. The Gestapo particularly wanted to know if Brown visited Ziegfeld at his home.[4] Brown, of course, was now fully alerted to Purdy's activities. So the two spies began keeping wary watches on each other from a careful distance.

The increasing frequency of the bombing raids on Berlin served as a constant reminder that the war was never far away.

On 6 June news reached Berlin that the first Allied forces had landed in Normandy. For Purdy and the other British traitors, it was a disturbing development. They had to consider the real possibility that Germany might be defeated in a ground war, in which case Britain was unlikely to overlook their treachery. Yet Purdy still believed he could rescue the situation for himself, if not for the Third Reich.

He still clung to the hope that the Germans would buy his secret plans for an anti-aircraft weapon that possessed the potential to decimate the RAF and American bomber forces. By happy coincidence, Purdy was sharing his accommodation at number eight with a British civilian radio engineer called Robert Louis Lindemere, who had fallen into German hands in France during the summer of 1940. Lindemere was a former drug addict whom the Germans had been trying to persuade to work for them. But Lindemere insisted that, other than repairing three German radio sets, he had withstood all the Nazi inducements and threats. Purdy decided to take the scientifically minded Lindemere into his confidence in the hope he could help him turn his anti-aircraft invention into a commercial venture. During their discussions, Purdy told Lindemere that he escaped from Colditz – not as a POW, but as a German spy 'condemned to death' by the British for passing on information. Lindemere says Purdy still appeared 'terrified about this'.

But if Purdy thought Lindemere was a fellow collaborator, he had badly misjudged his housemate.

Lindemere later told MI5: 'He [Purdy] told me he invented some kind of invention for shooting down night bombers which he was going to make a lot of money from and the Germans would probably start a factory for him. I pointed out that the night bombing was done by British planes and that if he sold his invention to the Germans he would be a traitor.'[5]

Their discussions became fraught and ill-tempered, culminating in Lindemere saying he would kill Purdy if he carried out his plan.

Purdy responded by threatening to report Lindemere to Heimpel for working for the British.

Lindemere called Purdy a 'dirty swine'.

Purdy first tried to have Lindemere locked up on grounds of insanity. But when that proved too difficult he plotted the British engineer's murder.

Fortunately, Lindemere overheard Purdy talking to a Gestapo officer about how they were going to arrest Lindemere and then 'dispose' of him.

Recalled Lindemere:[6] 'I left the house before the others were awake on the morning of 19 July 1944 and made my way to the Swiss Embassy where I told them I was a British subject who was going to be murdered.'

The diary in which Walter Purdy documented his time living and working in Berlin. On 4 March 1944, the week before he was sent to Colditz to spy on the British, he wrote: 'After a long sleep had a good lunch and afternoon walk with the only woman I can ever love – Gretel.' © The National Archives

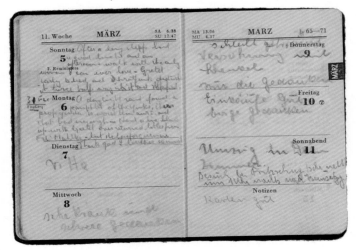

MI5 became increasingly worried about the threat posed by British POWs who had been recruited by the Nazis. In October 1944 Tom Shelford wrote to Roger Hollis who headed F Division warning that Walter Purdy was 'typical of the worst [traitor] cases.' © The National Archives KV-2-259 (1) p7

In May 1945 heads of MI5, MI9 and Royal Navy intelligence met to decide how best to detain Purdy. MI5 sent a cable to Allied Forces Headquarters in Italy asking to hold Purdy for as long as possible until it emerged his commission in the navy had ended upon the sinking of his ship in June 1940. © The National Archives KV-2-259 (1) p9

Alarm bells rang at MI5 when it dawned on the intelligence chiefs that Purdy was sailing for Britain before they had gathered enough evidence to bring about his prosecution. Lt Col Vivian Seymer described Purdy's case as a 'screaming baby'. © The National Archives KV-2-259 (1) p11

On Reception

On Discharge

(68 page 3)

Purdy was sentenced to hang but was granted an 11th-hour reprieve. He served just nine years of his life sentence. Within a year he had organised an escape from Wandsworth Prison but was betrayed by a fellow inmate. The governor of Parkhurst Prison on the Isle of Wight described Purdy as 'a devious twister of the worst kind' while an MI5 report said Purdy was the 'greatest rogue unhung'.

Colditz during the Second World War. © Getty

Colditz Castle today which hosts guided tours of the prison camp. The guides take great delight in ending the tour with the words 'for you Englanders the tour is over'. © Author

The attic room where the British officers tried to hang Walter Purdy. In the space above, the POWs built and assembled a model glider in which two officers planned to escape. The glider was never tested, as the castle was liberated by the Americans on 16 April 1945. © Author

Chapter 29

Paradeplatz 8

Military breakthroughs by the Allies in the late summer of 1944 meant the war was closing in on John Brown, Julius Green and Walter Purdy. Allied forces were driving towards Germany's capital city – the British and American armies from the West, the Russians from the East. In a matter of months Berlin, would be in range of Stalin's artillery.

Many Germans knew the war was already as good as lost, the Nazi high command leading the German people into a death spiral. On 20 July 1944, a group of high-ranking army officers carried out an attempted assassination of Adolf Hitler.

The plot was led by Claus von Stauffenberg, who smuggled a bomb in his briefcase into a staff officers' conference chaired by Hitler and taking place at the Wolfsschanze (Wolf's Lair), hidden in an east Prussian forest in modern-day Poland.

Stauffenberg made his excuses and left the Wolfsschanze before his bomb went off.

Several Nazis were badly injured and died of their wounds, but Hitler survived, shielded from the blast by one of the thick wooden table legs.

The failure of the assassination and the intended coup d'état that was to follow triggered mass arrests. The Gestapo was wholly distracted by the grizzly business of disposing of nearly 20,000 suspects, many of whom were publicly hanged, strung up on lamp posts by piano wire. Even Erwin Rommel, the Wehrmacht general whose daring Blitzkrieg of the summer of 1940 had ended the war prematurely for hundreds of thousands of British POWs, including John Brown and Julius Green and many of the Colditz veterans, was implicated in the plot, and later accepted the Nazis' offer of suicide rather than endure a show trial.

The Nazi dragnet and the military purge consumed almost all of the Gestapo's energies and resources, including those of Alexander Heimpel, who was now too preoccupied to follow up his suspicions about Brown.

Left alone at Genshagen, John Brown continued overseeing the surreal business of holidays for British prisoners who the Germans, facing defeat, still believed could be recruited to the Nazi cause.

Brown had orders from London to recover evidence against as many of the British Berlin traitors as possible. Unmolested by Heimpel, the artillery quartermaster was particularly determined that Walter Purdy, who had betrayed him to the Gestapo almost ending in his execution, should be held to account for his treachery.

After the war, he explained to James Davies of MI5 that although he knew he still had to be 'extremely careful' sending intelligence back to London, he 'felt a very strong desire' to find out about 'Purdy and the others working for the Germans'.[1]

In the first week of September 1944, Brown asked to speak to Dr Ziegfeld. Relations between the two men had cooled since the first days of Genshagen, and after Purdy's report from Colditz, Ziegfeld knew the Gestapo would be watching Brown closely. Nevertheless he agreed to see the British POW camp leader in whom he had invested so much trust and hope. Brown said that he had arranged for a number of German artistes to perform at Genshagen that week and asked if they could be accommodated in Berlin as the British air raids made travelling at night very perilous. Brown suggested the building next door to Ziegfeld's house and that Ziegfeld needn't worry about preparing the guests' accommodation as he would send a party of men to clear a couple of bedrooms and to tidy up the house. Ziegfeld, who still stubbornly clung to the hope that Genshagen would ultimately prove to be a success by helping to unite Germany and Britain at the end of the war, agreed. The property Brown had in mind was number ParadePlatz 8, the very same building in which Walter Purdy was living.

Brown selected a cleaning party of four of his most trusted staff with instructions to search the house from top to bottom looking for anything that might incriminate Purdy.

The party was led by Private Tom Savin of the Gloucestershire Regiment.[2] After a thorough root around the premises, one of the men found two torn-up letters left in a waste-paper basket in one of the bedrooms. When the men pieced together the letters they realised that they were part of a chain of correspondence between Purdy and a number of senior Nazis. Savin couldn't be sure that this was what Brown had in mind, especially as one of the letters was written in German, so they secreted the pieces of paper among themselves and returned to camp.

One of the letters turned out to be the memo Purdy had written in English to Reinhold Eggers after his Colditz mission informing the security officer he had managed to trace his letter to Berlin which he had sent from the camp using the secret POW communication system.

The second letter was written by Dr Wunsche of the Reich Ministry of Enlightenment and Propaganda who had responsibility for Colditz. It was addressed to Robert Wallace, Purdy's alias. 'Berlin,' wrote Wunsche, 'has received your message and someone responsible will be in touch soon. Heil Hitler.'

Brown was delighted with the finds, as he was now sure he had enough hard evidence to see Purdy hang for treason.

Concerned that with Purdy's help the Abwehr may have broken the British codes, Brown switched to sending messages in invisible ink written on the POW forms that kept the War Office informed about how much war pay each prisoner was entitled to while interned in Germany.[3] He used one of these forms to warn MI9 about Purdy's treachery and trusted status among the Abwehr double agents.

This still left him with the problem of getting the letters, the hard evidence against Purdy from ParadePlatz8, safely back to London. These would have to be physically brought back to Britain, and Brown instructed Reg Beattie to make microcopies of all Purdy's letters which he carefully concealed in a secret cavity in the heel of one of his shoes. Brown knew the original versions would be more valuable as they would be considered primary evidence in a court of law. But he could not risk Heimpel catching him with them in his possession. So Brown planned to give the original letters to the one agent he thought had the best chance of keeping them safe until the war was won.[4]

After his interrogation by Heimpel, Brown's freedoms had been partially curtailed and Ziegfeld had cancelled the Foreign Office travel pass he had used to get around Berlin. Brown was forced to fall back on his standard operating procedure, bribing the guards with chocolates and cigarettes to escort him on a comfort trip out of the camp to visit his girlfriend. On one of these trips he gave a guard enough cigarettes to persuade him to leave him alone with Gisela for the afternoon. The guard, sympathetic to the British sergeant's sexual needs, agreed to the arrangement and said he would come by in the afternoon to pick him up.

As soon as the guard had left, Brown slipped out of Gisela's apartment to a secret rendezvous with Margery Booth. Brown had with him all the collaborators' documents he had been hiding since he started his work with MI9. He explained to Booth how important it was that she should keep the Purdy letters until she could hand them to a trusted courier or, better still, take them with her to England herself. But he warned Booth to be very careful as the Gestapo was watching him very closely and he suspected they would soon have her under surveillance as well.

Booth couldn't be sure that her opera star status or even the patronage of the Führer meant she was above suspicion, so she decided to use her contacts with the German aristocracy to help cover her tracks. One of Margery Booth's foremost admirers was Crown Prince Wilhelm, the son and heir of the last German Emperor, the Kaiser Wilhelm II, and no friend of the Nazis.

Wilhelm, or Little Willy as he was known before the war, had been approached by the 20 July plotters as a possible interim leader after Hitler's assassination. He had tried to distance himself from the plot, refusing to play a role, but after the failure of the coup, the Gestapo kept Prince Wilhelm's stately home Cecilienhof under close watch. Booth decided to risk paying a visit to Cecilienhof,[5] although she judged it was too dangerous to confide in the prince the true intention behind her mission.

During a walk of the grounds she safely buried Brown's documents in a secret location from where she could retrieve them when the time came. After dining with the prince, Booth and her loyal housekeeper both returned to Berlin by car. She appeared to have given the Gestapo the slip.

Chapter 30

Who Will Lead the British Traitors?

One of the consequences of the failed plot to kill Hitler was that responsibility for the administration of all German POW camps was transferred from the Oberkommando der Wehrmacht, OKW, directly to the SS.[1]

Himmler gave this role to his trusted deputy Gottlob Berger.

The Waffen-SS commander now held responsibility for both Colditz and the British Free Corps, which he was keen to exploit for his own purposes. The unit of British traitors was of great interest to him and Berger requested from Heimpel an urgent update on the status of the BFC. Even the most sanguine account of the strength of the BFC put the British contingent at no more than 40 men, of whom Heimpel and Lange considered only half were suitable for combat operations.

The question of who should lead them remained unresolved. Lange suggested his old comrade Thomas Cooper, who had served on the Eastern Front and had been recruited to the SS before the start of the war. But Cooper was not an officer, and Berger, for propaganda and military reasons, insisted that it must be a British officer to take the British traitors into battle. Kommando 999, the 'officer holiday camp', had demonstrably failed to produce a suitable candidate for leader. The sole British officer signed up to the BFC was Lieutenant Allan Shearer of the 4th Seaforths. But Shearer's reason for enlisting turned out to be suicide. Shearer had suffered a nervous breakdown after capture in March 1943 and had expected the Germans would send the BFC to the Eastern Front where 'I hoped I would be killed by the Russians'.

It was decided to step up recruitment efforts at the Oflags, the officer POW camps. In the meantime, Berger appointed Hans Roepke to take temporary command of the unit. Roepke was highly educated with an excellent grasp of English from his time as an exchange student in America before the war.[2]

He had worked his way up the Nazi Party and was now an SS Hauptsturmführer, a senior Nazi Party member, whose military record and leadership qualities had so impressed Berger that he recruited him to SS-Hauptamt, the SS headquarters in Berlin.[3] With Roepke in temporary charge of the British, Berger redoubled the recruitment campaign.

In June 1944, two British soldiers dressed in SS uniforms and wearing the insignia of the BFC turned up at Colditz Castle and reported to Reinhold Eggers. They had orders from Heimpel to speak to any British officers who the camp commandant thought might be persuaded to switch sides. Eggers had one or two names in mind but after Purdy's hostile reception, he concluded that such an operation undertaken by two junior NCOs was doomed to failure.

'These two said they wanted a chance to talk to the prisoners with a view to getting some of them to join up to the BFC. This did not seem like a good idea to me... Anyone who knew Colditz could be certain that there would be 100% non-cooperation.'[4]

Eggers also feared a violent reaction in the camp prompting a crop of 'pseudo-volunteers' who would use the offer as a means of escape.

The Colditz security chief refused to escort the 'recruiting officers' around the camp. Instead, Eggers agreed to place the BFC leaflets with the prisoners' mail. The message conveyed on the leaflets encapsulated the familiar Nazi contention that the war was the work of the Jews and international finance, and amounted to a 'betrayal of the British Empire'.[5] The prisoners burnt all the leaflets, rather confirming Eggers's reading of the situation. Lieutenant Colonel Willie Tod demanded an explanation from the commandant as to who had authorised the placing of the BFC leaflets with the POW official mail.

Visits to other Oflags proved equally unsuccessful.

Gottlob Berger now realised that the recruitment of officers to the BFC represented a serious impediment to the formation of the unit. After the Allied breakthrough on D-Day, the task was made even more difficult.

An MI5 report[6] on the BFC in 1944 found that: 'censorship intercepts from POW mail provided ample and often amusing details of the general indignation felt within the camps and the persistent efforts by the Germans to secure recruits, including the sending of men into the larger camps to serve as decoys.'

Yet Berger knew that his standing among the Nazi high command would be greatly enhanced if he could be the first to inform Hitler and Himmler of the combat readiness of a British unit of SS soldiers.

Although the number of recruits was disappointing, Berger reasoned that once the ball was rolling, others would join from experimental recruitment camps like Luckenwalde, which used the shock of capture and blackmail to force Allied officers to switch sides. Berger's only stipulation for clearing the British fighters for combat was that there must be a minimum of 30 soldiers, enough for an infantry platoon.

Gottlob Berger carefully reviewed the BFC leadership candidates. The obvious choice was John Amery, the British aristocrat who had first come up with the idea of recruiting an army of collaborators to fight the Bolsheviks. But his louche character had alienated many of the men he had tried to rally to the Nazi cause. Moreover, although Amery had experience as an intelligence officer serving with Francisco Franco's nationalists during the Spanish Civil War in 1936, he was not a soldier.

Himmler and Berger could see little use for Amery in their BFC and he was funnelled into broadcasting and diplomacy work.

Then there was Lieutenant John Calthrop. He had been at Genshagen for several months and knew the BFC recruits well. He had already established a relationship with Cooper, who Berger thought would make an excellent second in command.

Berger elected to send a 63-year-old former British officer in the Royal Artillery, who had served in the First World War, to sound out his new BFC prospective commander. Dr Vivian Stranders moved to Germany between the wars when he was recruited as a spy, helping in the clandestine rearmament of the Reich. In 1932 he joined the Nazi Party, became friends with Hitler, and in 1944 was appointed by Berger as the Waffen-SS adviser on British affairs. When he met Calthrop in July 1944, Stranders emphasised his goal of uniting the two nations.

Calthrop claims he told Stranders he did not want to join the BFC, although he admitted later: 'I played up to Stranders and agreed with him in general principle. I was able to impress Stranders sufficiently well with my malleability to such an extent that I got from him an undertaking that he would take a personal interest in my case, follow my movements and see me again at a later date.'[7]

Even by Calthrop's account it was clear that the Germans considered him a key prize in their recruitment drive for the BFC.

Stranders said that Berger had so many schemes and plans concerning Calthrop that he (Stranders) 'couldn't keep up with them'.[8]

By now, Brown's secret message to MI9 warning of Calthrop's collaboration had arrived at Whitehall. But there was little London could do to prevent Calthrop from working with the Germans. Brown was the man on the ground, the MI9 spy-catcher, and it was up to him to make sure Calthrop played no part in the formation of the BFC or any other grand plan the Nazis had for him.

Brown accepted the mission. If he could keep Calthrop at Genshagen then he would be able to watch him much more closely. Once again he turned to Margery Booth for help.

Calthrop was infatuated with the Wigan songstress, boasting to her that he was a successful London theatre producer and promised to put her on the West End stage regardless of who won the war. Booth responded with personal invitations to watch her performances at the Berlin State Opera and evening trysts at her rehearsal rooms at Kaiserschloss and later to her apartment at Willander Strasse 10/11. Calthrop, who had swapped his officer's uniform for a smart German suit to attend the operatic performances, sat spellbound in the front row of the guest seats among the elite of the Nazi Party.

After one particularly intoxicating night at the opera, Calthrop declared to Booth that he was 'passionately in love' with her. She told him that she was thinking of leaving her husband, although she made him promise to keep their affair secret from the Germans. The following day Calthrop proposed and then confided to Brown that he must stay in Berlin so he could be with Booth forever.

The entrapment of the British officer was complete.

When Heimpel told Calthrop that Berger wanted to move the BFC to another camp away from the threat of Allied bombs and that Calthrop was to lead them, the British officer refused.

In his distracted love-struck state, Calthrop was in no position to take command of a Waffen-SS unit.

Berger and Heimpel would have to look for an alternative leader.

Chapter 31

Western Front

It had been a precondition of enrolment in the BFC that no British servicemen would be sent to fight his brother soldier on the Western Front. But towards the end of 1944, it was clear to Berger that the war in the east was already lost. There was no military value in the sacrifice of the BFC in the fighting against the Russians. So it was decided to dispatch members of the BFC to units in the west where they could carry out propaganda operations.

Corporal Francis Maton, a British commando captured in Crete, and Roy Courlander, a British-born New Zealander who served in the Western Desert and Greece, were the first of the BFC to be sent west.

After a deployment briefing at the SS headquarters in Berlin, the two men boarded a train for Brussels in the company of a Flemish Waffen-SS unit. They were to join the SS-Standarte 'Kurt Eggers', part of the Scorpion West, a black propaganda unit that broadcast directly to the enemy in order to sow confusion and sap the enemy's morale.[1]

When the two SS soldiers arrived in Brussels on 3 September, they found advanced elements of the British 2nd Army commanded by Field Marshal Bernard Montgomery were in control of large parts of the city, and the Germans were in the process of withdrawing. During the retreat, Maton and Courlander surrendered and became the first soldiers of the BFC to fall into British hands.

Although both men had discarded their SS uniforms and claimed to have escaped from the Germans, their capture was immediately reported to the War Office in London who in turn informed MI5.

For Colonel Seymer this was a significant breakthrough.

Seymer arranged for Courlander and Maton to be flown back to the UK and held at the Great Central Hotel in Marylebone Station in London. As soon as they had safely arrived, Seymer made sure he was the first MI5 officer to interrogate them. It was important that he saw for himself the character and disposition of the cast of British soldiers who were fighting for the Nazis. What he encountered was a curious mix of self-serving narrative and a deluded unwillingness to recognise the incriminating circumstances in which both men now found themselves. There was neither contrition nor acknowledgement of their treachery. Seymer instructed Jim Skardon, an experienced MI5 interrogator, who after the war led the interrogations of members of the Cambridge spy ring, to take as long as he needed with the traitors to find out as much as possible about the BFC and the identities of any of the other British renegades with whom they had been in contact.

Since late 1943, Seymer had received from MI9 a growing number of POW reports about the increasing efforts of the Germans to recruit British traitors from the prison camps. The notion of a BFC had been mentioned several times, and John Brown's own intelligence revealed the existence of the Genshagen and Zehlendorf holiday camps. But MI5 and Seymer could not be sure of the scale of the threat posed by the BFC.

Skardon's report rang some worrying alarm bells.

Maton had been left alone in his blacked-out hotel room for almost 24 hours. A guard had been posted outside and Maton had had nothing to eat since the day before. He knew he was in trouble, but what could they do to him and how much did they know? Maton still regarded himself as a POW who had escaped from Nazi captivity.

When the door opened and Skardon, accompanied by another suited MI5 officer, started his interrogation, Maton was soon reminded of just how grave his situation was. Skardon told Maton he was facing a charge of aiding and abetting the enemy while serving as a British soldier, a crime for which the penalty was death by hanging. Maton was visibly shaken.

It didn't take long for Maton and Courlander to start spilling the beans about what they had been a part of in Berlin, and the BFC duo were soon naming the names of their fellow collaborators in return for clemency.

Maton said he had been at Zehlendorf [Kommando 999] recruitment camp where he was able to give a first-hand account of the establishment of the BFC. He identified several senior officers, including Brigadier Parrington and Lieutenant Colonel Stevenson of the South African Army, who appeared to be compliant with the known aims of the holiday camp. Maton said he had also been at Genshagen at its inception in August 1943 and had witnessed the first wave of 200 British POWs arriving at the camp. Skardon further learned about the third BFC recruitment camp at Luckenwalde, where the Germans used subversive recruitment methods including blackmail and sexual entrapment. Many of these BFC recruits had been originally captured fighting the Germans in Italy.

Courlander's and Maton's testimonies, the first-hand confirmation of the existence of the propaganda camps, the seniority of the officer cadre and the high number of potential recruits to the BFC made for chilling reading.

The two traitors also provided intelligence about the individuals integral to the BFC. Maton had been a broadcaster at the Büro Concordia where he had met William Joyce and John Amery. He spoke admiringly of Joyce's idealism and his bravery in making live broadcasts from the Funkhaus during RAF bombing raids.

At Genshagen, Maton had also encountered John Brown. He was unaware that Brown was working for the British and included him in his list of traitors. He told Skardon: 'It was during this period that BQMS Brown and Bombardier Blewitt were brought to the camp by a German Sonderführer by the name of Lange to do the jobs of camp commandant and confidence man respectively. This action by Lange immediately aroused the suspicion of us because of the fact that they were already amongst us men senior in rank to either of these two men. These senior-ranking NCOs were subsequently got rid of on evidence of their anti-German feelings given to Lange by Brown and Blewitt, thus leaving the way clear for their complete domination of the forthcoming activities of the camp.'[2]

Maton said he suspected Brown of working for the Germans because on several occasions he witnessed him leaving the camp for the city in civilian clothes.

Since Brown was supposed to be an MI9 agent, Seymer made sure these suspicions about him were passed on to the sister agency. Of further concern was new intelligence regarding Thomas Cooper, who Maton and Courlander said was the leading light of the BFC. Maton described how Cooper had bragged about his service on the Eastern Front, and of being a guard at Dachau concentration camp and his involvement in the murder of Jews.

Cooper's name was already known to MI9 and MI5 but this first-hand description of the battle-hardened Cooper and his role in war crimes heightened the potential threat to Allied forces posed by the BFC.

There was another name that Seymer had heard of before. Maton said that while he was working at the Reichssportfeld he had got to know a radio broadcaster who had mysteriously and suddenly left the radio station. The Germans tried to cover up his disappearance by telling the Büro that the person concerned had had a fight with one of the German radio directors. His name was Lieutenant Walter Purdy.

Colonel Seymer distributed an updated report to the rest of the agency saying: 'The information that follows as to those responsible for founding the BFC, how it came into being, and the identity of its members, was obtained from corporals Courlander and Maton who were themselves members and who were found in Brussels at the time of its occupation in mid-September 1944. Right up to this time they had been actually serving in the Free Corp.'

But the truth was that Maton's and Courlander's intelligence was hopelessly out of date. Both men had been separated from the main force of the BFC in August before being sent to Brussels for their front-line propaganda mission.

There were far fewer BFC personnel than the hundreds of potential recruits that Courlander and Maton claimed were being indoctrinated at Genshagen. While at Zehlendorf, not a single suitable officer had emerged as a candidate to command the Corps.

In Berlin, Gottlob Berger had received a letter written by Walter Purdy while he was at Colditz requesting to join the BFC. But hopes for Purdy to lead the unit were quickly dashed after it became clear that even elements of the BFC regarded him as a 'rat'. Heimpel of course knew that Purdy's unique value to the Nazis was in espionage, not battlefield combat.

Gottlob Berger always believed that a few British soldiers serving with the Nazis on the Western Front would have a much greater disproportionate impact on the combat effectiveness of the enemy than sending them to their inconsequential deaths on the Russian front. Yet it was also obvious that only the most diehard British fascist could be persuaded to go into battle against his countrymen. Gottlob Berger, realising the BFC experiment had come to nothing, quietly abandoned the recruitment programme.

From the remnants of the 30-odd British servicemen, he asked Heimpel to select the most loyal who could follow Maton and Courlander to the Western Front for front-line propaganda operations.

The remainder were sent east to their deaths.

Chapter 32

Secrets for Sale

Robert Lindemere safely reached Sweden in September and was able to make a full report to MI9 about what he had found out while living in Berlin. The most disturbing part of his intelligence was what he had to say about Walter Purdy. If it was true that Purdy had discovered a secret anti-aircraft weapon which he was preparing to sell to the Germans, then the RAF faced a serious threat to their bombing operations. MI9 urgently made enquiries with the Air Ministry about whether they were aware of a new explosive device being tested by German fighters that used an electronic detonator. A top secret memo[1] confirmed the War Office's fears.

The British had been considering their own plans for such a weapon in 1940 but had not developed them as they were deemed 'impractical' in the Battle of Britain. By the end of 1942, the prospect of a return of mass German air raids against Britain had receded, so plans for a mid-air exploding bomb were mothballed. However, the Air Ministry was recently in receipt of its own intelligence revealing the Germans had taken up the invention and had started using it against RAF bomber formations.[2]

In his Air Intelligence report sent to MI9, Squadron Leader Oak-Rhind wrote: 'The Germans did attempt to carry out a certain number of attacks on our bombers with bombs trailed on a length of wire from fighter aircraft – these bombs were probably to be detonated electronically.'

Whether Purdy had successfully sold his intelligence to the Nazis or they had acquired the weapon by alternative means may never be known. But MI9 was able to tell MI5 that Purdy was much more than a run-of-the-mill collaborator.

Lindemere's intelligence also confirmed what Brown had already warned London about – that Purdy had been sent into prison camps and may have broken the British codes. Colonel Seymer urgently upgraded his security assessment of the naval officer.

Back in Berlin, Heimpel rewarded Purdy with a few weeks' leave for his spying endeavours. He spent the time with Gretel at home, walking in the Tiergarten and drinking in the bierkellers and hotels. The bombs may have destroyed some of his familiar haunts, but he found the Germans to be a resourceful people who had kept the city operational and most of the entertainment open.

Purdy and Gretel's lifestyle had hardly changed since they had begun living together the year before. The Joyces and their lively expat crowd were mostly still going strong, and in between the sirens there was always someone or something to see.

Gretel now had some important news which she had kept from Purdy while he was away in Colditz – she was expecting his child. Purdy was overjoyed. The prospect of becoming a father and starting family life in Germany would mean Purdy would be able to give himself completely to the Third Reich. He wrote to Heimpel asking if he could apply for German citizenship so that he could marry his German girlfriend. But the Nazi intelligence officer said he first required Purdy to complete one more important assignment.

Chapter 33

Escape From Berlin

The success of the British Intelligence operation that had tricked the Nazis into believing the D-Day landings would take place in the Pas de Calais and not Normandy had greatly enhanced the reputation of MI5. Now the Security Service turned its attention to the business of tracking down and catching the British traitors working for the Germans.

Major Edward Cussen was one of the key MI5 directors who helped ensure the Germans didn't find out about Operation Fortitude, the D-Day deception plan. It was Cussen who stepped in to prevent the wife of MI5's star double agent, Garbo – real name Juan Pujol Garcia – from blowing her husband's cover. Unhappily stuck in London during the war, Mrs Garcia had approached the Spanish authorities for their help to get back to Spain. Cussen called on the homesick Mrs Garcia and threatened to lock her up in prison should she ever whisper a word of her husband's espionage activities, which did the trick.

After the Normandy Landings, the MI5 sleuth was sent to the continent in the wake of the Allied advance through northern France.

On 9 September 1944, Cussen tracked down the British author P G Wodehouse and interrogated him over four days at his house in Le Touquet. Wodehouse had been on the Nazi payroll, and as late as July 1944 was still receiving the equivalent to a salary of £150 a month, a not inconsiderable sum at the time.

Taken in the context of his earlier broadcasts for the Germans, it appeared Wodehouse had a charge of treason to answer. Certainly, the British public and the newspapers thought so.

But on 28 September, Cussen filed his report describing Wodehouse's behaviour as merely 'unwise', and advised against further action. Theobald Matthew, the Director of Public Prosecutions, agreed and decided there was only misplaced public interest in prosecuting Wodehouse.

As the Nazis were rolled back across Europe, exposing German spy networks and collaborators, MI5's limited resources were better directed at much more dangerous traitors. A barrister before the war, Cussen held discussions with Roger Hollis who headed F Division,[1] the MI5 department investigating British fascists and other subversives working against Britain.

Top of the agenda was the detection, detention and prosecution of the POW collaborators – the British soldiers, sailors and airmen who had joined the Nazis. Cussen believed that while civilians like Wodehouse had acted foolishly, British servicemen who worked for the Germans deserved to be hunted down and put on trial for their crimes.

Cussen was now armed with Brown's secret reports, which identified at least 20 of the British traitors and showed precisely where in occupied Europe the Security Service might find them.

He told Hollis's deputy Tom Shelford that each case should be brought to the attention of the Attorney General, who would decide whether treason or court martial charges were appropriate.

Hollis and Shelford were already compiling a long list of suitable candidates.

Lieutenant Colonel Seymer, who remained in overall charge of all the investigations into the POW collaborators, attended a meeting with Brigadier Henry Shapcott, the senior military lawyer, Officer in Charge, Military Department, Office of the Judge Advocate-General, War Office, to establish exactly what kind of evidence would be needed to secure a conviction. Shapcott advised MI5 that the test of whether a court martial charge should be raised was the extent to which the suspect had acted voluntarily in the service of the enemy.[2]

In the first years of the war, Cussen, Hollis and Shelford had all been involved in the investigation of a number of suspected Fifth Columnists in Britain who had been identified by agents like Eric Roberts, better known as Agent Jack. They had success uncovering a few genuine spies, but all three had expressed misgivings about using an agent provocateur like Roberts to entrap housewives, local loudmouths and village idiots into agreeing to work for the Nazis.

These British-based subversives seemed far removed from the collaborators who had joined the SS or were working as spies for the Gestapo in Germany. A slew of memos flew between the desks of SLB3, B4 (prisoner of war renegades) and F3 (civilian renegades).

On 24 October 1944, Shelford wrote to Hollis and Lieutenant Colonel Seymer: 'You may like to see this case of Lt Walter Purdy whose inclusion in the Surrender List I am going to suggest. It is typical of the worst B4a cases.'

A few days later, Major Headley White of MI9 passed a report to MI5 containing everything MI9 had collected on Walter Purdy over the past two years.

The intelligence pointing at the Royal Naval sub-lieutenant painted a picture of a diehard Nazi collaborator who threatened Allied operations on a number of fronts.

The race was on to catch Purdy and his fellow collaborators before they could do any more harm to British interests – especially as the war in the west reached a critical military phase.

General Bernard Montgomery's 2nd Army had broken out of Belgium, and was preparing to cross the Rhine and attack the Nazis' industrial heartland in the Ruhr.

To the south, US General George Patton's 3rd Army had already crossed the Moselle near Metz with the obvious possibility of achieving a breakthrough into Germany's economically critical Saarland.

But a lack of urgency and bitter rivalry between the two generals gave the Germans, who were outnumbered 20 to 1 in tanks and aircraft, time to dig in and halt the Allied advance. Montgomery proposed Operation Market Garden, a parachute landing behind the German positions in Holland to secure the vital bridges across the Rhine. But the bold operation proved to be a bridge too far, and the British-led force was captured when it ran into heavily armoured Panther units based near Arnhem.

Hitler now planned one of the most audacious counter-attacks of the Second World War. The Germans mustered nearly half a million troops, 1,400 tanks and 1,000 combat aircraft in the area of the Ardennes. This combined force was meant to strike back against the Allies, leading a thrust towards Antwerp which would split the British and American lines in two. One of the key elements of what became known as the Battle of the Bulge was Operation Greif, involving a Waffen-SS unit of English-speaking commandos dressed in Allied uniforms, who were given the job of infiltrating enemy lines, spreading confusion and carrying out acts of sabotage.

In November, the call went out to all SS Corps for English-speaking soldiers to take part in the mission. Members of the BFC were obvious candidates. A CIA intelligence report[3] confirms that Hans Roepke, the then leader of the BFC, was recruited to Operation Greif.

It was only after the war, when Roepke applied for a visa to visit America, that the full extent of the part played by the BFC on the Western Front in 1944/45 became clear. Refusing his visa application, the sceptical Americans wrote: 'Mr. Roepke has also done a good job of minimising his role in the formation of the Britisches Freikorps. It is clear that sometime between March of 1943 and November of 1944, while working for the Germanische Leitstelle (Berger's department in the SS-Hauptamt) he was put in charge of developing the Britisches Freikorps. There is a letter dated 2 August 1944, from Gottlob Berger, head of the SS-Hauptamt to Himmler, proposing that the 20 members of the Britisches Freikorps should be committed to the front for action, and that Roepke, because of his past involvement in the programme, should be made their leader.'[4]

A second letter, dated 18 November 1944 from an SS-Standartenführer (Colonel) Sparmann in the Amtsgruppe (an office of the Wehrmacht High Command) of the SS-Hauptamt, requested an English-speaking officer for the Britisches Freikorps.

The secret files show that on 15 November, Roepke was transferred to the SS-Führungshauptamt, administrative and operational headquarters for the Waffen-SS that was responsible for the organisation, equipment and order of battle of SS combat units.

The American files conclude: 'From this date, Roepke states that he was assigned to a commando unit of an SS Jagdverband (SS special forces) and that he participated in the Ardennes counter-offensive. This innocuous statement may explain why Mr. Roepke is so reticent about his past.'[5]

The recent capture of Courlander and Maton served as a warning to British intelligence that the deployment of POW collaborators was not restricted to the Russian front. At least four other British members of the BFC were sent to the Western Front. One of them was Walter Purdy, who joined the Waffen-SS Kurt Eggers's propaganda unit after Heimpel had authorised the transfer of his star agent to front line operations.

The timing of Purdy's deployment suggests he was assigned to a counter-intelligence operation during the Battle of the Bulge. Purdy was no commando, but his valuable broadcast skills would have been put to good use in sowing confusion among the British and American forces as the disguised German saboteurs infiltrated the Allied lines. In the event, the defenders withstood the German onslaught of the Battle of the Bulge, ending Hitler's last hope of a successful counter-offensive. Purdy has never disclosed which operations he took part in while serving with the SS but he remained on the front line with the SS for at least four more months.

London had located a number of traitors identified by Brown and confirmed by Maton and Courlander. But at the turn of the year, the whereabouts of Walter Purdy were unknown.

Chapter 34

Gestapo HQ: Prinz-Albrecht-Strasse 8

The German preoccupation with the Ardennes offensive left Brown and his staff facing another winter as prisoners of the Germans. 'In all the full horror of the final death throes of the Nazi regime we POWs were forgotten,' Brown later recalled.

Berger could only muster a handful of BFC soldiers to send to the Western Front, exposing the woeful state of the British Waffen-SS unit. It was clear to Gottlob Berger, his boss, Himmler, and now the Führer himself that the BFC would never be an effective fighting force.

Responsibility for such abject failure rested with Major Alexander Heimpel. It was a failure which was about to have serious repercussions for John Brown. Heimpel had for a long time suspected there were forces at play that had sabotaged the Genshagen experiment. Once again suspicion fell on Brown, and this time, neither Ziegfeld nor any of the British quartermaster's other German friends would be able to protect him.

In late December, after the Allies had beaten back the German offensive in the Ardennes, the Gestapo finally remembered Brown and the Genshagen contingent.

It was early morning in Genshagen and John Brown, Reg Beattie and Jimmy Newcomb were sitting in their room chatting through the progress of the war. Suddenly the door was thrown open and a detachment of soldiers accompanied by two Gestapo officers barged their way into the British quarters. Brown was just about to demand what was going on when Heimpel strode in and stood between the guards and the quartermaster and his men. He ordered the guards to turn over the room. This time the Gestapo found enough contraband to justify individual body searches of all the British prisoners. Brown had to think quickly.

'I was determined they would never search all my personal papers, many of which would be needed in England after the war. One by one they took us from the room. At last only four of us were left – Jimmy Newcomb, Reg Beattie, Ian Ryburn and me.'

The Germans made short work of Newcomb and Ryburn before approaching the two remaining POWs, who were standing to attention by their beds.

Brown whispered to Beattie to try to distract the guard who was standing by the window. Beattie did what he did best and started gently baiting the German, forcing him to come away from the window. As soon as the guard moved, Brown lifted his suitcase, in which he had hidden a great deal of incriminating evidence, and flung it out of the window into the arms of the waiting Newcomb. When the Gestapo officers came to conduct a body search of Brown, he confidently told them: 'I've nothing to declare, Heil Hitler!'

But Heimpel wasn't going to let Brown escape a second time. The Nazi had seen enough and ordered the arrest of Brown and all his men.

They were taken by truck and then train to the notorious 'house' prison of the Gestapo at Prinz-Albrecht-Strasse 8, in Charlottenburg, north Berlin. Here, thousands of enemies of the Nazis – communists, Jews, German traitors, even soldiers who had once loyally served the Reich – had come to a sticky end. In a dark back room, the Gestapo had erected a beam serving as gallows for up to eight victims at one time. It was here that a number of the 1944 Wolf Lair plotters were taken to be hanged.

It looked like the resourceful Brown, who prided himself on always being one step ahead of the dozy Germans, would shortly join them.

The British POWs were first detained in a crowded holding prison close to the Gestapo HQ. The Gestapo were world leaders in extracting confessions by removing fingernails and toenails, or applying strangulation and suffocation techniques, or hanging victims from their wrists and beating them senseless. Brown realised that it was only a matter of time before he was called for his interrogation. Every man had his breaking point, and he couldn't be sure that he wouldn't talk.

Even if he held out against the torture, he knew his secrets weren't safe. In the cavity of the heel of his shoe was the list of British collaborators, and next to each name, the treachery they had committed against Britain. A full Gestapo search was bound to discover the concealed document. While Brown languished in his cell awaiting his fate, Heimpel started rounding up other members of the British Berlin spy network. There was one other high-profile suspect who Heimpel was particularly interested in speaking to. He had enough circumstantial evidence to place Margery Booth at the centre of the spy ring, but he did not have anything concrete to lay before Himmler and the other Nazi chiefs. So he decided to get it.

Two Gestapo officers in black leather coats and wide-brim felt fedoras arrived by car at Booth's Berlin apartment. They rapped on the door, which was eventually answered by the housekeeper.

'Where is the lady of the house?'

The woman asked if they had an appointment, playing for time while Booth, in her bedroom and aware of the nature of the men's business, was desperately destroying or hiding any incriminating evidence. The Gestapo men eventually ran out of patience, brushed past the housekeeper and found Booth in her bedroom.

'You must come with us.'

Booth didn't waste any energy protesting at the intrusion; instead, she steeled herself for what she feared was to come.

Margery Booth, who had risked so much to help Brown, was taken to Prinz-Albrecht-Strasse 8 where she was thrown in a cell.

Soon Heimpel arrived to personally conduct the interrogation about her association with Genshagen and the British camp leader. The Gestapo man had plenty of questions for the British opera singer who had for so long enjoyed the personal protection of the Führer.

Why did John Brown secretly visit her flat and the Berlin State Opera House? What part had she played in helping to send messages to England? What did she know about the truth of John Brown's background?

Margery Booth denied working with Brown or helping any of the British prisoners. She insisted that her only dealings with John Brown were restricted to putting on entertainment at Genshagen as the Germans had requested.

Then Heimpel showed his hand: 'We know that Brown is an English Secret Service agent, so you need not tell us any more lies. He is under arrest and has revealed the method he employed for getting messages home.' Leaning over the frightened opera singer, Heimpel excitedly told Booth: 'His confession has implicated you. We are going to shoot Brown and then deal with you later – as a German citizen – in the People's Court.'[1]

Any mention of the People's Court conjured images of show trials followed by the defendant being slowly strangled with piano wire.

Booth must have been terrified. But she showed immense courage and continued to dismiss Heimpel's allegations as fanciful. She reminded him that she was a personal friend of the Führer and called Heimpel's bluff by demanding to be taken to Brown so she could confront him with his lies. There was a stand-off. Heimpel knew that the Gestapo had not yet started interrogating Brown and was not ready to produce him.

Reluctantly he released Booth, although not before warning her that she would be watched closely and very soon would indeed be introduced to Brown.

For three weeks over Christmas and the new year, Brown and his men were left to rot in their cells, not knowing whether they would meet their ends at the hands of the Gestapo torturers or by RAF bombs that were targeting key Nazi infrastructure. All the time Brown was desperately working his magic on the guards. Brown still had good contacts among the Gestapo who were regular guests at the shows he arranged in Genshagen. To the German guards, Brown was a likeable British rogue whose fondness for schnapps was matched only by his interest in the Fräuleins. He showered Red Cross goodies on the Germans like confetti, and at the Cafe Vaterland used his German currency to hire female favours for some of the goons. Now he needed to draw down on his investments. By chance, one of the more corruptible officers was in charge of the prison guard detail. Brown managed to get his attention and offered him enough Red Cross parcels to fill his bierkeller if he would let him escape. The officer agreed, and even forged Brown an SS pass with Himmler's stamp.

It was once again a very lucky escape for the Royal Artillery quartermaster. Reg Beattie, who hadn't been able to evade the Gestapo interrogators, was not so lucky, and had his front teeth ground down with an iron file. The Brighton gunner survived the war, but the torture took a terrible toll on his mental health.[2]

Chapter 35

Death March

In Berlin, Brown was reunited with Jimmy Newcomb, who had escaped after the first search of Genshagen. The two POWs boarded a train full of British prisoners being sent east to Lamsdorf Prison in Upper Silesia where the front line was just 10 miles away. When they arrived, they found the Russian air force was mounting hourly sweeps over the camp; German air defences were almost non-existent, so no German fighters or anti-aircraft fire were sent up to counter the enemy intruders.

Camp conditions were just as dire. Food was extremely scarce, and the camp commandant was rationing the water supplies for both the prisoners and his own men.

The Russians were now only a few miles away, and the commandant, finally succumbing to the inevitable, prepared to abandon the prison and march the prisoners west in the thick of winter. Brown later recalled: 'I can never forget watching that motley crew walking through those gates… I wondered how many would make it home… Few POWs were fit for a normal walk, let alone a 600-mile trek across Germany in the worst possible winter conditions, harassed by Allied bombers and the ground-strafing fighters by day and at night huddling together in a snow-clad field.'[1]

Despite all this, the German guards managed to retain a semblance of discipline, although they knew they couldn't push the POWs too far. The thin, brittle line of authority which separated the prisoner from his guard was close to breaking point.

Brown and Newcomb had no choice but to join the end of the column of the two thousand POWs, trust in God, and pray for the arrival of General Montgomery.

Brown soon discovered he had more than bombs and the harsh German winter to contend with.

After his escape from the clutches of the Gestapo, Heimpel had no doubts that Brown was the British agent he always suspected he was.

At Genshagen and Stalag III-D HQ, Brown had been given unprecedented access to the German intelligence and security apparatus. Heimpel, Hesse, Ziegfeld and Lange had all trusted him with secret details about Nazi operations. Brown could name names and would be able to attribute war crimes to individual Nazis. Heimpel no longer cared about the sabotaging of the BFC and Genshagen or even Brown's spy network. The Germans were about to lose the war and the Nazi chief of POW counter-intelligence faced the prospect of soon being a prisoner of the Allies. The theft of the Red Cross parcels alone would be enough to see Heimpel hang.

It was a matter of the gravest importance that Brown was caught and executed before he got back to the British lines.

Heimpel arranged for an order signed by Himmler to go out to all POW camps stating that POW 11953 BQMS John Brown was a British spy who must be detained and returned to Gestapo headquarters in Berlin.

Equally, the British had much to lose should their double agent fall into the hands of the Gestapo. Brown not only held the secret codes used to contact London, he also knew the names of the British agents who were using them. If he was caught, dozens of lives would be in danger.

The situation at Lamsdorf was far too chaotic for the commandant to follow up on the Himmler order. But there would be many stopovers at other camps on the 600-mile trek where thorough POW checks would be carried out. Brown thought about changing his name by switching identity discs, but he was already too well-known a figure among the POWs, most of whom regarded him as a collaborator, and he feared being handed over to the Germans by his own side. Contemplating his impossible situation, Brown lamented: 'There was no one I could go to for advice, for by now it had become "each man for himself" and soon it would be "survival of the fittest".'[2]

Until he could come up with a better plan, he would stay with the marchers. The deep snow and Russian air attacks meant progress was slow; the number of sick and wounded quickly started to mount up. And all the time, the Russian front line was getting nearer and nearer. On the second day, it was the turn of Allied bombers, who mistook the long lines of POWs for retreating German soldiers.

The next day, the column reached a POW camp where the men rested and collected more prisoners.

Addressing the new arrivals, the camp commandant tried to reassure his prisoners by promising them they would all be protected by the Reich and eventually handed over to the British authorities. But first he said it was imperative that he made contact with one of their number: 'I have a message for a prisoner if he is here – BQMS John Brown?'

The British sergeant was so surprised to hear his name being called out he was about to step forward until Newcomb had the wit to pull him back. When no one came forward, the commandant warned them: 'We cannot wait now to check all identity discs, but at a later stage of the journey there will be a full check with photographs.'[3]

Brown was a marked man, rations were low and the Russians were getting closer every day.

Busty decided he would have to leave the marchers as soon as possible, and he asked Jimmy Newcomb to come with him. Newcomb, who had been close to Brown at Genshagen where he had helped run the camp's black market, was not going to be left behind to face awkward questions about his absent friend. He had come to rely on Busty to always get them out of the stickiest of situations. When all seemed lost and he feared the Germans were about to rumble them, Brown somehow found a way to turn the tables.

Outside the protection of the German prisoner escort, the British escapers faced vengeful attacks from the Volkssturm, SS extermination squads operating at the rear of the German lines, and trigger-happy Russians. But Newcomb had no hesitation – 'I'm with you, Busty.'

On the second day of the second stage of the march, Brown and Newcomb made their move.

In the afternoon, another Russian air attack sent the guards and their prisoners diving for cover. Brown saw that most of the Germans had their heads buried in the snow as the bombs dropped all around them. He grabbed Newcomb.

'Let's make a run for those pine trees – a German bullet would hurt no more than a Russian bomb.'

The British soldiers jumped up from their positions and ran as fast as their tired legs could carry them through the deep, sinking snow until they reached the cover of the first trees. Brown expected to be picked off at any moment – if not by the camp guards, then by an SS unit lurking in the forest waiting for deserters and Russian reconnaissance units. But miraculously not a single shot was fired at them. The Germans were too concerned about their own survival to worry about escaping British prisoners who were risking far more by running from the safety of the POW detachment into the frozen wilderness towards the enemy.

Brown and Newcomb laid low in the thick of the trees until they felt it was safe to move on. The weather was bitterly cold and their summer uniforms could not protect them from impending hypothermia. Moreover, they had very little food, perhaps enough for three more days.

Brown told Newcomb that they had to keep moving, otherwise they would die in the open.

They decided to break cover, and emerged from the forest close to a road which they followed to a small, eerily quiet village. The two men approached tentatively, and after passing the first houses, abruptly stopped in their tracks. There on a side road they saw a large German staff car parked outside one of the houses.

This was their chance. Brown told Newcomb that if the keys were still in the ignition they could steal it before attracting the attention of its owner. It was too good an opportunity to miss. Brown carried out a reconnaissance walk past the car and just as he had hoped the keys were still in the ignition. Brown crept back to rejoin Newcomb at the end of the road.

After a few minutes' conference, they decided Brown should break in through the car window, start the ignition and drive back to collect Newcomb who would be keeping watch, ready to sound the alarm. It would be a piece of cake. But just as Brown was climbing into the car, the door to the house on the opposite side of the road opened and a man appeared wearing the uniform of an SS colonel. The Nazi officer immediately saw Brown, who was now halfway through the car window, and began fumbling for his revolver buttoned in his leather holster. With a Luger in one hand he rushed forward to get a closer shot at the car thief. Jimmy Newcomb had already seen the danger and was racing towards the Nazi from the other side of the street. Before the German could squeeze off his shot, Newcomb had rugby-tackled him in the middle of the road and thrown him on to his back, knocking the gun from his hand. Brown heard the shouts and turned round to see the two men wrestling in the snow. He threw open the car door and dived on the rolling bodies twisting in the snow. The SS man fought fiercely, punching, kicking and pushing at the British soldiers, who were now pummelling him with all the strength they could muster. Finally the German's resistance weakened, and

Brown and Newcomb were able to rain blows on to his face until he was dead.

They pulled the dead body on to the grass verge and then drove the car west – Brown dressed as an SS colonel and Newcomb wearing the uniform of a Wehrmacht soldier which he had found in the back of the car.

Their route took them past Blechhamer, their old camp, where they intended to head southwest to Slovakia in the direction of Switzerland. Blechhammer looked almost deserted as the German staff car sped through the town. Two remaining residents, who had decided to take their chances with the Russians, stood by the roadside and obediently gave a Nazi salute to the SS colonel as he swept by.

Chapter 36

Downfall

The fate and safety of all the British POWs was in the hands of Gottlob Berger, the Nazi leader of the Waffen-SS responsible for countless atrocities across Nazi-occupied Europe. Hitler now pressed him to defend the Reich by executing select groups of POWs in the hope of bringing the Allies to the negotiating table. Berger, who was more concerned with his own self-preservation, resisted, and instead tried to reach out to Britain.

He ordered Vivian Stranders to find Lieutenant John Calthrop and bring him to his offices in Berlin. Calthrop had been dividing his time in the German capital between working for a Nazi propaganda film unit and wooing Margery Booth.

When he arrived at the SS headquarters, the German general told him he wanted to send him on a peace mission to Britain.[1] Berger confided in Calthrop that his daughter had been raped by 'Bolsheviks', and his two sons had been killed on the Eastern Front. He said he would 'fight to the death' against the Russians but would not fight the British or the Americans. Berger instructed the bewildered Calthrop that once he was in London he was to contact the British Cabinet and tell them to make preparations for the receipt of 500 British officers held as POWs by the Germans. This was to be Berger's gesture of his good faith. In return, he expected the British to reciprocate by repatriating German prisoners to help Berger in the Nazis' last stand against the Russians.

On 12 April 1945, Calthrop crossed the German border into Switzerland posing as a Hungarian electrician and was promptly arrested and flown back to Britain.

The British officer was taken to Room 055, MI5's interrogation centre in Whitehall, where he was greeted by Lieutenant Colonel Seymer who began questioning Calthrop about his role with the Nazis.

Calthrop tried to pretend he had been stringing the Germans along and that he had only been waiting for the right moment to escape. His mission to London to seek a German/British prisoner exchange was just such a chance and he had grasped it. If anything, he expected to be rewarded for his efforts. But the smug Calthrop hadn't reckoned on how much MI5 knew about him. Brown's secret reports were now in British hands, and they painted a very different picture.

Having listened to Calthrop's less than convincing account, Seymer decided it was time to 'make his position clear to him'.[2]

Seymer pointed out that Calthrop's 'story did not match' Brown's intelligence about his 'activities now coming into our hands'.

The MI5 director noted afterwards 'he does not appear in the least to appreciate his position and throughout his story there is a curious failure to recognise the difference between fraternisation in peace and war.' Seymer concluded that Calthrop was a 'collaborator' whose 'statement stank' and he recommended him to be court-martialled.

After waiting more than a month and hearing nothing from Calthrop, Berger was left to surmise that his overtures had been rebuffed by the British.

However, Berger had one more important card to play in his efforts to save himself from a war which he knew the Germans were about to lose.

At the same time that Berger's British peace envoy was cross-ing the German/Swiss border, American forces had reached the outskirts of Colditz town. Colonel Willie Tod and his senior officers had been expecting rescue for many weeks. Waiting for the Allies to push through the German defences of depleted SS units and Hitler Youth only added to the tense atmosphere inside the castle. The POWs could sense their captivity drawing to a close, but also feared being caught in a murderous crossfire in the Nazis' last stand, or getting massacred by the Gestapo like the RAF officers who had taken part in the Sagan great escape.

Julius Green, who had been waiting much longer for the Germans to repatriate him to Britain on grounds of his faked insanity, described the prison conditions as the worst he could remember. He had not received a Red Cross parcel for months, and the men were now so hungry the guards were able to charge the British inmates £10 for a single egg. Green said he was so hungry he would have handed over his life savings for a piece of non-kosher bacon.[3]

Tod had received the MI9 instruction not to undertake any more escape attempts. But the presence of the prominente made all the prisoners' situation more perilous. Rumours about the real value of the prominente to the Nazis, and more importantly their intended fate, had been closely followed in London.

Julius Green and the other MI9 agents had been told that the British believed the prominente were to be held as hostages to be 'exchanged for Nazi chiefs' who had already fallen into Allied hands.

But as advance American forces began approaching the town, Green had picked up intelligence that the Germans were now planning to transfer the most important prisoners to Hitler's Bavarian redoubt where they were to be used as human shields. Their predicament could not have been graver.

Green and the other Colditz coders tried to convey this message to London as quickly as possible using the usual secret lines of communication.

In February, Gottlob Berger ordered a detachment of soldiers to Colditz town where they were to await his orders.

For Julius Green, the situation was especially dangerous. He was a Jew who had taken particular interest in the Nazi concentration camp near Blechhammer, details of which he had passed back to his MI9 handlers. In Colditz town there was another concentration camp for Hungarian slave labourers who were being worked to death in the nearby kaolin quarries. On a rare escorted trip to the town, Green had caught glimpses of their bag-of-bones bodies and pathetic expressions. He could see they were being worked to death just like the Poles and Jews at Blechhammer. When the Americans reached the outskirts of the town, the SS guards began massacring the workers. Green was determined that the Nazis should pay for their crimes, and in those last weeks of the war he let the Germans know it.[4] He was playing a very risky game. His certificate of insanity would not protect him from the vengeful Gestapo.

Lieutenant Colonel Cecil Merritt and Lieutenant Colonel George Young, the two officers in charge of security, were still concerned that a Colditz spy might be working for the Germans. Should the POWs have to defend themselves against the SS, they would first need to wrest control of the castle from the Wehrmacht guards. They had to mitigate the possibility that a traitor was feeding information to the Germans who could betray their plans. The two British counter-intelligence officers reviewed the situation. The self-confessed spy Purdy had been removed from the camp nine months ago. Dr Mazumdar, whose open hostility to the British had left Merritt no choice but to treat him as a high-security risk, had also gone. Yet the Germans had continued to make regular finds, and no one had escaped from the castle in nearly 18 months.

Merritt and Young now considered all the potential suspects. Alec Ross, whose place on a separate repatriation programme had been vetoed by Bader, had a genuine axe to grind against the officers and Bader in particular.

There were two more officers of whom many of the prisoners remained suspicious.

Micky Burn had been allowed to work with Rupert Barry, taking shorthand notes of BBC radio broadcasts, but he remained committed to Bolshevism and refused to take part in any escapes.

Questions were also hanging over Ralph Holroyd, who had been allowed a visit from his mother bearing a letter personally signed by Hitler.

Shortly after his arrival at Colditz, the Poles had bequeathed him the POWs' secret camera which had proved very useful in faking escape documents. But while the camera was in Holroyd's possession, a German security guard had discovered its secret location, setting back a number of escape plans.

In March 1945, Reinhold Eggers informed Willie Tod that the SS were to take charge of the camp and he was to be relieved of his responsibility for the Colditz prisoners. He had received orders that preparations were to be made for the prominente to move out of the prison. It seemed the POWs' worst fears were about to materialise.

In London, Major Miles Reid, who had been repatriated from Colditz the previous year, was briefing security chiefs at the War Office about the special dangers now facing the prisoners. Reid, older brother of Pat Reid, one of the first British POWs to make a Colditz home run, was familiar with the character of the British POWs. He knew which ones were trustworthy and which ones still had questions to answer.

Miles Reid shared his security concerns with the War Office and proposed a paratrooper rescue operation.[5] He had an intimate knowledge of the prison layout and was willing to personally lead such a mission. But in the event, a rescue operation was deemed too risky and too late in the day. It was left to Willie Tod to vigorously protest to Commandant Prawitt about German plans to move the prominente. Prawitt said his hands were tied, and showed him a letter written by Himmler setting out the 'marching orders' for the Allied VIPs. Tod warned him that if anything happened to them, Prawitt would answer in a court of law. Prawitt just shrugged his shoulders.

Under the cover of darkness at 1:30 a.m, 13 April 1945, the prominente left the prison with their SS escort. Hopetoun and Haig were too ill to make the onward journey and so were left behind.

Driven in two buses, the party headed towards Hitler's Eagle's Nest, in the Bavarian mountains. They first reached Königstein Castle on the River Elbe before continuing to Laufen, close to the border with Austria. The senior British officer, John Elphinstone, became uneasy about what the Germans were planning for them, and when the prominente reached the camp at Laufen the prisoners refused to disembark. After a stand-off with the SS, the Germans agreed to take them to Tittmoning Castle where some of the other POW officers had begun their captivity.

A few days later, Berger was called to a meeting with Hitler where the Führer discussed the fate of the VIP prisoners. During this meeting, Hitler ordered Berger to execute all the prominente and to tell him as soon as it had been carried out.

Early on the morning of 15 April 1945, Julius Green and the rest of the prisoners left behind at Coldtiz were disturbed by the sound of sporadic machine-gun fire. Green watched from his cell window as the SS troops quartered in the town and a group of mostly elderly and lightly armed Volkssturm retreated across the Colditz town bridge over the River Mulde. When the Germans failed to blow the bridge, American Sherman tanks trundled into the middle of Colditz and fanned out along the streets.

Green anxiously waited for either the SS to storm the castle and slaughter all inside or the Americans to rush over the bridge and liberate the POWs. Instead, Green found himself diving for cover as a couple of loose rounds fired by the US artillery hit the castle just above Douglas Bader's quarters. Then silence. A few minutes later the castle gates opened and a single American GI,[6] unshaven, chewing gum and with his helmet straps dangling around his chin, appeared in the courtyard. Within seconds he was being mobbed by the jubilant prisoners until he became overwhelmed and was forced to wave his machine gun in the air to clear his path.

'It is over!' declared Julius Green. In a matter of seconds the Wehrmacht guards had deserted their posts and were being replaced by armed British officers.

For the next few weeks, the secrets of Colditz were proudly given up to the Allied press corps who were arriving at the castle to grab interviews with the high-ranking prisoners.

The famous Colditz Glider had never taken to the air but its construction was a remarkable feat of British engineering and POW ingenuity. Perhaps the Germans had been tipped off about its existence in the attics but thought it better to do nothing, hoping the work would keep the captives fully occupied so they couldn't take part in other escapes more likely to succeed. In the last two years of Colditz, not a single prisoner had managed to escape from the German fortress.

Julius Green, Alec Ross, Micky Burn and Ralph Holroyd would soon be back in Britain. The senior British officer, Colonel Tod, who had kept detailed files on a number of sensitive issues at Colditz including the case against the traitor Walter Purdy, began making his final report.

But it was Captain Birendra Mazumdar who arrived in Britain first. After going on hunger strike, he had been transferred from Colditz to a prison for Indian POWs where he had escaped and crossed the Swiss border. He would be first of the Colditz 'spies' to be questioned by MI5:

'They questioned me for two days. When I had nothing to say, they told me, "You are ruining your chances of getting a medal." I burst out laughing. "Do you think I escaped and went through all this to get a medal?"'

Back in Germany the fate of the prominente was still hanging in the balance. A convoy of vehicles left Tittmoning and headed south up the Austrian mountains towards Berchtesgaden, Hitler's mountain-top headquarters. Progress was held up by columns of retreating SS units coming down the mountain. On 28 April they stopped at Markt Pongau, a run-down prison camp, where all the prisoners spent the night.

The next day, a large black Mercedes pulled up in the courtyard. Out stepped a weary-looking SS-Obergruppenführer who walked purposefully towards the entrance to the POWs' new quarters. Reprising the speech he had given to Lieutenant Calthrop shortly before sending him on his peace mission to London, Gottlob Berger told the gathered officers and aristocrats that he had no quarrel with the British. He had only ever wanted to defend Germany against Bolshevism, and the war between Germany and England was a mistake. Then he handed out cigarettes and glasses of whiskey before explaining that the Third Reich was finished and that in the chaos he could not guarantee their safety. He told them that Hitler had ordered him to execute them but he had refused.

Delivering his speech in dark theatrical tones, Berger said it was he who had rescued them from Laufen, but he added menacingly: 'When the whole German people are weeping, the English Royal Family should not be laughing.'[7] An uncomfortable-looking John Elphinstone, better known as the nephew of King George VI, shuffled in his chair.

On 30 April news reached Berger that Hitler, who had retreated to his Berlin bunker, had taken his own life, dramatically changing the closing chapter of the war. No longer fearing the Führer's death squads, Berger immediately arranged for the prominente to be handed over to an American unit of the 53rd Division that had reached Innsbruck. In yet another parting speech, the puffed up Berger impressed upon the Allied POWs how much he had personally risked to bring them to safety. A few weeks later, Berger surrendered to the Americans.

Chapter 37

Hostile Reception

On 1 May 1945 John Brown reached Erfurt, a medieval town just 70 miles west of Colditz, also in American hands. There he was treated to the full hospitality of the American army, where the US equivalent of Women's Amry Corps served him his first cup of real coffee for nearly five years. That night, Brown and some other newly released POWs were invited to a party hosted by the German-American actress Marlene Dietrich who, in her US army uniform, sang songs and doled out the drinks.

Brown, finally safe from Heimpel and the Gestapo, was able to reflect upon his good fortune while paying proper attention to the female American soldiers. Sitting under canvas on a table laden with drink and food, the MI9 agent reached down to remove his left shoe and prised open the heel to reveal a tightly folded set of micro documents. These were his secret records of all the British traitors and their role in their service to the Nazis. Here were all the names, ranks, army numbers and POW identity logs which had been so carefully copied by Reg Beattie. This miniature charge sheet would prove to be of great interest to MI5 and the Attorney General, who were building the case for the prosecution of the traitors. Brown persuaded himself that British intelligence wouldn't begrudge him staying a little longer, enjoying the feminine hospitality of the American army before he returned to England and did his duty to British justice.

So he hung around for three more days before being flown to the British POW reception centre in Brussels. The lines of arriving

British soldiers were directed to busy processing desks where military clerks were waiting with pens and paper to collect information about their time in captivity. Brown was given a form asking him to identify any German guards who had mistreated the prisoners, any British soldiers who had worked for the Nazis and anyone suspected of being a member of the British Free Corps. Brown figured that the intelligence he possessed was too sensitive to be collected in this manner, so scribbled across the form 'have additional information available when I reach England' and then handed it back to the clerk.[1]

The other POWs arriving at the reception centre were far less circumspect when their turn came to inform the military who they thought had been working for the Germans. Some of them remembered Brown and his men from their days at Blechhammer or Genshagen, when the quartermaster and his gang had been living it large and cosying up to the Germans. Unaware of Brown's secret agent work, they naturally volunteered Brown's name as someone who should be added to the traitor list.

It didn't take long for the British military police to link the battery quartermaster's name and service number with the reports they had received from other servicemen returning from German captivity. Only a few months earlier, British forces in Brussels had captured the traitors Courlander and Maton, who had both named Brown in their statements as a possible collaborator, while others were convinced he had been stealing Red Cross parcels for himself. The case against Busty Brown appeared damning. While Brown stood in line patiently waiting for instructions for his repatriation, he was approached by a military police sergeant who told him to accompany him to the guard house where he was arrested on a charge of aiding the enemy. His seat on the next flight to England was cancelled and he was placed under house arrest and held in a cell familiar to ones he had shared in his first days as a German POW.

Chapter 38

Soldier Spy

In the aftermath of German army's failure to break out from the Ardennes, Walter Purdy's SS unit was moved to forward positions between Krefeld and Kempen in western Germany, close to the front line on the River Rhine.[1] Purdy was now under the command of Sturmbannführer Anton Kriegbaum and Sturmbannführer Hans Damrau, two seasoned officers of the SS Standarte (paramilitary) detachment who had seen action on the Eastern Front. The Rhine basin was going to be where the final and decisive battles on the Western Front were to be fought. The Germans clung to the belief that even at this late stage in the war they could make use of crude propaganda to fool the Allies into thinking a force of 5,000 renegades was waiting on the other side of the Rhine. Damrau ordered Purdy to make a number of[2] recordings of an 'Englishman' singing national songs that could be broadcast over radio speakers close to the British front line, which he did.

A few weeks later Purdy, and the rest of the Kurt Eggers company were pulled back from the front line. Purdy, proudly wearing his SS uniform, returned to Berlin on leave, desperate to be reunited with the pregnant Gretel. But when he arrived at their apartment on 20 March 1945 he found it empty and Gretel nowhere to be seen. A note on the kitchen table told him she had been taken to Dr Lessing's maternity clinic 100 kilometres north of Berlin.[3] Purdy wasted no more time and raced to the station to catch a train to the hospital. He made it in the nick of time, and found Gretel lying in a bed in one of the public wards being cared for by the midwives. Gretel had heard nothing from Purdy during his months away on the Western Front, and was overjoyed to be reunited with him in time for the birth of their child. Purdy still couldn't quite believe that amid all the murderous chaos and mayhem of the war, he was going to be a father. The maternity ward was an oasis of calm and his mental strain of the last few months gave way to dreams of a new life with Gretel after the war.

But no sooner had he settled down in the hospital than he received an urgent message from Major Heimpel telling him to report to Stalag III-D immediately. He phoned the Stalag protesting that his wife was about to go into labour and begged for a few more hours' leave. Heimpel laughed and told him that the war couldn't wait for his baby to arrive. Resistance was futile. It would be another 18 months before he saw Gretel again.

Purdy was told to report to the SS headquarters in Berlin. On 7 April he was sent to northern Italy where he was once again put to work in a propaganda unit broadcasting to the Allies. The fighting in Italy had entered its last weeks and the Germans were preparing to make their final stand. This was also where John Amery was holding meetings with the Italian leader Benito Mussolini, hoping to broker an 11th-hour peace deal between Germany and the Allies.

In truth there was little to negotiate, and the British and American armies were busy preparing a new offensive, Operation Buckland, in northern Italy.

The capture of Bologna, a vital communication hub, was the key prize eyed by the British and American forces.

Purdy joined an SS unit supporting the XIV Panzer Corps, where he was once again involved in a last-ditch defence. The British naval officer thought he had come too far and sacrificed too much already to end up as a random casualty in a hopeless military campaign waged against his own country.

It was time to change sides. On 23 April 1945 Purdy swapped his SS uniform for Royal Navy dress and with a Dutch POW made an escape on a stolen motorbike, reaching the US 88th Division in Bologna.[4] Six days later, the German forces in Italy capitulated.

Both Brown and Purdy were now in Allied hands; neither had stories that stood up to the scrutiny of the military police who were on the lookout for spies and traitors. Brown was under house arrest suspected of working for the Germans, while the treacherous Purdy was presenting himself as a bona fide POW escapee.

After reaching American lines, Purdy was transferred to Mediterranean Royal Navy headquarters in Naples where, in line with War Office protocol for returning POWs in the field, he was interviewed and asked to account for his movements. Purdy told the interviewing officers that after his ship had sunk off the Norwegian coast, he had been taken prisoner and had made his escape on motorbike. This very short and selective version of his story was true.

Nevertheless, Purdy's name was already known to Naval Intelligence, and the senior officer sent a message to London with news of the renegade's sudden reappearance in Naples. Diana Barnes at MI5 wired back a telegram urgently instructing the Royal Navy security office not to impede Purdy on his journey back to Britain. MI5 were still building their case and needed more time to locate and interview prosecution witnesses. As far as MI5 was aware, the only witness who was in British hands and had evidence against Purdy was Lieutenant John Calthrop, who had told MI5 he had known the naval officer while working for the German Foreign Office in Berlin. While this was damning, Calthrop was a tarnished witness who was facing his own court martial. The defence would make mincemeat of the prosecution case if Calthrop took the stand. The two key MI9 agents in the case, John Brown and Julius Green, had not been located. Green would soon be home to be reunited with his family and his MI9 handlers. But Brown, unknown to MI9, was still being held by British forces in Brussels on false accusations of collaborating with the enemy.

In London, Lieutenant Colonel Seymer (SLB3) and Lieutenant Colonel Sinclair (SLB1) hastily arranged a conference with Lieutenant Commander Ricketts, one of the heads of Naval Intelligence, to discuss the best way to proceed with Purdy's case.

They gathered at the Admiralty naval law offices in Queen Anne's Mansions, together with MI9's Naval Liaison Officer, Lieutenant Commander Andrews.[5]

Purdy was a serving naval officer and the Navy was determined to take charge of his interrogation. Seymer objected. Walter Purdy was one of the names at the top of his traitors' list and he insisted that the conduct of Purdy's case was 'entirely a matter for MI5 interrogators'. He said it was important that nothing should be done to alert Purdy that he was under suspicion as MI5 needed more time to get their evidential ducks in a row. In the meantime the Navy should treat him as an ordinary naval officer returning to Britain. Ricketts relented.

On 18 May, Purdy was allowed to board a ship bound for Britain. The week-long voyage gave him plenty of time to prepare his story. After his confession to Colonel Tod in Colditz, he knew he would have some questions to answer – but how much did MI5 know about his activities in occupied Europe? Purdy hoped to rely on the fog of war to avoid any uncomfortable scrutiny by the British secret services.

While Purdy was at sea, the Admiralty made an alarming discovery. Because Purdy was a merchant seaman (before he was commissioned into the Royal Navy under war time regulations), naval jurisdiction over him ceased upon the sinking of his ship in Norwegian waters in June 1940. It seemed the military might not even have the power to detain Purdy when he reached British territory.

Seymer wrote to Shelford: 'Sorry to have to pass you this screaming baby. The worst of it is that he turns out to be a civilian, already on the high seas, whose entry into this country cannot be prevented. This is not our fault since his status depended upon which form of contract covered his service with the RN. You will see from the first minute at 78a that the Admiralty discovered yesterday that Purdy's subjection to naval law ended with the sinking of his ship, so as a merchant seaman and civilian he becomes your case.'

MI5 would have to act quickly if they didn't want Purdy to disappear forever as soon as he discovered he was no longer subject to naval military discipline.

Chapter 39

The Loyal Traitor

Thomas Shelford alerted the local police forces to Walter Purdy's imminent arrival and ordered James Davies, a senior investigating MI5 officer seconded from Scotland Yard, to conduct Purdy's interrogation. But they had to find him first. Davies discovered that it wasn't even certain at which port Purdy's ship was due to dock, so he arranged for officers to wait for him at Liverpool and Glasgow. Purdy's hope to take advantage of British confusion at the end of the war appeared to be justified.

Purdy eventually turned up at Glasgow where he was treated as an ordinary returning naval POW and transferred to the Royal Naval College at Greenwich. He was informed he would be held for only a few days while the authorities prepared his POW release papers. Davies, however, planned to keep him there as long as possible, until MI5 had sufficient evidence to charge him.

But within hours of his arrival on 25 May, Purdy asked to see a member of Naval Intelligence as he had some very important information he wished to disclose to them.

The next morning, James Davies travelled to Greenwich to speak to Purdy.

Davies was taken to Purdy's room and without knocking opened the door:

'We are officers of the Intelligence Service. I understand you want to see a Naval Intelligence officer about something.'

Purdy, who was writing at his desk, seemed unperturbed by Davies' abrupt entrance.

'Yes, it is about my interrogation in Italy,' Purdy replied, not getting up. 'All that I said then is not true as I did not think them to be the proper authorities to tell the story to.'

'What information do you have?' asked the MI5 officer.

'I have important information I wish to pass on to the proper authorities.'[1]

The implication was that Davies was too junior an officer for Purdy to deal with. Davies decided it was time to put Purdy under some pressure: 'I have reason to believe, that amongst other things, you have done broadcasts and propaganda work for the Germans.'

Purdy appeared completely unsurprised by Davies' sudden direct accusation.

'That is true,' said Purdy, 'but it is linked with the sabotage. I will tell you about it and how I came to be linked up with the Germans.'

Purdy then explained that he had been secretly working for Britain and that his broadcasts contained coded messages that warned the RAF about the weather conditions in Berlin. He had also written coded letters to his mother and sister which were intended for the Air Ministry where his nephew worked. He did not deny meeting William Joyce nor working at the Büro Concordia. He only hoped his broadcasts and letters had been of value to the War Office.

Purdy said he had also carried out acts of sabotage in Berlin including, under the cover of an air raid, firebombing the 'night fighter headquarters of the Berlin Defence system' and the Siemens factory that was making parts for the V-1 rockets. On two occasions he even claimed he had tried to assassinate William Joyce, once throwing a hand grenade into a train compartment in which Joyce was travelling.

He explained to Davies that he had let the Germans believe he was a traitor so that he could carry out these actions against the enemy. Purdy said he was arrested by the Gestapo on 7 March 1944 and sent to Colditz, where he was mistaken by the British for a German spy and handed to the camp authorities.

He claimed he was placed in solitary confinement before being taken to the nearby town of Rochlitz, where the Germans sentenced him to death. He was told that if he didn't carry out propaganda work for the SS they would execute his girlfriend.

Purdy insisted this was the true account of what had happened to him, adding, 'although I can see now what a fool I have been.'

Davies was not in a position to challenge anything that Purdy had told him. Hostilities had ceased only two weeks earlier on 8 May, and Europe was still in a state of chaos. The war-weary British forces had to marshal and administer hundreds of thousands of captured soldiers and refugees as well as repatriate their own servicemen.

The security and intelligence services of MI5, MI6 and MI9 were also facing new challenges, confronting the threat from Russia and the start of a Cold War.

There was political pressure as well. The public wanted retribution and vengeance on the traitors who had served Hitler while the Luftwaffe was bombing them in their beds. Now the war was won, the newspapers were whipping up a frenzy of hatred against William Joyce and John Amery. No one had heard of Walter Purdy, although many in the service believed he had done just as much to endanger British lives as the better-known traitors.

Davies wrote up his report to Cussen and Shelford setting out the evidential position.

It included evidence from another witness, the radio engineer Robert Lindemere, who Davies had discovered had been in England since 1944 after he had escaped from the Gestapo and taken refuge in the Swiss Embassy. Lindemere's statement[2] against Purdy appeared damning: 'I have no hesitation in saying Purdy is a traitor. I told Purdy I could get him out of the country if he wanted to go but he refused and said, "I can't go now; I am up to my neck in it and I would rather kill myself than be taken back to England."'

But further interviews with Lindemere revealed years of captivity in Germany had taken a terrible toll on his mental health. He was a drug addict, and Davies strongly advised against calling him as he would be an 'appalling witness'.

The only other significant witness he had been able to interview was the captain of Purdy's ship, the *Vandyck*, who was also the senior British officer at Marlag. Captain 'Tug' Wilson had no hesitation in saying that he suspected Purdy of working for the Germans, and had recounted how he had personally admonished the British officer when he discovered that he had requested and received a signed copy of Joyce's book *Twilight Over England*.

Wilson also handed Davies the letter Purdy had instructed Lieutenant George Thorpe, the camp paymaster, to give to the senior commanding officer of the camp when Purdy left for Berlin in July 1943. In it, Purdy said that any work he did for the Germans was done only to help secure his escape. Wilson thought this was damning, but Davies knew this actually corroborated the story Purdy had told him at Greenwich.

Davies had more success with Lieutenant Jolly, one of the officers whom Wilson had instructed to keep an eye on Purdy at Kommando 999.

Davies wrote to his MI5 bosses: 'There is one interesting point about Jolly's statement. After Purdy's departure [from Kommando 999] his mail was readdressed to "% of Major Heimpel" which was a most unusual procedure as normally such mail was directed to the camp to which a prisoner was sent.'[3]

In conclusion, Davies said: 'In my view a clear case of collaborating with the enemy exists against Purdy… I am inclined to believe that his story of the alleged sabotage activities is totally untrue, and merely put forward at this stage in an attempt to excuse his collaboration.'

Davies may not have believed a single word Purdy had told him, but until MI5 had located its key witnesses, there was insufficient evidence upon which to hold the British traitor.

Reluctantly the MI5 officer informed Purdy he was free to go home to stay with his mother in Barking, where he was to report any change of address to his local police station.

Within days, Purdy had moved into a flat at 20 West Cornwell Road, Earls Court, and was enjoying his new-found freedom in London. With the help of a Royal Naval works programme he took a job as a machine tool salesman at an engineering firm in Putney and applied for membership of the exclusive King George's Officers' Club in Piccadilly.

Very soon he was frequenting his old Soho haunts and dating a series of women whom he entertained with his war stories of daring escapes and encounters with the Gestapo. The naval officer became particularly close to a telephonist he chatted up when he made an enquiry at the Cunningham Telephone Exchange in Hall Road, NW8. Her name was Betty Blaney from St John's Wood, and she soon became involved in a relationship with the dashing young naval officer who had impressed her with his story of his 'escape' from Colditz Castle. The couple went out for dinner almost every night and at least twice a week took in a West End show. Betty Blaney became fascinated by the young naval war hero and his Walter Mitty stories about life as a POW in Berlin working for British intelligence.[4]

Purdy made no mention of the mother of his child in Germany, whom he had sworn to marry as soon as the war was over.

His life had moved on, and any claims Gretel and his son may have had upon him were conveniently forgotten. He had also had enough of the Navy and visited a hospital where he convinced doctors he was suffering from acute anxiety brought on by his detention in a German POW camp. This diagnosis enabled him to be medically discharged from the Navy on a full war disability pension. After five years he was finally free from the British military.

While Purdy spent the summer of 1945 posing as a brave serviceman celebrating the end of the war, MI5 continued the painstaking business of locating the missing witnesses they hoped would bring the curtain down on the adventures of the 'British POW hero' Walter Purdy.

The testimonies of Maton and Courlander led Davies to strongly suspect Purdy had been a member of the SS but he was unable to prove it. He knew that all members of the Waffen-SS had a blood tattoo, a small black mark underneath the left arm denoting the soldier's blood group. If Purdy had one, then it would be irrefutable evidence of his membership. But how was Davies going to find out? Purdy was a free man and could refuse a request to bear his arm. Then, Davies had a major piece of good fortune. Purdy had entrusted Betty Blaney with a copy of a self-serving statement that explained his actions in the war. He intended it to be the draft for an autobiography entitled 'The Loyal Traitor'. Blaney, who was more broke than she was in love with Purdy, immediately recognised the incriminating nature of the writing and threatened to sell his story to the papers unless he paid her some money.

But Purdy turned the tables on Blaney and went to the police, who had no choice but to charge her with blackmail. The notes on his prospective autobiography were little more than an embellishment of the statement he had already given to MI5, but the case gave Davies an idea. He realised he had another way of discovering whether Purdy carried the SS tattoo – he could question Betty Blaney. When Blaney told Davies she was pretty sure there was no such tattoo[5] or any other distinctive marking on Purdy's body, Davies began to wonder whether Purdy would ever stand trial for treason.

Chapter 40

Green and Brown

The USAF Dakota flying Captain Julius Green home to Britain touched down at an airfield near Amersham in Buckinghamshire. Five wasted summers had passed since the dentist and MI9 agent had left Scotland for France. Two and a half stones lighter and mentally exhausted, Green knew he would never be able to expunge from his mind the acts of barbaric cruelty he had witnessed as a POW. Tightly strapped into the belly of the aircraft on the bumpy flight home, the Army dentist consoled himself by reciting his wartime medical inventory: 4,700 patients, 1,500 fillings, 2,350 extractions and 500 dentures.

An army truck was arranged to transport the Colditz dentist to a special reception centre at a country house three quarters of an hour's drive from the airport. There, a 'delicious-looking blonde' made a beeline for Green and asked him to identify himself. The bottle green Wren in question was in fact an MI9 officer who had orders to ask Green a series of security questions. When it became clear that he was indeed the same Green who had been sending coded messages to London throughout the war, he was told to report to the War Office in Whitehall the same evening.

Green was one of MI9's most prolific coders, and had visited more POW camps than any other agent. What he had to report would be of vital importance.

During his debriefing Green had been careful to show the interviewing officer a tiny scrap of paper which he had faithfully kept with him since 1942. On it were the details of everything he could remember about the murder of Private Skett. MI5 thanked Green for his excellent work on this matter and gave him assurances that everything would be done to bring those responsible to justice. Nevertheless, the Security Service had another even more sensitive case they were keen to put to him.

The next morning, a Special Branch officer picked Green up from his London billet.

The green Hillman Minx turned into Old Bond Street, then into Savile Row and stopped outside one of the many gentleman tailor's shops enjoying an upturn in business at the end of the war. Green got out and followed the Special Branch officer to the shop door which he opened with his own key. Behind the racks of suits was a concealed door which the officer also unlocked, and led Green into a room where a typist and a man were sitting at a long desk. 'Good morning, Captain Green; thank you for coming,' James Davies greeted the army dentist.

After a short exchange of pleasantries, Davies got down to business.

'You were in the Naval POW Camp Marlag Sandbostel in 1941 and later in Sonderlager Colditz in 1944?'[1]

'Yes, I was,' replied Green.

'You knew sub-lieutenant Walter Purdy?'

'Yes.'

'Can you pick him out from these?' asked Davies, pointing to a selection of 100 photographs of British servicemen neatly laid out on the large table.

Green took just a few seconds to find the man who had caused him so much trouble. Now he was very curious to know what had happened to him.

But first Davies asked Green to tell him all he knew about Purdy and his meeting with him at Colditz.

Green didn't hold back, explaining how he had rumbled Purdy as soon as he arrived at Colditz, how he had befriended him and then turned him over to the commanding officer, who interrogated him before handing him back to the camp authorities.

When Davies asked Green how he could be so sure that Purdy was a German spy, he recounted in great detail the way the Germans had located the tunnel and the POW cache of currency and escape equipment.

But how had Green come to suspect Purdy in the first place? Green explained that a battery quartermaster sergeant called John Brown had come to visit him when he was in Blechhammer camp especially to warn him about Purdy.

If Davies wanted to know any more about what Purdy was up to in Berlin, then he would have to find Brown and ask him himself.

In fact, the MI9 agent had been forgotten; just another one of the hundreds of British POWs held in Brussels for desertion, insubordination or some other camp misdemeanour. The dejected Brown was under guard and refusing to answer questions. He would say nothing more until he was put in contact with the proper authorities: 'I tried to keep a level head. Doubtless, several men who knew me or my name in Blechhammer or Genshagen had already passed through Brussels and described me as pro-German… but my instructions had been clear; only in England and then only to somebody in authority could I talk about my work.'[2]

It was Brown's unbending devotion to his duty that had made him a prisoner of his own side. The weight of evidence against him was heavy, and in his darkest moments he wondered if he might end his days in front of a British firing squad.

After Davies's interview with Green, Seymer began making enquiries with a multitude of military agencies urgently seeking Brown's whereabouts.

When MI9 discovered his name on a list of suspected collaborators being held in Europe, Seymer dispatched an officer to Supreme Headquarters Allied Expeditionary Force to seek his immediate release. The commanding officer apologised to Brown for the mix-up, and within 12 hours Brown was lying flat out in the bomb bays of a Lancaster flying back to London. He would soon be crossing the English Channel.

As he looked down through the bomb bay window at the patchwork quilt of green fields and hedgerows laid over his beloved county of Surrey, tears began rolling down the burly quartermaster's cheeks.[3] Brown couldn't believe he would soon be in the loving embrace of his wife and daughter and supping warm beer in his local pub. But most of all he felt the relief of never having to worry about all the 'suspicious eyes' watching his every move, every waking day.

At a reception centre near Horsham in Sussex, Brown was deloused, given a new uniform and taken to a tent for a welcome-home hot meal.

The British agent was on British soil, home and safe. But while Brown was tucking into his first English supper for five years, he became deeply unsettled by the presence of two former POWs sitting at a nearby table laughing and joking. They hadn't noticed Brown, or if they had they didn't feel they had much to fear from the Nazi-friendly quartermaster. Brown recognised them from Genshagen. The sight of men who he knew were among those who had signed up for the traitors' corps was bad enough, but the thought that they had been allowed to freely waltz back home to England unchallenged was almost too much for him to bear. Especially after all he had been through.

Seymer informed Davies that Brown had been located and was about to be driven to an office in Whitehall for his interview with MI5.

But when Davies enquired with Special Branch, who were arranging the MI5 interviews, what time he could see Brown, he was told that Brown had gone AWOL.

Brown was still upset by the hostile treatment he'd received in Brussels, and was further enraged by the presence of BFC men quietly returning home unmolested after he had risked so much to catch them. Nancy was worried sick about her husband. She knew from Jimmy Newcomb that 'Busty' had arrived in Brussels so why wasn't her man back home with the other POWs? When he finally reached her on the camp telephone, she burst into tears and begged to see him as soon as possible. So instead of waiting for the staff car to take him to London, Brown exited the camp and hitched a lift with an army lorry to Horsham train station. On the way up to Waterloo he found a paper in one of the carriages and saw for the first time the shocking images of mass extermination at the Nazi concentration camps.

'The pictures were of Belsen camp where great piles of bodies, male and female, had been starved and then half cremated. A cold shudder ran down my spine. I recalled Heimpel's threat. "We will send you to Belsen!" I had been much luckier than I realised.'[4]

At Waterloo station, Brown caught a train to Kempton Park. As he strolled down the road towards his old house he noticed a set of sentry boxes and hundreds of German soldiers being held behind barbed wire. It took him a few minutes to comprehend what he was seeing before he realised that he wasn't suffering from hallucinations – Kempton Park racecourse had been turned into a German POW camp. His tender reunion with Nancy and his daughter was everything he had dreamt it would be. The long-suffering Nan sat him down in the front room, took off his boots and told him to sit there for as long as he liked while she plied him with home-cooked food, beer and newspapers.

It was a whole week before Davies managed to track down Brown again.

Finally, the dogged MI5 officer was sitting in the same room as the elusive MI9 agent. As he studied the thick-set smiling battery sergeant, he couldn't help wondering whether he had got the right man. Could this really be the MI9 agent who had run a spy ring right under the Nazis' noses in Berlin; who had fooled the Gestapo and broken up the Nazi plans for a British Free Corps?

Without a word, Brown removed his left shoe and tapped the side of the heel to reveal a cavity from which he recovered his microcopies of the letters Walter Purdy had written to his German spymasters. He now proudly presented them to Davies. Brown told Davies that he had given the original documents to a very brave agent called Margery Booth who he suspected may have been arrested by the Germans and was probably dead. Davies told Brown that Booth had indeed been arrested and tortured by the Gestapo, but had said nothing, and later managed to escape from Berlin with the help of a lady called Gisela Maluche. Brown didn't try to hide his delight and smiled with relief knowing the two women he had relied on so much in Berlin had managed to save themselves. Davies said that Booth had suffered terribly at the hands of the Germans and was still in Germany, mentally incapable of giving evidence. After her interrogation by the sadistic Heimpel, she lived in constant fear of the Gestapo even though the war was over and the Nazi torturers had been arrested or executed.[5] She had saved many lives and risked a great deal, but now could barely write her own name, he said.

It took three days of almost continuous scribbling before Brown had set down everything he had witnessed in Blechhammer, Genshagen, Berlin and elsewhere during his adventures in Nazi Germany. Having done his duty and unburdened himself of his intelligence, Brown quietly returned to his job as a clerk at the Truman brewery in London.

James Davies considered there was enough evidence to prosecute many of the British collaborators, including William Joyce, John Amery and Thomas Cooper. Davies was particularly satisfied that Brown, who would be able to testify against all these traitors, had also provided the missing evidence that he hoped would hang the Nazi agent Walter Purdy.

Chapter 41

Treason Charge

On 18 October at Westool Ltd, Deodar Road, Putney, the engineering company's sales director rang Walter Purdy in his upstairs office to inform him two gentlemen wanted to speak to him. Purdy cannot have been too surprised to see James Davies accompanied by a Metropolitan police officer waiting at the reception counter.

When the police officer asked Purdy for his address he replied: 'Barking, and true British and would never be anything else.'[1]

Davies produced a charging document and told Purdy he was under arrest. He then read out a charge of high treason under the Treason Act 1351, a crime for which the punishment was death by hanging.

Purdy was handcuffed and led out of his workplace into a waiting police car.

He was held at Brixton Prison and later granted legal aid at a short hearing at Bow Street Magistrates, where he was only asked to confirm his name and address, and entered a plea of not guilty.

He was later moved to Wandsworth Prison, joining William Joyce, John Amery and Thomas Cooper, the three other traitors who were also facing the death penalty in what became known as the Old Bailey 'treason trials', which took place at the end of 1945 under new laws[2] rushed through Parliament earlier in the same year. A thousand miles away in Nuremburg, the senior Nazis who had overseen and carried out the Final Solution and other atrocities of the war were being forced to answer for their own war crimes.

The case against Walter Purdy was supposed to be open and shut. But Purdy had contrived to weave a series of truths, half-truths and lies to justify his collaboration with the enemy.

Throughout his interrogation with MI5, he hadn't wavered from his claim that he had been working for the British all along and that his propaganda broadcasts from Germany contained codes which would have helped the Allies in the war effort. James Davies still had nagging doubts about the strength of the prosecution case. There were a number of key German witnesses, including the Colditz commandant Lieutenant Colonel Gerhard Prawitt, the camp's security chief Captain Reinhold Eggers, and the shadowy military intelligence Gestapo link, Major Alexander Heimpel, whom he had failed to locate and so couldn't call in support of the Crown's case. Investigations at the Büro Concordia revealed that the Germans had burnt all the incriminating documents. In the rush to leave Colditz, Colonel Tod's own file on Purdy had been left behind and was now likely in Russian custody.

The defence had an array of potential witnesses who might be able to speak in favour of the defendant. One of them was Purdy's German girlfriend Margarete 'Gretel' Weitemeier. While on remand, Purdy had written to Gretel begging her to agree to come to England to appear in court and save him from the hangman's noose: 'Darling, please go and fetch the diary and bring it to England for the next High Court, then we shall know definitely whether I am to live or die.'[3]

But he had had no reply.

On the morning of 18 December 1945, Walter Purdy was brought by police van from prison to the cells at the Central Criminal Court colloquially known as the Old Bailey. Purdy knew that his old friend William Joyce had already been convicted of treason and sentenced to hang in the new year. Joyce's barrister had put up a valiant defence arguing that Joyce was an American citizen and therefore not subject to Britain's treason laws. But the jury had rejected this argument. The only silver lining was that the conviction allowed Purdy to distance himself from Joyce without any fear of retribution from his one-time mentor and fellow Nazi collaborator. Purdy must have also been aware that John Amery's trial on 28 November had taken just eight minutes. After Amery's lawyers were unable to establish a claim to Spanish nationality or support a defence of insanity, Amery pleaded guilty. Amery was due to hang the next morning.

The judge ticketed to hear Purdy's case was Mr Justice Travers Humphreys, a distinguished legal figure who had once acted for Oscar Wilde in his libel case against the Marquess of Queensberry, as well as having prosecuted Crippen, 'brides in the bath' murderer George Joseph Smith, and the Irish spy Sir Roger Casement for treason.

None of this mattered to Purdy, who was morosely fixated with Judge Travers Humphreys's two most recent cases; Humphreys had presided over the short trial of John Amery, whom he sentenced to hang, and been a member of the High Court panel that had dismissed William Joyce's 11th-hour appeal, effectively sending him to the gallows.

At 8 a.m. sharp, Purdy was visited in his cell by his barrister, J P Eddy, King's Counsel.

Eddy, 63,[4] was experienced counsel who had represented many capital cases at the Bailey. He came with good news. Humphreys had been replaced at the last minute by the younger Roland Oliver, a judge with a much more lenient track record on sentencing. However, Eddy didn't linger on the fact that Oliver had been Humphrey's pupil when he was training for the bar and Oliver had returned the favour by agreeing to be pupil master to Humphreys's own son. Instead he focused on the positive, reassuring Purdy that his case was not as serious as the two condemned traitors, Joyce and Amery. He told Purdy he wasn't as well known and so had avoided much of the public vitriol that the other traitors attracted. He also sensed a mood among the public that the British people felt they had had their pound of flesh.

Eddy may not have believed Purdy's far-fetched line of defence, but he was going to run it as hard as he could. He had watched Joyce's trial[5] and saw how much Lord Haw-Haw had damaged his own defence by refusing to enter the witness box. When Purdy said he too was reluctant to give evidence, Eddy persuaded him that everything depended on how the jury responded to Purdy's character. And Eddy had one critical evidential card up his sleeve, which he intended to play well before the jury retired to consider their verdict.

Just before 10 a.m., the Old Bailey jailers unlocked Purdy's cell and brought him up the short iron staircase which led from the cell block to the dock in the middle of the famous Number 1 Court. Purdy was wearing a grey, double-breasted woollen lounge suit with a sober brown tie, a bespoke suit he had had tailored in Berlin. He shuffled into the dock and then took his time fixing his gaze on the judicial bench in front of him, and then on the 12 members of the jury empanelled in their wooden box. Below the jury he could make out the solemn faces of his mother, sister and brother-in-law sitting in the public gallery.

Purdy was asked to affirm his name and address.

The court of the clerk read out the charge:[6] 'You are charged with the following offences. High treason by adhering to the King's enemies elsewhere than in the King's realm to wit in the German realm contrary to the Treason Act 1351. On the second day of August 1943 and on divers other days thereafter and between that day and the first day of May 1944 being then to wit on the said several days, a person owing allegiance to our Lord the King whilst on the said several days an open and public war was being prosecuted and carried on by the German Realm and its subjects against our Lord the King and his subjects then and on the said several days traitorously contriving and intending to aid and assist the said enemies of our Lord the King and his subjects did traitorously adhere to and aid and comfort the said enemies.'

There were three counts on the indictment: i) making broadcasts for the Germans; ii) providing information to the enemy while at Oflag V-C, which led to the discovery of a tunnel and wireless set and endangered the life of a British agent; iii) serving with an SS propaganda unit.

'How do you plead to count one?'

'Not guilty.'

'How do you plead to count two?'

'Not guilty.'

'How do you plead to count three?'

'Not guilty.'

The judge beckoned Purdy to be seated.

Sir Hartley Shawcross KC, the recently appointed Attorney General, rose to his feet. Leaning towards the jury he began his opening remarks, saying that he would show that Purdy had taken money from the Germans in return for broadcasting propaganda against Britain and later 'deliberately and callously betrayed' the lives of other prisoners of war.[7] Shawcross said the man the jury could see before them sitting in the dock today was a hardened fascist and a member of the British Union of Fascists before the war. He had associated with William Joyce in London and then sought him out again in Germany when he was a prisoner of the Germans. The Attorney General said that Purdy had already admitted broadcasting for the Germans, and the Crown had witnesses testifying to having seen him doing so.

Purdy, said Shawcross, had collaborated with the Nazis because he thought they were going to win the war, and when the tide of the war turned he contrived to make out that he had remained loyal to Britain all along: 'He is an arrogant, vain man who put self before country.'

Shawcross's approach was invested in the belief that the jury reflected the feelings of the British public who, after five long years of war, was in no mood to let traitors off the hook.

This desire for revenge was certainly felt by the recently liberated prisoners of Colditz, many of whom had spent almost the entire war behind the walls of Germany's high-security fortress. In their dribs and drabs they had returned to Britain to resume their old lives. Some of their friends, like Lieutenant Mike Sinclair, the Red Fox of Colditz, had been killed trying to escape while others had suffered badly at the hands of their captors. Many of them blamed Purdy for Sinclair's death, believing the Germans' discovery of Crown Deep had been the final straw which had pushed him over the edge.

When officers from MI5 and Special Branch began contacting the Colditz POWs, there was no shortage of witnesses willing to testify against Walter Purdy, the 'rat of Colditz'.

At least a dozen Colditz 'krieges' had agreed to give evidence, and Shawcross intended to contrast the Colditz heroes with the 'traitorous' Purdy.

'Call Captain Julius Maurice Green.'

The Colditz dentist, in a new suit and sporting a fashionable English moustache, was led into court by the usher and took his position in the witness box. Shawcross had made sure that the clerk would ask Green whether the witness wished to swear on the Jewish Bible.

He took the Tanakh in his right hand and affirmed to tell the truth, the whole truth and nothing but the truth, and then made sure he looked Purdy square in the eyes. It was the first time the two men had seen each other since March the previous year, when Green had befriended the naval officer and taken him on a tour of Colditz before denouncing him to the senior British officer. He and the other officers had found Purdy guilty for his treachery and had expected Purdy to hang for his crimes in the Colditz attic. How Green must have relished his second chance to make sure justice was finally done.

'Please, Captain Green, tell the court how you became a POW.'

Green recounted his capture at Saint-Valery in 1940 and his detention at various prison camps, as well as his work fixing the teeth of the prisoners and one or two Germans.

'Captain Green,' said Shawcross, 'without disclosing any official secrets, can you say whether you had any dealings with the British intelligence services while you were a prisoner.'

'Yes, I did.'

'And can you say whether your work helped the British war effort.

'Yes, I was told that it had.'

'Captain Green, have you ever met the defendant before?'

'Yes, I know the defendant.[8] I saw him first in Marlag Sandbostel, Berlin, in May 1941. I was in the same camp as him until I was moved, in October or September, to Marlag und Milag. Later I was with him at Oflag IV-C. This camp was in Colditz. I saw the defendant there. He arrived sometime early in 1944, towards the end of March or the beginning of April I think it was, but I can't be certain as to the time.'

'Did you speak to the defendant at Colditz?'

'After he arrived I had some conversation with him. He told me he had escaped from a camp in Berlin, had been at large for some time and had been recaptured.'

'Did he say which camp he had been in?'

'I think it was one of what we used to call the propaganda camps he escaped from – either Genshagen or another I don't recall the name of.'

'What did you speak to him about?'

'He asked me why I had been sent to Colditz and I told him that it was because the Germans thought I was a Jew. At the time I knew a prisoner of war called Brown and he [Purdy] said he thought Brown was too friendly with the Germans. I told the defendant not to be troubled by this as Brown was doing an excellent job of work and he had to appear to be friendly with the Germans.'

'What else happened between you and the defendant?'

'In our camp we had a wireless set which was hidden away. One or two officers were appointed to listen to the news and to take it down and then it was read to us by one of the officers.... On his first day in the camp I think it was, the defendant was present at such a reading of the news.'

'Anything else?'

'Soon after he arrived he wanted to send a postcard to the Red Cross notifying his change of address, and I took him to find Captain Leah, the postal officer. While we were looking for him we saw on the first floor of the Kellerhaus in the corridor an officer emerging from the entrance to a tunnel.'

'Who knew about this tunnel?'

'Up to then I knew there was a tunnel and that it was on the first floor, but I didn't know exactly where the entrance was. I think, although I cannot be certain, that the Germans had searched the camp after my arrival but before the defendant's arrival.'

'Please tell the court what happened to the tunnel, Captain Green.'

'Some few days after the defendant left the camp, this tunnel was discovered by the German search party, who also discovered a wireless set and a hide for escape equipment.'

'Thank you, Captain Green, that will be all for now.'

The next witness called was Lieutenant Ian Maclean, the officer whom Purdy had seen emerging from the Colditz tunnel entrance. Maclean said he was certain that Purdy's treachery had led the Germans to find the tunnel. But Mr Justice Oliver interrupted Maclean, telling the jury they must decide the case on the facts and the law only. The judge told them to discount the officer's assertion that it was Purdy who had informed on them to the Germans as this was merely Maclean's opinion.

Shawcross then called Lieutenant Colonel Charles Merritt, the Canadian Victoria Cross hero of the raid on Dieppe, who had interrogated Purdy after he had been rumbled by Green.

Colonel Merritt said that he and Lieutenant Colonel Young had interrogated Purdy for several hours at Colditz. 'The defendant contradicted himself many times,' said the Canadian officer, before Purdy 'admitted that his whole story was a fabrication, that in fact he had left Marlag to go to a German propaganda camp from which place he had agreed to broadcast in English on behalf of the Germans.'

Shawcross's next prosecution witness was Colonel William Tod, the senior British officer at Colditz. Tod's cool and measured leadership of the POW camp at the end of the war, when the prisoners had faced down the SS and the commandant, had earned him much respect from his fellow officers and the British public.

Tod said that Purdy had been brought to his room after Merritt and Young had reported the admissions Purdy had made in the afternoon about his work for the Germans. Tod said Purdy had made a long, grovelling speech about how he had 'been a traitor and a rat' and how he had begged Tod to give him one more chance.

'I asked him if the Germans sent him back to Berlin and to the woman I understood he was living with, in return for telling them about anything he may have seen at Colditz, would he then tell them? He said he would.'

Chapter 42

Witness for the Prosecution

The next witness Hartley Shawcross intended to take the stand had already helped to convict four British traitors. BQMS John Brown was the Crown's star witness, but he was also the most problematic for the intelligence services. The ending of the war had not ended the role of MI9 in using prisoners held by hostile states to feed Britain with vital intelligence. If an iron curtain was to descend across Europe, Lieutenant Colonel Sam Derry, the new head of MI9, wanted to be absolutely sure that all of his agents operating in Russia-controlled territory would be able to correspond secretly and safely with London[1].

Derry had sought assurances from Shawcross that no MI9 spycraft would be exposed during the trial.

Shawcross knew what John Brown had to tell the jury was a key part of the prosecution's case. He may have been confident that the Crown would be able to establish beyond doubt that Purdy had been working for the Germans and that he had betrayed his comrades, but without Brown's evidence, how could he prove that Purdy's actions had caused any direct harm to British citizens?

Derry said he would only permit Brown to testify if his testimony was 'in camera' and Brown was not named.

Shawcross was happy with this arrangement; the jury would still hear how Brown had been interrogated by the Gestapo after Purdy had betrayed him. So they agreed to apply to the judge to have Brown's evidence given in secret.

But the 'treason trials' had become so highly charged that they were the subject of intense debates in the House of Commons,[2] where it was argued that now the war was over it should be only in very exceptional circumstances that proceedings were conducted in camera. MPs argued that justice must be seen to be done, otherwise it would look like some kind of secret Nazi justice. The Director of Public Prosecutions had been forced to give his assurance to the Commons that he would ensure all future war trials would be held in open court.

Brown's previous evidence had been given behind a cloak of national security secrecy. He had testified at both Joyce and Amery's trials. And he had been sent to a military camp in Margate to testify against the ringleaders of the British Free Corps, Francis Maton[3] and Roy Courlander, who were sentenced to prison terms of 10 and 15 years respectively on charges of 'voluntarily aiding the enemy'. Although Brown had been mobbed by reporters after the Margate court martials, he had refused to comment or disclose his identity. Brown had been warned by the War Office that under no circumstances must he reveal what he had done for MI9 in the war.

After leaving the army, John Brown had found the return to civilian life hard. Rumours that he had been working for the Germans continued to dog him at the brewery office where he had been effectively sent to Coventry. One of the directors who had come back from a POW camp had picked up rumours about Brown spying for the Germans and passed them around the office, but he had then died from the privations he had endured as a POW before Brown could confront him about these stories. He was even shunned by the clientele in his local pub because they thought he had been a Nazi stooge. For the affable, sociable Brown who had risked so much, this ostracism must have been especially hard to bear. He complained to his government handlers about his predicament but 'they told me to suffer in silence until the treason trials were over and then they would clear my name'.[4]

The DPP's new instruction to Sam Derry, effectively bringing Brown out of the shadows, brought matters to a head and left MI9 with a tough call to make. Did the conviction of Purdy justify risking the operational safety of the newly created secret service for escapers and evaders? They had worked hard to nail Purdy and his conviction would be a feather in their cap. But was the conviction of one traitor worth jeopardising the chances of catching many more? It looked like Purdy was to walk free and escape punishment for his crimes without having to utter a single word in his own defence.

On the afternoon of 20 December, the ushers waiting outside Number 1 Court had their hands warmly shaken by a jovial lump of a man dressed in a double-breasted grey suit. His bald head gleaming under the courtroom lights, John Owen Henry Brown was led past the lawyers' benches and the jury seats to the entrance to the witness box. He opened the metal catch on the wooden door and stepped inside. Making no eye contact with Purdy, Brown confidently took the King James Bible in his left hand and swore to tell the whole truth and nothing but the truth.

The clerk asked Brown to provide his name, rank and address, and then Hartley Shawcross introduced his star witness to the jury.

'Sergeant Brown, I understand you have been on demobilisation leave and are now working at the Truman brewery in east London?'

'That's right, sir.'

'After bravely fighting in France in June 1940 you were taken prisoner by the Germans. Can you please tell the court what happened after that?'

'In February 1942 I went to a prisoner-of-war camp, Stalag III-D in Berlin. I was interviewed there by a German officer named Heimpel whose rank then was Rittmeister, equivalent to a cavalry captain. He was in charge of counter-intelligence in prisoner-of-war camps.'[5]

'Without telling the court the methods and techniques you may have used, were you at any time helping the British war effort?'

'From about the end of 1942 I was able to get information back to this country and I did so.'

Pointing at Purdy, Shawcross asked, 'Do you recognise the defendant?'

Brown didn't have to look up but he paid the court the courtesy of doing so. The two men, once fellow prisoners of war, coldly held each other's gaze.

'Yes, I have seen the defendant, Purdy. I first saw him I think in the summer of 1944 at number 8, ParadePlatz, Tempelhof, Berlin, which was a house belonging to Dr Ziegfeld. I didn't speak to him. He was in civilian clothes and was not under any form of escort. He was then living at the address I've given.'

'Since he wasn't wearing a British uniform or under any guard, what did you decide to do?'

'Sometime after this I went to that address; it was in August or September 1944. I had sent Private Savin to this address about this time to help me in obtaining information where possible. Savin and other soldiers handed me certain documents in the form of letters and also a photograph. In the presence of Savin I had copies made of the documents. In November 1944 I handed these letters to an Englishwoman in Berlin who was married to a German. I do not know where she is now. The copies which I had made I retained and I brought them back to England. There were two letters – one copy of each – and when I got back to England I handed these copies to Mr Davies.'

'Where did you keep these copies?'

'In the heel of my shoe.'

Shawcross gestured to the usher to collect a bag marked exhibit 1 and to hand it to the jury.

'Is this the shoe in question, Sergeant Brown?'

'Yes, sir, I believe it is.'

'And are these documents the copies of the two letters?'

'Yes, they are.'

'Sergeant Brown, without disclosing any secrets that might help an enemy of this country, did anything unusual happen to you around the spring of 1944?'

'In March 1944 I was interrogated by the Germans about my activities. Between the end of 1942 and that date I had not previously been so interrogated. It was between 14 and 20 March 1944 that I was interrogated and it was Heimpel who was then a major, Dr Ziegfeld (a member of the German Foreign Office) and another man who I was told was a member of the Gestapo. After this interrogation I was unable to continue for a time sending information back to this country as I knew I was under suspicion.'

'Why do you think the Gestapo interrogated you?'

'They had been given a report written by Walter Purdy while he was in Oflag IVC which incriminated me and my operations in Berlin.'

Shawcross thanked Brown for coming to court and released him from the witness box. 'My Lord, ladies and gentlemen of the jury, that is the case for the King.'

Outside the court, John Brown was mobbed by reporters and publicly congratulated by senior members of MI9 and MI5. At least his story could now be told. For Brown, who had been a hair's breadth away from being stood up against a wall and shot – by both sides – it was a welcome moment of public vindication. Now he was a national hero with photographs of 'Berlin Brown' splashed all over the newspapers. His boss at the brewery called him in to praise him for his brave work on behalf of the war effort and reassured him that no one in the office ever really believed the traitor stories about him. He was even welcomed back with open arms by the regulars of his local pub.

Chapter 43

The Noose Tightens

It was now Walter Purdy's turn to take the stand and state his name and address.

When Purdy was asked how he wished to affirm, he enthusiastically clasped the Bible and brushed away the clerk's attempt to make him use the prompt card. It was the first time the jury had heard Purdy speak and his rich, overstrained voice didn't disappoint.

'Mr Purdy,' began Eddy, 'were you ever a member of the British Union of Fascists?'

'Yes, I think I joined when I was just 16 years old and then remained a member for only a month.'

'What work did you perform?'

'I am a single man and was a ship's engineer... On 3 December I voluntarily joined the Royal Naval Reserve... On 9 June 1940 whilst engaged in the evacuation of Allied troops from Narvik, Norway, my ship, Her Majesty's armed cruiser *Vandyck*, was sunk and I was captured by the Germans[1] and about one month later taken to Germany.'

'I think you have already said that you did some broadcasting for the Germans?'

'I was taken to Berlin to meet William Joyce.[2] In this interview at a block of offices, Joyce repeated the offer made by the Sonderführer from Marlag that if I made 10 broadcasts over a period of five weeks I would be allowed to escape to a neutral country. I asked for this to be put in writing and later the assurance was given to me in writing by a German soldier in Stalag III-D. My working for the Germans was only done so that I could in the first place get out of Germany. Unfortunately, having got some secret information, I knew it would be impossible to go out of Germany with that information. So I decided I would do everything I possibly could to hinder the German war effort. Sabotage was my only means. Broadcasting was purely the means of fulfilling my work of sabotage. I just wanted to have another crack at the enemy.'

'What sabotage did you perform?'

'On 3 September 1943 there was a heavy night raid on Berlin when bombs were dropped in the vicinity of the Reichssportfeld. Before the all-clear was given I made my way from the Reichssportfeld.... I walked past a particularly damaged building. Having a bottle of lighter fuel in my pocket I made an incendiary bomb by wrapping a piece of my handkerchief soaked in petrol and oil mixture around the neck of the bottle, I lighted this and threw it through the broken windows of the building. This building was the night fighter headquarters for the Berlin defence system. Two days later I learned from a German air force officer that important machinery and documents were destroyed as result of the fire caused in this building.'

'Did you carry out any other acts of sabotage?'

'About 10 days later the Parachute Division's wooden buildings in the vicinity of Pichelsberg railway station in Berlin were hit with incendiary bombs and I added to the fire by throwing in two bottles of petrol. About the beginning of November 1943 I was in the vicinity of the German Navy house in Kaiserdamm when a large bomb dropped behind the drawing offices of the German Navy. I threw a lighter bottle of petrol into this wooden building and entered it through a door and removed from a drawing board and the table a number, 11 in all, of drawings of naval craft. I took these drawings to Reich Strasse 6 and borrowed a camera from Frau Weitemeier together with the rolls of films and made exposures of the drawings, without the girl's knowledge. I hid the films in an earth tube to a radio set outside the window of the rooms occupied by Frau Weitemeier. Another set I hid in a suitcase lid between the layers of leather which to my knowledge is still at the Reich Strasse 6 in the room of the flat occupied by me. A third set I've always had in my pocket and the fourth set was given to Fräulein Otband residing at 28 or 29 Geisburgstrasse, Berlin. I cannot produce any copies at the moment. The ones I had in my possession I later threw away when arrest was imminent. In addition I committed about 15 similar acts of sabotage. I was never given any assistance by any British soldier, hearing they might be unreliable.'

'How did you try to get this secret information back to Britain?'

'During my stay at the Reichssportfeld I was allowed to write home through normal prisoner-of-war channels. By this means I tried to convey information to the Air Ministry, Admiralty and Scotland Yard of some activities of mine. I know definitely that two such letters did arrive in England as my mother Mrs Alice E Purdy forwarded them to the Air Ministry...'

'Did you try any other ways to pass on information to Britain?'

'During my working at Radio National before closing down for the night, it was usual to say "Goodnight" or "Goodnight all".[3] I deliberately varied this closing sentence. When the weather was bad, poor visibility etc., I would say, "Goodnight all," but when the weather was suitable for raiding purposes I said, "Goodnight everybody, goodnight," laying stress on the word "everybody" and leaving a longer space than was necessary between everybody and the last goodnight.'

By now Shawcross had heard enough and sought to cross-examine Purdy on this part of his evidence.

'It is not true that these broadcasts were recorded live, is it? They actually went out a few days afterwards. So your clever system for alerting the RAF to weather conditions over Berlin was completely useless, if indeed that was ever your intention at all.'

Eddy resumed his examination in chief: 'Thank you, Mr Purdy. Now, can you tell the court about your relationship with William Joyce or Lord Haw-Haw? Mr Shawcross has said that you were in daily contact with him.'

'I loathed him and in fact tried to assassinate him on two occasions. Once with a bomb placed on his door handle but I had to abandon it because I wasn't sure whether it would kill him and not someone else. And then again on a train in Berlin when with the help of a Dutchman I placed grenades into his compartment but they failed to explode.'

'You have also heard Captain Green give evidence today. Did you meet Captain Green at Oflag IV-C?'

'On or about 12 March 1944 a bogus Captain Green was placed in the next cell to me and conversations were held through the thin dividing wall. The genuine Captain Green of the Dental Corps is a very old friend of mine and I recognised that the voice of the person was not that of the Captain Green whom I knew. He told me that if I were to work with agents who would contact me in Berlin he would see that when I return to England nothing will happen to me. Knowing this man to be an imposter I reported all this to the German camp authorities. I was able to see this imposter later in the day and I am certain that he was not English but a German soldier who was wearing a German Army uniform.'

After a short lunch break, Eddy called Mrs Alice Purdy to testify that her son's POW letters had reached her and that the contents concerned her so much that she gave them to the Air Ministry.

Shawcross then recalled James Davies to the witness stand.[4] The MI5 officer, who had so thoroughly prepared the evidence against Purdy, assured the court that the defendant's letters had been carefully analysed by cryptographers [IS9Y] who could find nothing in them which suggested Purdy was trying to secretly pass on intelligence. He also said that his own investigations had failed to establish the identity of another Captain Green at Oflag IV-C.

J P Eddy got to his feet and addressed the judge: 'At this juncture, my Lord, I wish to make an application in the absence of the jury.'

Once the jury were cleared from the court Eddy informed the judge that his client intended to argue duress as his defence to treason.

'My Lord, the defendant will say that the Germans had sentenced him to death and it was on pain of death and torture that he later acted as he did.'

Shawcross objected to Purdy relying on the defence of duress, arguing that it was not open to a defendant accused of high treason to be able to say his crime could be excused by a threat to his own life. He prayed in aid the seventeenth century regicide trials of those who carried out the execution of King Charles I. They had failed to defend themselves against the charge of treason even though they attested to have faced the death penalty should they have disobeyed Parliament's order.

Eddy responded with the Oldcastle case concerning a 1419 rebellion against King Henry V in which a group of men who had assisted the uprising by supplying food to the rebel soldiers were acquitted because they had been under threat of death. Eddy said this case was upheld in 1745[5] when participants in the last Jacobean rebellion against King George II were allowed to argue that the threats against their property and livelihoods had compelled them to take up arms against the King.

Final determination rested with Mr Justice Oliver.

Should the judge accept Eddy's legal argument, then he would be allowing scores of British traitors, including many of the BFC, to avail themselves of the defence of duress. There was enough in the statements taken by MI5 to show a number of broadcasters and collaborators would be more than happy to take opportunistic advantage of his ruling by relying on Nazi death threats they claimed were made against them.

The judge adjourned to consider the law and its implications before delivering his ruling on the point.

When he returned he recalled the jury and asked both counsel to stand.

'Having given the argument sound thought, I have come to the conclusion that fear of death could indeed be a defence to a British prisoner of war who was charged with high treason in having assisted with German propaganda in the Second World War.'

Oliver had shown that he was not a judge who was willing to deny a defendant a legal defence purely because there was public clamour for revenge.

Eddy now asked Purdy to retake the stand.

'Mr Purdy, when you were in Germany as a prisoner of war, why did you help the Germans with their propaganda and join an SS propaganda unit on the Western Front between November 1944 and April 1945?'

Purdy took a few seconds before gathering his thoughts and seizing his opportunity: 'On the night of 17 March[6] [when Purdy was at Colditz], I was removed under guard to Rochlitz for a preliminary court martial and given a Portuguese lawyer to act as my representative. The result of the court martial was that all findings would be sent to a higher court and as I was charged with sabotage and espionage I would in all probability be sentenced to death. On the morning of 20 March I returned to Oflag IV-C. On 7 June I was removed from solitary confinement and sent to Berlin with a guard. This had been arranged by the SS who had prepared a cell for me at Prinz Albrecht Strasse [Gestapo HQ] for four days. On the second day after refusing to answer questions put to me by an Unterscharführer, I was hit and beaten. Towards the end of November I was sent to Berlin Zehlendorf and told by two SS officers that if I did not do a little work for them with the SS Standarte Kurt Eggers, I and my friend Frau Weitemeier would be sentenced to death. They also explained that the final court had already passed that sentence. There was no alternative for me but to accept the offers made and I started to work as an interpreter at an SS organisation called Scorpion West.'

Shawcross asked Purdy that if he had been charged with sabotage and faced a court martial, why hadn't he said so when he was being questioned by Merritt, Young and Tod at Oflag IV-C?

'Oh, but I thought I had,' Purdy replied.

'And can you explain why, according to other statements you have made to the authorities, you spent the summer of 1944 as free as a bird in Berlin?'

'That's not correct, sir.'

Mr Justice Oliver adjourned proceedings until the next morning and Purdy was led back to his cell. A few minutes later the jailor appeared at Purdy's door with a clinking of keys. In walked a bewigged Eddy who had rushed down from the courtroom. Behind the barrister, accompanied by a police matron, stood Gretel Weitemeier.

She had received Purdy's letter and had come to London to testify in his defence after all. The couple tried to embrace but the police matron came between them.

'Frau Weitemeier,' explained Eddy, 'is being held at Holloway Prison as an enemy alien. Tomorrow she will appear in Court Number 1 as a witness in your defence. And then she will go back to Germany.'

'Thank you, Gretel, for coming,' was all Purdy could say before she was whisked away for another night in her own cell in Holloway Prison.

The next morning, Gretel appeared as promised. Please give the court your full name: 'My name is Margarete Weitemeier, née Heumeyer, and I live in Berlin-Charlottenburg, Reich Strasse, 6.'

'Do you know the defendant standing in the dock?' asked Eddy.

'I know an Englishman who is called Robert Wallace.[7] Robert Wallace is the father of my son, Stephan Robert Willy Heumeyer, who was born on 5 April 1945.'

'How do you know the defendant?'

'I got to know him in November 1943 when he came to live in this house. He lived here until 1 April 1944... in April 1944 he and I were arrested by the Gestapo. Why Robert Wallace was arrested I do not know. I was asked to give information about him. I was released on the afternoon of the same day.'

'What happened to the defendant, the man you know as Robert Wallace?'

'Herr Wallace was sent back to a prisoner-of war-camp and in May I received a letter from him. The letter was on plain paper which was marked with a big red stamp. In it he wrote to me that he was in a British camp at Colditz. In June and July he visited me often at home and also in the Funkturmgarten where I worked. After that I did not see him again until my birthday on 21 November. I do not know where he lived in the meantime.'

'Did the defendant speak of his work?'

'He never spoke to me about his work. I have a feeling that perhaps he works secretly for the British government.'

'Thank you, I think Sir Hartley may have some questions.'

'Frau Weitemeier, do you own a camera and film?'

'Yes.'

'Did you ever give this film to the defendant?'

'I never gave him the film and I never lent him the camera. But it could be that he borrowed the camera and film without my knowledge.'

Gretel caught Purdy's eye. He was pleased with the loyal Gretel.

It was at this moment that Eddy decided to play his last evidential cards:

'Please recall Captain Julius Green.'

'Captain Green, you told the court that you informed the defendant when you met him at Colditz that the reason the Germans had sent you there was because you are Jewish. After telling Purdy that this was the case, did the Germans ever arrest you for being a Jew or send you to a concentration camp?'

Green told Eddy that although the Germans suspected him of being a Jew, and had even carried out a medical examination on him, they had not been able to prove it.

Eddy turned to the jury: 'It does seem odd if the defendant was really working as a German spy in Colditz the Germans didn't find out about Captain Green's Jewish faith.'

'I now wish to recall Lieutenant Colonel William Tod.'

Shawcross, the jury, even Mr Justice Oliver must have wondered what Eddy could possibly hope to achieve for his client by recalling the senior British officer at Colditz who had already testified that Purdy was, by his own words, a 'rat and a traitor'.

'Colonel Tod,' began the wily defence barrister, 'we have already heard how you interviewed the defendant in Oflag IV-C after Colonel Merritt and Colonel Young. What happened after that?'

'About 10 March 1944 I went to the German commandant, Lieutenant Colonel Prawitt, and told him that Purdy had admitted having worked for the Germans and that in consequence we no longer considered him a British officer and also it would be an insult to us if Purdy was allowed to remain. I said if you don't take Purdy into your custody I won't be held responsible for his safety in the camp. After some argument the German commandant agreed to have Purdy removed and a few hours afterwards Purdy was taken away.'

'Where was he taken?'

'Purdy was taken away from that part of the camp in which we were and was put into a cell in a building outside the main camp building.[8] I think he was there for about a week or more. We could see him being exercised at different times of the day. During this period he was allowed to go for a walk for perhaps an hour or so, but with one unarmed escort.'

'Before you are released from your evidence I have two final questions for you. Colonel Tod, were you aware from your time at Colditz that the defendant had any sympathies towards fascism?

'I have no personal nor hearsay knowledge as to Purdy being a member of the British Nationalist Socialist Party or the British Union of Fascists before the war.'

'And to your knowledge, did Walter Purdy disclose any Oflag IV-C camp secrets to the Germans?'

'My answer to this question is that nothing that took place afterwards made any of us suspect that Purdy had disclosed any of our camp secrets. I feel quite certain, too, that Purdy had no opportunity to discover any Oflag IV-C camp secrets.'[9]

'Thank you, Colonel Tod, those are all the questions I have for you. You may go.'

A stunned silence fell over Court Number 1. The implication of Tod's last answer was that Purdy was not responsible for the Germans discovering the prisoners' tunnel, the radio set and the cache of money and escape tools. And if Purdy hadn't told the Germans about this then how could the jury be sure that he had informed on John Brown, Julius Green and the coded messages?

Shawcross tried to mitigate the damage caused by Tod's testimony by reminding the jury of Brown's evidence of Purdy's treachery and how badly the British agent had suffered at the hands of the Gestapo.

In his closing speech, Shawcross said:[10] 'Is not the true explanation of this preposterous nonsense that the defendant has been a weak and vain man who, having decided to sell himself to the enemy, had misgivings and began to wonder whether after all Germany was going to win the war and if so what was going to happen to him – this is a man who wanted to run with the hare while he was hunting with the hounds. By his own words he is a "rat and a traitor".'

It was now up to Mr Justice Oliver to sum up the case for the jury:[11] 'Evidence has been given to show that the defendant was 100 per cent pro-British and wanted us to win the war. But that is not the point. The point is whether he fell to taking money from the Germans in order to benefit himself – to get a more liveable existence. We've only his word that he was condemned to death by the Germans. Would a man who was condemned to death be allowed to live freely in comparative luxury in a Berlin flat? The defendant, according to his own statement, wrote offering his services in the British Free Corps. That was a Corps the Germans tried to raise of English renegades to their country to fight for the Germans against one of our Allies – not a very savoury type of thing for any Englishman to be associated with.'

The judge then asked the jury to retire to carefully consider their verdicts on all three counts, reminding them that only they could decide who was telling the truth. He told them to take as much time as they needed.

The jury took just 17 minutes before returning to court, causing the ushers to scramble to alert the lawyers, jailors and the public that the verdicts were about to be delivered.

The court of the clerk asked the jury foreman:

'On count one, making broadcasts for the Germans, how do you find the defendant?'

'Guilty.'

'On count two, serving with an SS propaganda unit, how do you find the defendant?'

'Guilty.'

On count three, providing information to the enemy while at Oflag IV-C which led to the discovery of a tunnel and wireless set and endangered the life of a British agent, how do you find the defendant?

'Not guilty.'

The clerk then addressed the jury: 'You find him guilty on the first and second count of high treason and not guilty on the third count; and those are the verdicts of you all?'

'Yes they are,' replied the foreman.

Purdy was then told to remain standing: 'Prisoner at the Bar, you stand convicted of high treason. Have you anything to say about why the court should not give judgement of death according to the law?'

Purdy's broken and crushed expression said everything he was capable of saying.

Mr Justice Oliver reached beside him and took the square black cloth, the black cap, from the box and placed it on top of his wig:

'Walter Roy Purdy, you will be taken hence to the prison in which you were last confined and from there to a place of execution where you will be hanged by the neck until you are dead and thereafter your body buried within the precincts of the prison and may the Lord have mercy upon your soul.'

The jailors clasped Purdy by the arms and prepared to walk him back down the stairs. At the same time, a scream rang out from the public gallery, momentarily freezing all three men in the dock.

Walter Purdy's sister Millicent shouted out at the judge, 'My God, my God,'[12] before a police officer tried to restrain her. 'I must stay to the end,' she protested and then collapsed to the floor. Purdy was forced down the stairs looking back all the time at the place where his sister had fainted. As he did so he had a final glimpse of Julius Green, who had been sitting at the back of court, watching proceedings. From across the well of the court, Walter Purdy shouted to the man whom he ultimately blamed for his downfall: 'I'll get you, Green.'[13]

Chapter 44

A Twist in the Rope

The newspapers had a field day with the Purdy trial. The traitor's German lover, the Colditz betrayal, secret agent John 'Busty' Brown and the Betty Blaney blackmail case made for days of lurid headlines.

Purdy was sentenced to hang on 8 February at Wandsworth Prison, where Amery, despite his father's special pleadings to the Cabinet, had been hanged on 19 December. William Joyce was set to join him on 3 January.

Purdy spent Christmas Day sitting in his cell, clinging to the desperate hope that his 11th-hour appeal would save his life. But on 12 January, he heard that the jury in the case of Thomas Cooper had come to the same verdict as his own and found Cooper guilty of high treason. Cooper was sentenced to be hanged a few days after Purdy.

The former naval officer prepared himself for his fate, and wrote his last letters to his mother and sister who had stood by him until the end. There is no record of him writing a final letter to Gretel, only legal correspondence asking for her help to find evidence in his forthcoming appeal, which his lawyers eventually abandoned.

Then on 6 February, just two days before the day of his execution, he was visited by J P Eddy.

The usually unflustered barrister appeared excited. In his hand he held a scroll of paper which, without any introduction, he proceeded to read to Purdy: 'Walter Purdy[1] was convicted of high treason for which by law he is liable to suffer death, but His Majesty having been graciously pleased to extend his grace and mercy unto the said Walter Purdy and to grant him a pardon for the said crime on condition that he be kept in penal servitude for life.'

Eddy explained to Purdy that his conditional pardon[2] had been granted because he had been acquitted of the most serious charge: informing on the prisoners at Colditz and betraying John Brown. It had significantly lessened his treachery in the eyes of the Crown.

After Colonel Tod's testimony flatly denying any links between the discovery of the tunnel and Purdy's actions in Colditz, the jury had little choice but to acquit Purdy on this count.

A closer examination of Tod's statement suggests he may have changed or added to his evidence a few weeks before the trial. In the MI5 files marked secret, Tod's critical sentence 'I believe Purdy did not pass on intelligence to the Germans' is overwritten in bold typeface on much brighter white paper.

Which all begs the question, what motivated Tod to alter his account and go against the testimonies of all the other Colditz POWs?

There are perhaps two explanations.

At Purdy's trial, the jury were not given any details of the POW court martial at Colditz or told of the attempted lynching by his own side. To this day, the MI5 files remain selectively sieved so that the event is not officially recorded.

It was a grim moment in the history of Colditz, and even in December 1945, when Purdy was brought to trial, it reflected badly on the British POWs, who had always claimed to hold themselves to higher standards than those of the Nazis. If Tod was able to alter his testimony and now say there was no reason to suspect Purdy of treachery at Colditz, then it would help the prosecution by under-mining any claim Purdy's lawyers may allege about a kangaroo court and a British death sentence. It would deny Eddy the oppor-tunity to argue that Purdy was acting not only under the duress of a German death sentence but also a British one.

Among the hundreds of official documents relating to Purdy's case there are only two references to the court martial, which both evaded the government weeders. One is by Robert Lindemere who recalled how Purdy told him the British had tried to kill him at Colditz. MI5 discredited Lindemere as a drug addict and an 'appalling witness'. The other is in a letter handwritten by Margaret Joyce to her husband just before his own hanging. In it she says Purdy had been subject to a 'comic court martial' by the British in Colditz.[3]

The absence of any official record of the incident also raises the prospect that the prosecution had done a deal with Purdy. In return for Purdy not referring to the British death sentence, did the Crown ask Colonel Tod to say he did not believe Purdy had betrayed them to the Germans and thereby save him from the gallows?

By Purdy agreeing to keep his silence about his attempted lynching in Colditz, his barrister JP Eddy may have been able to extract a promise from the Attorney General not to oppose a plea for clemency. Certainly, Eddy abandoned Purdy's appeal mid-application.

It has been claimed that the Crown had come to a similar arrangement[4] with William Joyce, who by refraining from revealing his early contacts with MI5 before the war received assurances that his wife would not be prosecuted for any offence relating to her own treachery. Margaret Joyce remained the only member of the group of British traitors to avoid any criminal charges.

With the war crime trials in Nuremberg looming, and Sir Hartley Shawcross appointed to be the lead British prosecutor, it was important to Britain that its own double dealings with traitors did not harm its reputation on the international stage, nor offer the Nazi war criminals the scintilla of a defence in the charges arraigned against them. It was the same with Purdy – the attempted lynching of a prisoner by British officers without due process not only undermined the rule of law but showed the heroes of Colditz in a different light.

There is another reason why the Crown might have agreed to a clemency deal. A War Office file[5] from 1946 shows that the British had begun an investigation into the shooting of Lieutenant Mike Sinclair at Colditz in 1943 during the Franz Joseph escape attempt. Three German soldiers were accused of this war crime but the British case looked weak. MI5 needed help identifying and locating the suspects. Walter Purdy's name appears on the top secret file as someone who could provide intelligence to bring the German suspects to justice. If Purdy, a collaborator at Colditz for three months, was able to help the war crimes prosecutors in their case then the Attorney General may have been able to look upon his sentence favourably.

The second explanation is that the British officers' failure to carry out the hanging had placed the lives of Brown and Green in danger and risked the security of the Berlin spy ring. It may also have ended whatever hope Mike Sinclair and the others had left of escaping. The whole affair was an embarrassment, and Tod had good reasons to want to protect his own reputation and the reputation of his fellow prisoners who were now lauded as national heroes. It was far safer for him to testify that he believed Purdy had not passed on any intelligence so that no one could accuse the Colonel of placing British lives at risk by handing Purdy back to the Germans after the naval officer had told him he fully intended betraying them should the Gestapo threaten his relationship with Gretel. Tod may well have tried to mitigate the damage caused by the information Purdy gave to the Germans by supporting Julius Green's claim to be medically insane, throwing the intelligence Purdy was passing along into doubt. But none of this would play well in an open court. It was better to say nothing at all about what really happened in Colditz. It would also explain why none of the organisers of the hanging party were asked to testify against Purdy. Rupert Barry and Gris Davies-Scourfield were conspicuous by their absence at the Old Bailey trial. They both wanted Purdy to hang and they didn't care who knew it.

Epilogue

Had the death sentence been carried out on Purdy, he would have been the last man in Britain ever to be hanged for treason. Instead, that grim record is held by William Joyce. Purdy had now twice escaped the hangman – once in Colditz and once at the Old Bailey. An MI5 report describes Purdy as the 'greatest rogue unhung'.

Purdy's life as an inmate in a British prison would turn out to be almost as duplicitous as his time as a POW in Germany.

The governor of Parkhurst prison on the Isle of Wight described Purdy as 'a devious twister of the worst kind who pretends to cooperate but is really not and is always trying to reopen his case. He is anti-British and stirs up trouble.'[1]

But perhaps the greatest justice done to Walter Purdy was on 21 May 1946, when he tried to organise a mass escape from the laundry room in Wandsworth prison. The plot was discovered in time after another prisoner informed on Purdy, for which the informant was paid '28 penny pieces'.

Before Purdy left prison in 1954, he applied for the return of his passport. In his submission to the Foreign Office, he said he intended to travel to Berlin to be reunited with his Gretel. MI6 and MI5 advised[2] withholding permission to travel to Germany on the grounds he might be recruited by the Stasi or the KGB.

Margarete 'Gretel' Weitemeier never gave up on Robert Wallace, who she always believed was really working for the British. She travelled to London to give evidence in his defence and after the verdict begged the judge to let her see Purdy one last time. Permission was refused and instead she was imprisoned as an illegal alien and sent back to Germany. Her picture was splashed over the front pages of the British newspapers, dubbed the Nazi lover who begged for the life of the British traitor.

When Walter Purdy finally walked free from Wandsworth prison after serving nine years of his life sentence, Gretel was waiting for him. She may have never given up on her British lover, but she now revealed that she could not marry him. During their separation, she had fallen in love with Eric Rowlins, Purdy's nephew and the RAF serviceman to whom Purdy had claimed to MI5 he had sent his secret messages while he was in Berlin.

Eric and Gretel settled in Essex and married in 1955. None of their family or neighbours knew the events which had brought them together, and despite great efforts, the British newspapers were never able to find Gretel, wrongly believing she had remained in Germany.

On the same day Walter Purdy was released, the Glasgow dental practice of Julius Green received a strange phone call from a man who said he knew Julius 'and he was coming to see him'. According to Alan Green, Green's son, his father believed this was Purdy coming to carry out his courtroom threat. 'My father phoned the police and went to the top of the house with his gun to keep watch on all approaching visitors. But it turned out to be an old army colleague of my father who was passing by and just wanted to drop in to say hello.' Purdy never did carry out his threat to 'get Green'.

In 1957 Purdy provocatively changed his name to Robert Wallace Poynter, a combination of the name he used while making his Nazi broadcasts and the alias Alexander Heimpel had given him. The same year, he married a woman he had known before the war, Muriel Anslow, but she died three years later. In 1961 Purdy married again, this time to a divorcee called Veretta Wallace. The Poynters and Gretel and Eric Rowlins lived close to each other in Essex for the rest of their lives. Purdy, who never told his wives what he had done in Colditz, ended up working as a quality control inspector at Ford's car factory in Dagenham.

A former colleague of Purdy still remembers mechanic inspector Robert Poynter: 'As a person who worked with this man at the factory in Essex, I can assure you he was not a very nice man. He was, in his role as an inspector, always quick to drop people in it. He was, in factory parlance, as crafty as a shithouse rat. So I suppose the old adage that a leopard never changes its spots is true of him.'

Walter Purdy died peacefully in 1982 in Southend after a short battle with lung cancer.

Thomas Cooper also had his death sentence commuted to life imprisonment days before he was due to hang. He was released a year earlier than Purdy in 1953 and reportedly settled in Tokyo, converted to Buddhism, and became an English language teacher. Conflicting reports suggest he returned to England and died either in 1987 or in the late 1990s.

John Boucicault de Suffield Calthrop escaped any punishment for his collaboration. He continued working as a film producer, but in 1967 he ran into serious financial trouble and was declared bankrupt.

After the war, Reinhold Eggers returned to Halle,[3] then under Soviet control. Eggers claimed he had never joined the Nazi party and was allowed to resume his career as a teacher. But in September 1956 the Russians were given intelligence suggesting Eggers had worked with the Gestapo to plant agents in Colditz and to threaten the prisoners. Charged with crimes against humanity, spying and supporting a fascist regime, he was sentenced to 10 years' hard labour in Sachsenhausen prison and then at Torgau prison. He survived, and after his release moved to Lake Constance where he spent the last years of life, dying at the age of 84.

Hans Werner Roepke tried to return to America to capitalise on his English language skills, but his war record caught up with him and he was refused a visa. In 2002 a documentary film crew tracked down the former SS captain to a Frankfurt suburb and questioned him about his time with BFC.

Gottlob Berger was arrested by the Americans in May 1945 but he wasn't tried for his war crimes until April 1949. Berger claimed that he had not been aware of the Final Solution until after the war, but the court found ample evidence to prove that he was compliant with the programme to exterminate Jews. The court also found Berger to be responsible for atrocities carried out by the Waffen-SS. In his defence, Berger argued that the aims of the Cold War echoed the Nazi war against 'Jews and Bolsheviks', and raised the possibility that the US would also have to fight the Soviet Union in the near future.

Berger was sentenced to 25 years' imprisonment, later reduced to just 10 years after a judicial review accepted that he had saved the lives of the Colditz prominente who Hitler had ordered to be shot. He was released in 1951, serving a shorter sentence than Walter Purdy. Berger took a job as a manager of a curtain rail factory in Stuttgart, had four children and continued to speak up for former members of the Waffen-SS. He died peacefully on 5 January 1975 in Gerstetten.

Alexander Heimpel was wounded fighting the Russians in Berlin in 1945 and was taken to a hospital in Rüdersdorf. But in June 1945 when the Russian military police started making enquiries of the patients, he discharged himself and crept back to his apartment in Kleinmachnow, eight miles north of Genshagen. All four Allied powers were hunting him. As head of the Gestapo for the German POW camps he had plenty to answer for. On 2 November 1945, four French soldiers came for him at his apartment and took him to Berlin-Tegel, then a high security prison in the French sector of the city. According to German records[4] Heimpel knew one of the officers, possibly one of his victims. Many French prisoners had died under his torture programmes and Heimpel spent nearly two years in French custody.

According to his wife Helene, who instructed a lawyer to find out what had happened to him, Heimpel was released in 1947, only to disappear again. Initial reports suggested that he may have hanged himself in prison or that he had been handed over to the Russians. What really happened to the diehard Nazi intelligence chief was still a mystery.

In 1961, after years of unsuccessfully trying to locate him or confirm his death, his sister contacted the German Red Cross.[5] They informed her that they had tracked down a Berlin lawyer who had some information but because of the legal oath of confidentiality to his client he could not share the information with the family. The trail appeared to have gone cold again. Then, in 1967 the Central Office of the State Justice Administrations for the Investigation of National Socialist Crimes (Zentrale Stelle der Landesjustizverwaltungen) opened a war crimes investigation concerning the activities of Stalag III-D. One of the principal suspects was Alexander Heimpel.[6] The investigators contacted some of the military staff who served with Heimpel at Stalag III-D. Many of them remembered the Abwehr officer who worked closely with the Gestapo but either claimed he was dead or didn't know what had happened to him.

Five years later the federal investigators interviewed Dr Wilhelm Wieck, one of the doctors at Stalag III-D. He told the inquiry that he had heard reports that Heimpel, perhaps using an alias, had returned to live peacefully in his city of birth, Frankfurt am Main. Wieck's report was partly substantiated by Gerhard Zuhl, another of Heimpel's officer contemporaries, who said he thought Heimpel had been receiving food and clothing parcels from his relatives for some time after his release from Berlin-Tegel.

But the most intriguing interview was with Eberhard Stein,[7] another soldier at Stalag III-D, who said he believed that after Heimpel's release he had begun working for the Americans.

In 1976, without any further leads, the inquiry into Alexander Heimpel was officially closed:[8]

'Major Heimpel was indicated by most of the witnesses for the entire period of the camp's existence as an Abwehr officer. But it has not been possible to determine where Heimpel is living or any more files relating to him... Carrying out further investigations is not promising.'

I have since been told by a German researcher that Heimpel may have moved to Innsbruck with his second wife where he lived out a peaceful retirement until his death. There appears to be as many theories about the fate and whereabouts of Alexander Heimpel as there are of Hitler's henchman Martin Bormann.

Margery Booth escaped during one of the air raids on Berlin, reached Bavaria, and sent this message[9] to MI9:

'I protected and gave comfort to my fellow countrymen. I hid papers on my body for them. Had these papers been found on me I should have been shot. I am so proud, for I did my bit, and proud to have been able to do so. In my house I had a Jewess for three quarters of a year and helped other Jews as well. Had this been found out it would have meant death. Now the terrible reaction. I had a terrible time. I was threatened with the concentration camp. I had to go twice a month to the secret police – two hours each time. They wanted to find out about prisoners of war. I always acted like I had no idea. One slip from me would most likely have meant the death of a good many countrymen of mine.'

Booth was eventually picked up in Bavaria by the Americans and returned to Wigan. After the war she divorced her German husband, but she could not escape her association with the Nazis, which blackened her character and forced her to live in a seedy bedsit in Southport. In 1951 she emigrated to New York where she died of cancer one year later. It was a sad end of a life of a very courageous woman.

Julius Green was demobbed in 1946 and, after flirting with a number of commercial enterprises, including an offer of gun-running in Israel, returned to dentistry. He married the same year and had two children. He died in 1990.

When he published his autobiography in 1971 it was first the time the public was told of the operation of MI9's secret codes.[10]

In 1974 Green was contacted by one of the MI9 letter writers whom he knew as 'Philippa'. Enclosing some of his wartime letters he had sent to MI9, she wrote: 'When I think what all you chaps went through – & what a state the country is in now – it makes me wonder what it is all about, Mary Trevor [Philippa's real name].'

Julius Green kept his Colditz certificate of insanity and occasionally waved it at his wife when he found himself in a spot of domestic hot water.

John Henry Owen Brown may have started out as a war-time black marketeer working closely with the Germans to make his life as a POW as comfortable as possible. But his subsequent acts of bravery made a significant contribution to the British war effort, and his achievements in Berlin helped forestall the political and military complications of a Britisches Freikorps. MI5 and MI9 were certainly grateful to Brown and repeatedly referred to his counter-espionage efforts in files now held at the National Archives.

After the war, John Brown gave evidence in 20 treason trials. Yet he was never completely trusted by other former POWs and he didn't help himself by continuing to enjoy the company of the Germans he was friendly with in the camps.

He kept in touch with Waldemar, Prince of Hohenlohe Oehringen, his old camp commandant at Blechhammer and even invited him over to visit him in England.

Brown and his family left London in 1946 and moved to Newcastle, where he opened a home brewing shop in Jesmond. After making a few bob on the black market, he retired to live quietly running a pub in Wimborne in Dorset. John Brown died on September 15 1965 at the age of 56 leaving his widow Nancy his entire estate worth just £4767.

His friend, Captain John Borrie, the medical officer at Blechhammer who helped Brown in the early days of his captivity and remained a loyal family friend, said this of[11] the proud working class John 'Busty' Brown: 'Had John Brown been an aggressive

British officer he would have spent the duration of the war in Colditz and his story would never have been told.'

For his service to Military Intelligence in the war, John Brown was awarded the Distinguished Conduct Medal.

The citation on his medal reads: 'Despite the very real danger involved, he pretended to be working for the Germans, whilst at the same time he was really using the comparative freedom accorded him to further the cause of the Allies. Even when the Gestapo became suspicious B.Q.M.S. Brown did not hesitate to continue his work. Acting as he did entirely on his own initiative, he fully realised that in all probability he might be suspected of betraying his own country. This did in fact happen, but it has now been established without question that he did acquire and transmit to this country valuable information.

'Through his continuous efforts the British Free Corps, which the Germans hoped to expand from the men sent to Genshagen, gained few recruits and eventually the project became a complete failure. In addition B.Q.M.S. Brown used the frequent change of personnel at the camp to establish inter-camp communication, passing on information and escape aids. It is remarkable that whilst busy with all these activities, he did not neglect his duties as senior N.C.O. Genshagen was excellently run and men who had been there have shown marked respect and esteem for B.Q.M.S. Brown.'

Acknowledgements

There are many people to whom I owe a debt of gratitude.

Alan Green, son of Captain Julius Green, can to this very day recall the alarm caused in the Green household when Walter Purdy was released from prison in 1954. Alan has kindly provided records, photographs and memories of his father's time as a POW and an MI9 agent.

Trevor Beattie is the son of Reg Beattie, John Brown's trusted 'lieutenant', who suffered so terribly at the hands of the Gestapo. Trevor wrote down his father's story from the diaries he had smuggled out of Germany and then published them in an excellent account called *Captive Plans*. Reg Beattie kept many of the photographs from the Blechhammer and Genshagen camps and of the British POWs and Trevor has kindly given me permission to publish some of them in this book.

Robert McIntosh of the Museum of Military Medicine in Mytchett and Colonel (retired) Quentin Anderson, former Colonel Commandant Royal Army Dental Corps, were both extremely courteous and helpful during my research concerning Julius Green.

I wish to say thank you to Steffi Schubert and Alex Kalinowski, both experts in their field, who helped unlock the secrets of Schloss Colditz. Steffi was an excellent guide who took me to the site of the Crown Deep tunnel, the dentist quarters, Colonel Tod's room and the attic where the British tried to hang Walter Purdy.

I also wish to pay tribute to Steffi Schubertm, Heike Bohnstengel and Phoebe Garthwaite for their help in the translation of the German files.

Thank you also to Corolla Voigt-Allinger and Jorg Allinger for their warm hospitality when I was staying in Colditz. I am equally grateful to all the staff at Schloss Colditz where I stayed for five days researching that part of the book. I was given my own key to the main castle gate and on one night, during Covid restrictions, I swear I was the only guest staying in the prison.

Special thanks to my editors at Welbeck, Oliver Holden-Rea and Ajda Vucicevic. And to Tanisha Ali for her assistance with the plates.

But most of all I wish to acknowledge the contribution of Piers Blofeld, who helped me to distinguish the wood from the trees. 'Agent' does not come close to describing his many roles in ensuring *The Traitor of Colditz* saw the light of day. It was much more than 10 per cent.

References

The British files

The Military Intelligence and judicial documents relating to the investigation, prosecution and trial of Walter Purdy are held at the National Archives in Kew. They run to well over 1,500 pages, tracing MI9's first warnings about Purdy working for the Germans through to the MI5 investigations (KV-2-259), his Old Bailey trial (KV-2-261 (1 and 2) CRIM 1/1738), his judicial appeal (KV-2-261), eventual pardon (CRIM 1/585/141) and the nine years he spent in a series of high security prisons (HO336/8).

These court papers, interrogation transcripts, MI5 and MI9 memos, minutes and intelligence reports all forensically catalogue a treachery that led to him twice being 'sentenced' to hang. Purdy's diary of his time spent in Berlin in 1944 can be found at KV-2-261 (1).

KV-2-261 includes photographs of Purdy in Berlin when he was working for the Abwehr and the Gestapo, and HO336/8 contains a selection of his prison mugshots when he was detained at Her Majesty's pleasure.

Buried at the bottom of a brown box left to the Imperial War Musuem by MI9 officer Mabel Howat (documents: 16229 box no 08/111/1) is the original contacts book for all the MI9 directors and staff, itself coded as the '919 M.A.I.N Officers' Dinner Club', and underneath it a rare photograph of Headley White and Leslie Winterbottom, who helped hunt down Walter Purdy and the other traitors. Further MI9 files are at WO 208/3450 (MI9

Establishment 1939-42) WO 208/3569 (IS No 9 West Europe area: history) and WO 208/3572 (MI9 re-organisation).

The British Library holds many contemporaneous news reports of the trial of Walter Purdy, and there are further accounts in Rebecca West's *The Meaning of Treason* and C. E. Bechhofer Roberts's *The Trial of William Joyce* (which includes details of all the treason trials), both published shortly after the war. R v Walter Purdy (1946 10 J Crim L 182) remains the lead treason case for a defendant who wishes to plead the defence of duress when they are under threat of death, and it has been cited in a number of Northern Ireland terrorism trials.

Prosecution and defence documents relate to the blackmail case against Purdy's English girlfriend Betty Blaney (KV-2-261), while MI6's objections to him travelling to Berlin to visit his German girlfriend Margarete Weitemeier after his release from prison are at FO 371/109708.

Margarete Weitemeier's own application to the Home Office to live in the UK can be found at HO 334/636/34200.

BSQM John Brown's witness statements are found in the files of more than 20 traitors and renegades prosecuted after the war, including William Joyce (CRIM 1/483); Walter Purdy (see above); John Amery (CRIM 1/1717); Thomas Cooper (KV-2-254); John Calthrop (KV-2-439) and Richard Paul Francis Maton (KV-2-264). Brown's intelligence also appears in other MI5 reports relating to those POWs who were suspected of collaborating with the enemy.

There are four MI5 files on the British Free Corps (KV-2-2828) which include information passed on by Brown.

Captain Julius Green's documents (RADC/1942/18 and RADC/1944/17) are held at the Museum of Military Medicine at Keogh Barracks, Mytchett Place Road, Mytchett, Surrey, GU12 5RQ. These include a series of coded letters and replies he wrote to MI9 as well as the solutions to the codes. The museum retains Green's Colditz uniform, one of its most treasured exhibits.

The principal files for Colditz are in the National Archives (Kew) and the Imperial War Museum (London). The official camp history (AIR 40/1910) was compiled by the War Office after the war. It is supplemented by further files; WO 208/3288; WO 32/111; WO 361/1798 (court martial records of Colditz); WO 361/1838 (reports of the International Committee of the Red Cross).

The Imperial Museum in London also has a copy of the official record (Documents.2412) as well as many audio interviews with individual prisoners.

New documents relating to a 1946 war crimes investigation into the shooting of Michael Sinclair at Colditz during the 'Franz Joseph' escape were released to me by the National Archives under a Freedom of Information request (WO 311/145/1).

Texts

John Brown's memoir *In Durance Vile* and Julius Green's *From Colditz in Code* were the two most important texts in the development of *The Traitor of Colditz*. They sometimes needed reconciling but were crucial in the telling of the story. I also leant on the work of Henry Chancellor's *Colditz: The Definitive History*, Adrian Weale's *Renegades* and Reinhold Eggers's *Colditz: The German Story*.

The German and Swiss files

The quest for original documents about the German POW camps unearthed hundreds of pages of documents from the German archives. The bulk of the material came from the German Federal Archives or Bundesarchiv (BArch) in Koblenz and Berlin, including the only photographs of Alexander Heimpel. At Colditz Castle there is a small archive and museum dedicated to the POW years which contains information about escapes and the administration of the camp (https://www.schloss-colditz.de/en/events-and-exhibitions/exhibitions).

There were also fruitful finds at the German Federal Military Archive in Freiburg (Militärarchiv Freiburg im Breisgau), mostly dealing with the military service and war record of Alexander Heimpel. Research at the Schweizerisches Bundesarchiv Bern led to the release of Red Cross files for Stalag III-D, including inspection reports of Genshagen written in German and English. The Bundesarchiv Berlin holds YMCA reports relating to Kommando 999, the officers' holiday camp.

Enquiries at the war crimes investigation branch in Ludwigsburg (Zentrale Stelle Ludwigsburg Az. VI 302 AR 1212/68 Landesarchiv Baden-Württemberg, Dept. Staatsarchiv Ludwigsburg, EL 48/2 I Bü 2551) uncovered more than 200 pages relating to Stalag III-D and the ultimately unsuccessful attempt to find and prosecute Alexander Heimpel. Many of those interviewed by the investigators in the 1960s and 1970s remembered Heimpel from his days as military intelligence chief at Stalag III-D, but no one could say for certain what had happened to him after his capture by the French in 1945 and his release from prison in 1947.

The personal papers relating to Alexander Heimpel are held at the National Archives of Germany in Koblenz. Here we recovered legal papers in the case of Hedwig Kappelhöfer v Alexander Heimpel. 1936-41. (Heimpel/Bundesarchiv Koblenz Auftr No: 3534 R9). This file also contains information about Heimpel's legal disputes over his army benefits, details of his officer expenses, correspondence with Joseph Goebbels and the guardianship of his 'homosexual' nephew.

None of this would have been possible without the assistance of Philipp Steinhoff M.A., who worked from Berlin to help me track down these documents.

List of German and Swiss archives used:

Bundesarchiv – Abteilung Militärarchiv, Freiburg
Bundesarchiv – Abteilung PA, Berlin
Bundesarchiv – Berlin
Bundesarchiv – Koblenz
Institut für Zeitgeschichte München – Berlin
Landesarchiv – Berlin
Fritz Bauer Institut (Frankfurt am Main)
Bayerisches Hauptstaatsarchiv – München
Schweizerisches Bundesarchiv – Bern

It still amazes me that I was able to find out so much about the life of the Nazi Gestapo torturer Alexander Heimpel from the German archives, yet there is so little official British recognition of John Brown, Britain's brave spy who risked his life to avert a military intelligence catastrophe in Berlin.

The American files

Files concerning the British Free Corps and its leadership were released under the CIA Freedom of Information Act and the Nazi War Crimes Disclosure Act.

These referred to Hans 'Hermann' Roepke (ID: 19799241) and the SS chief Gottlob Berger (ID: 129175910).

Bibliography

Brown, John, *In Durance Vile* (Robert Hale 1981)

Brickhill, Paul, *Reach for the Sky: the story of Douglas Bader* (William Collins Sons 1954)

Burn, Michael, *Turned Towards the Sun* (Michael Russell Publishing 2003)

Champ Jack and Colin Burgess, *The Diggers of Colditz* (Kangaroo Press 1998)

Chancellor, Henry, *Colditz: The Definitive History* (Hodder & Stoughton Ltd 2001)

Court, John, *The Security Service 1908–1945: The Official History* (Public Record Office 1999)

Davies-Scourfield, Gris, *In Presence of my Foes* (Wilton 65 1991)

Eddy, J.P., *Justice of the Peace* (Cassell 1963)

Eggers, Reinhold, *Colditz: The German Story* (Robert Hale 1961)

Eggers, Reinhold, *Colditz Recaptured* (Robert Hale 1973)

Farndale, Nigel, *Haw-Haw: The Tragedy of William and Margaret Joyce* (Macmillan 2005)

Foot, M.R.D. and J. M. Langley, *MI9 Escape and Evasion 1939–1945* (Bodley Head 1979)

Fry, Helen, *MI9: A History of the Secret Service for Escape and Evasion in World War Two*, (Yale University Press 2020)

Green, Julius, *From Colditz in Code* (Robert Hale 1971)

Hunter, Robert, *Agent Jack: The True Story of MI5's Secret Nazi Hunter* (Weidenfeld and Nicholson 2019)

Ormerod, David, *Smith and Hogan's Criminal Law* (Oxford University Press 2019)

BIBLIOGRAPHY

Martland, Peter, *Lord Haw-Haw* (Public Records Office Publications 2003)

McNally, Michael, *Colditz: Oflag IV-C* (Osprey Publishing 2010)

Neave, Airey, *Saturday at M.I.9.* (Hodder & Stoughton Ltd 1969)

Platt, J. Ellison, *Padre in Colditz: The Diary of J Ellison Platt*, ed. Margaret Duggan (Hodder & Stoughton 1978)

Reid, Miles, *Into Colditz* (Michael Russell 1983)

Reid, Miles, *Last on the List* (Leo Cooper 1974)

Reid, P.R., *The Colditz Story* (Hodder & Stoughton 1952)

Reid, P.R., *The Latter Days* (Hodder & Stoughton 1953)

Reid, P.R., *Colditz: The Full Story* (Macmillan Publishing 1984)

Reid, Patrick and Maurice Michael, *Prisoner of War: The Inside Story of the POW From The Ancient World to Colditz and After* (Hamblyn 1984)

Roberts, C. E. Bechhofer, *The Trial of William Joyce* (Jarrolds 1946)

Romily, Giles and Michael Alexander, *The Privileged Nightmare* (Weidenfeld 1954)

Schädlich, Thomas, *Colditzer Schloßgeschichten: Die Geschichte des Oflag IV C in Colditz nach dem Tagebuch des Georg Martin Schädlich* (Swing Druck GmbH 1992)

Seth, Ronald, *Jackals of the Reich* (New English Library 1973)

Stein, George, *The Waffen SS 1939–1945: Hitler's Elite Guard at War* (Cornell University Press 1966)

Tate, Robert, *Letting the Side Down: British Traitors of the Second World War* (Sutton 2003)

Tunstall, Peter, *The Last Escaper: The Untold First-Hand Story of the Legendary World War II Bomber Pilot, 'Cooler King' and Arch Escape Artist* (Duckworth 2014)

Weale, Adrian, *Renegades: Hitler's Englishmen* (Pimlico 2002)

West, Nigel, *The Guy Liddell Diaries* (Routledge 2005)

West, Rebecca, *The Meaning of Treason* (Orion 2000)

Wilson. Patrick, *The War Behind the Wire* (Leo Cooper 2000)

Wood, J.E.R., *Detour: The story of Oflag IVC* (Falcon Press 1946)

Notes

Prologue

1 Davies-Scourfield, Gris, *In Presence of my Foes* (Wilton 65, 1991), pp.216–17

2 Pat Reid says 11 March.

3 https://www.nationalarchives.gov.uk/help-with-your-research/research-guides/courts-martial-desertion-british-army-17th-20th-centuries/#2-what-is-a-court-martial

4 They knew there were strict rules for the discipline of servicemen accused of breaking British military and civil law. Ref: Reid, Patrick and Maurice Michael. Prisoner of War: The Inside Story of the POW From The Ancient World to Colditz and After. (Hamblyn 1984)

5 Davies-Scourfield, Gris, *In Presence of my Foes* (Wilton 65, 1991), pp.216–17.

6 KV-2-259 (3) and CRIM 1/1738 Colonel Tod's statement to MI5

7 Foot, M.R.D. and Langley, J.M., Pp.35–37 *MI9 Escape and Evasion 1939–1945*.

8 Neave, Airey, *Saturday at M.I.9.* (1969).

9 Foot, M.R.D. and Langley, J.M., *MI9 Escape and Evasion 1939–1945*.

10 Schädlich, Thomas (1992), *Colditzer Schloßgeschichten: Die Geschichte des Oflag IV C in Colditz nach dem Tagebuch des Georg Martin Schädlich*.

11 Schubert, Steffi and Kalinowski, Alex. Museum Schloss Colditz (Oflag IV-C).

12 November 1943 tunnel revealed by British informant placed in the camp, AIR 40/1910, pp.10 and 42

13 Eggers, Reinhold, *Colditz: The German Story* (Robert Hale, 1961), p.141.

14 McNally, Michael, *Colditz: Oflag IV-C* (Osprey Publishing, 2010), p.33.

15 27.10.41 UK was concerned about contingent of French and other Jews isolated in camp. FO916/16.

16 Reid, P.R., *Colditz: The Full Story* (Macmillan Publishing, 1984), p.109.

17 Imperial War Museum. Camp History of Oflag IVC. Documents 2412 Box no: Misc164 (2537)

18 Moran, Michael, IWM reel 8 https://www.iwm.org.uk/collections/item/object/80004773.

19 KV-2-259 (3) and CRIM 1/1738 Colonel Tod's statement to MI5

20 Davies-Scourfield, Gris, *In Presence of my Foes* (Wilton 65, 1991), pp.216–17. Memoirs of Gris Davies-Scourfield.

21 Chancellor, Henry, *Colditz: The Definitive History*, pp.284–286.

22 Davies-Scourfield, Gris, *In Presence of my Foes* (Wilton 65, 1991), pp.216–17. Sinclair and Littledale when they crossed the Turkey–Bulgaria border, Royal Green Jackets Museum. https://www.youtube.com/watch?v=z6giQShi7vw

23 WO311/145 WO311/145/1. The author used the Freedom of Information Act to access NA files to shine new light on the incident. This Colditz file also includes Michael Sinclair's personal statement about the shooting written shortly afterwards and not previously published. It shows that the War Office was preparing a war crimes charge against the German guards and were working with the American Justice Department to locate Franz Joseph. Sinclair says his hands were raised when he was shot. In 1946 the UK Government named three suspects: Pilz, Krantz and Brentner.

24 Imperial War Museum. Camp History of Oflag IVC. Documents 2412 Box no: Misc164 (2537)

25 Green, Julius, *From Colditz in Code*, p.143.

26 Davies-Scourfield, Gris, *In Presence of my Foes* (Wilton 65, 1991), pp.216–17. Chancellor, Henry, *Colditz: The Definitive History*, pp.284-286.

Chapter 1

1   National Archives MEPO 2/10978 Press cuttings and reports from Special Branch outlining the injuries sustained by those present at Olympia, followed by descriptions by three medical doctors in attendance. There are also cuttings from the Daily Worker protesting about the broadcasting of Oswald Mosley's speech by the BBC and a pamphlet of eyewitness accounts prepared in the aftermath of the meeting. Among those providing accounts were the authors Naomi Mitchison, Aldous Huxley and Vera Brittain.

2   Metropolitan Police report on Walter Purdy's background. HO336/8.

3   Met Police report HO336/8.

4   MI5 report on Walter Roy Purdy. KV-2-259 (1, 2, 3 and 4).

5   KV-2-259 (1, 2, 3 and 4).

6   HO336/8 Metropolitan Police report.

7   HO336/8.

8   KV-2-259 (2 and 4) Walter Purdy's statement to MI5.

9   Ibid.

Chapter 2

1   CRIM 1/1738 John Brown's witness statement in prosecution of Walter Purdy, December 1945.

2   Census records 1911.

3   Census records 1911.

4   Brown, John, *In Durance Vile*, p.49 MI5, KV-2-439 (2) Brown's conversation with Lt Calthrop.

5   Dorothy Oakley and John Brown marriage certificate, MXJ 161738.

6   Brown, John, *In Durance Vile* (Robert Hale, 1981), p.71.

7   Nancy Mason and John Brown marriage certificate, MXJ 142117.

8   KV-2-439 (2) Brown's conversations with Lt Calthrop.

9   CRIM 1/1738 John Brown's witness statement in prosecution of Walter Purdy, December 1945.

10 Fry, Helen, *MI9: A History of the Secret Service for Escape and Evasion in World War*, Yale University Press (8 Sept. 2020).

11 Foot, M.R.D. and Langley, J.M., *MI9 Escape and Evasion 1939–1945* – only three servicemen out of 50,000 captured by the Germans had been taught the secret codes (BCA, 1979), p.60.

12 'It was the biggest convoy yet, stretching from Calais to the Belgian border. Our contempt for the Germans increased to a dangerous complacency.' Brown, John, *In Durance Vile*, p.16.
13 Brown, John, *In Durance Vile*, p.16.
14 Brown, ibid.

Chapter 3
1 Green, Julius, *From Colditz in Code*, p.49.
2 Green, Julius, *From Colditz in Code*, p.67.
3 RADC/1942/18 Papers of Captain Julius. Records at the Museum of Military Medicine, Keogh Barracks Ash Vale Aldershot GU12 5RQ.
4 Howat, Mabel. Imperial War Museum. Documents: 16229 box no 08/111/1. Howat says this very rarely happened and she was unable to name a single example. It was more likely that on very dangerous operations individuals would have been given the codes because there was a high likelihood of capture.

Chapter 4
1 Brown, p.17.
2 Brown, p.19.
3 Brown, p.20.
4 Brown, p.21.
5 Brown, ibid.

Chapter 5
1 http://ww2talk.com/index.php?threads/merchant-navy-war-grave-photos-for-reference.32890/page-3
http://ahoy.tk-jk.net/Letters/BrotherwasaboardBritishPe.html
Skett, 23, was a skilled communications officer and may have been able to help Green in his coded messaging.
2 Army Medical Services Museum. RADC/1942/18. RADC/1944/17.
3 Green, pp.219–220.
4 Green, p.182.
5 Army Medical Services Museum. RADC/1942/18. RADC/1944/17, Green, p.219.

Chapter 6
1 KV-2-259 (2 and 4) Walter Purdy's statement to MI5.
2 Lt Commander James Michael Moran. Interview with the IWM reel 8. Catalogue number 4816. https://www.iwm.org.uk/collections/item/object/80004773
3 K-2-259 MI5 witness statements from former Marlag prisoners.
4 KV-2-259 (3) Lt George Thorpe (from Liverpool) was on board *Vandyck* when it was sunk by the Luftwaffe.
5 Lt Commander James Michael Moran. Interview with the IWM reel 8. Catalogue number 4816. https://www.iwm.org.uk/collections/item/object/80004773.
6 Captain Graham Wilson's statement to MI9 KV-2-259 (2).
7 Green, p.99.

8   Green, p.113.
9   Green, p.128.
10   Green, p.112.

Chapter 7
1   Brown, p.21.
2   Brown, p.25.
3   Brown, p.30.
4   Brown, p.31.
5   Brown, p.57.
6   Brown, p.32.
7   Brown, p.33.
8   Brown, p.34.
9   Brown, p.36.
10   The Camp POW, 7.9.141, Brown, John, *In Durance Vile*, pp.149–52.
11   Brown, pp.150–152.

Chapter 8
1   Green, p.107.
2   Brown, p.64.
3   Green, p.121.
4   Green, p.120.
5   Bundesarchiv – Abteilung Militärarchiv, Freiburg.
6   Bundesarchiv – Abteilung PA, Berlin.
7   Bundesarchiv – Abteilung Militärarchiv, Freiburg.
8   Legal papers in the case of Hedwig Kappelhöfer v Alexander Heimpel.
     1936-41 Bundesarchiv Koblenz Auftr No: 3534 R9.
9   Legal papers in the case of Hedwig Kappelhöfer v Alexander Heimpel.
     1936-41 Bundesarchiv Koblenz Auftr No: 3534 R9.
10   Private papers of Alexander Heimpel, Bundesarchiv – Koblenz
11   Stalag III D war crimes files. Zentrale Stelle Ludwigsburg Az. Bundesarchiv
     Außenstelle Ludwigsburg. KV 2/2828 – MI5 report on Stalag IIID and the
     British Free Corps.

Chapter 9
1   Brown, p.67.
2   Brown, p.69.
3   Lord Haw-Haw and Brown's statement (KV-2-259 (2)) about Joyce, p.197.
4   Brown, p.74.
5   Brown, John, *In Durance Vile*, p.78.
6   Brown, John, *In Durance Vile*, p.79.

Chapter 10
1   Davies, James, MI5 report on Walter Purdy, 5.7.1945, p.1, KV-2-259 (3).
2   KV-2-259 (3) Lt George Thorpe says Purdy later met a German officer outside
     the camp.
3   Wilson, Captain Graham 'Tug', Witness statement to MI5. 20.6.1945. KV-2-
     259 (3).

4   Wilson, Captain Graham 'Tug', ibid.
5   KV-2-259 (3) Purdy's letter to Wilson explaining his decision to work for the Germans.
6   Lt George Thorpe KV-2-259 (3).
7   KV 2/2828 Col Vivian Seymer's MI5 report on the BFC. 27.4.1945.
8   Christensen, Erik, Head office for German YMCA. June 1943 Stalag III-D Kommando 999 YMCA Bundesarchiv MSG 194/64 Fol 1.
9   https://kar.kent.ac.uk/65227/3/__gort_WHR_tl54_My%20Files_Steward%20BJR.pdf
10 Stalag IIID Berlin. Red Cross Swiss legation visits. 1940-45. Bern Archives.
11 Officers' description of Kommando 999. KV-2-439 (2). Weale, Adrian, *Renegades*.
12 Bundesarchiv MSG 194/64 Fol 1.

Chapter 11
1   Farndale, Nigel, *Haw-Haw: The Tragedy of William and Margaret Joyce* (Macmillan, 2005), p.200.
2   MI5 reports on Walter Purdy KV-2-259(2).

Chapter 12
1   BBC monitoring report of broadcasts by 'POINTER', pp.55–61, KV-259 (1).
2   Farndale, Nigel, *Haw-Haw*, p.176.
3   KV-259 (2) Statement by Private Robert Burridge, a batman at Stalag IIID.

Chapter 13
1   KV-2-259 (2) Burridge statement to MI5.
2   Burridge ibid.
3   K-2-259 (1) Margaret Joyce correspondence with husband William Joyce.
4   KV-2-260. Purdy's leather-bound 1944 diary.
5   West, Rebecca, *The Meaning of Treason* (Orion, 2000), p.106.

Chapter 14
1   Brown, p.90.
2   Brown, ibid.
3   Brown, p.91.
4   Brown, ibid.
5   Brown, ibid.
6   KV-2-439(2), John Calthrop statement to MI5 p.15.
7   Brown, p.96.

Chapter 15
1   Joseph Seward was killed in 1945 when he was caught in the crossfire between German and Polish positions.
2   Red Cross report Stalag III-D, Rudolph Denzler, 1943, Berne, pp.81, 193, 427 and 456.
3   Brown, pp.100–101.
4   Bundesarchiv Koblenz.

5 Bundesarchiv Koblenz. Alexander Heimpel correspondence with German authorities.
6 Brown, p.110.
7 Brown, John, *In Durance Vile*, p.110.
8 Brown, p.111.
9 Brown, p.112.
10 Brown, p.117.
11 Brown, p.119.

Chapter 16

1 Court, John, *The Security Service 1908–1945: The Official History*, Public Record Office, p.306, 1999, The Guy Liddell Diaries, edited by Nigel West, 2006.
2 Thomson's career ended in scandal when he was caught propositioning a prostitute in Hyde Park in 1925. Vivian Seymer had changed his name and tried to escape the shadow of his father. After the war he became an architect and an appointed Fellow of the Royal Institute of British Architects. But he soon grew tired of civvy life and offered his services to Military Intelligence before eventually finding a berth with MI5.
3 Rupert Barry in *Colditz Recaptured*, compiled by Reinhold Eggers, describes how MI9 sent messages asking for information on suspected traitors, p.43, Robert Hale, 1973.
4 Brown, John, *In Durance Vile*, p.119.
5 A Lt Commander Purdy did serve with the Royal Navy in WWI.
6 Brown, p.120.
7 Brown, p.122.
8 Museum of Military Medicine Cpt Julius Green. Codes and papers. RADC/1942/18.
9 Green, p.132.
10 Green, p.136.

Chapter 17

1 Colditz Recaptured, Rupert Barry, p.43.
2 Interview with Colonel (retired) Quentin Anderson of the Royal Army Dental Corps Association. Cooper had been the dentist for Stalag III-D before his transfer to Colditz. Red Cross files, Berne.
3 Burn, Michael, *Turned Towards the Sun*, 2003.
4 Mazumdar, Birendra Nath (Oral history) Imperial War Museum https://www.iwm.org.uk/collections/item/object/80016245.
5 Mazumdar's wife Joan later said: 'The Germans were desperate to get him to join the movement and to broadcast propaganda to India. He was offered all sorts of inducements: money, women, a flat and a wonderful life.'

Chapter 18

1 Mabel Howat also wrote several times to Green's family in 1942 about Green's work with MI9.
2 Museum of Military Medicine, Cpt Julius Green, Codes and papers. RADC/1942/18.
3 KV-2-259 (4) and KV-2-260. Brown's evidence.

4 KV-2-259 (4) MI9 report from repatriated POW.
5 KV-259 (4) Police and naval answers to MI9 enquiries made by Major Hedley White.
6 KV-2-278 MI5 file on Abwehr officer Emile Kiemann.

Chapter 19
1 WO 416/42/404.
2 Britten recovered and was court-martialled in England and sentenced to prison but released when he suffered another flare-up of disease which doctors diagnosed as Crohn's but by now was probably advanced bowel cancer. He died shortly afterwards.
3 Brown, p.94, Brown knew Britten as Oscar England.
4 Brown, ibid.
5 KV-2-2828 MI5 Report on the BFC 27 March 1945.
6 KV-2-2828 ibid.
7 Stalag IID War Crimes investigation. Landesarchiv Baden-Württemberg, Dept. Staatsarchiv Ludwigsburg, EL 48/2 I Bü 2551 Zentrale Stelle Ludwigsburg Az. VI 302 AR 1212/68.
8 Seymer, Colonel Vivian, MI5 report on establishment of BFC circulated to all departments August 1945. KV 2/2828.

Chapter 20
1 https://www.feldgrau.com/ww2-german-wehrmacht-british-volunteers/.
2 Maton, Francis, KV 2/264.
3 Landwehr, Richard, *Britisches Freikorps: British Volunteers of the Waffen-SS 1943–1945* (3 ed.) (Merriam Press: Vermont, 2012) p.77.
4 Brown, pp.92–94.
5 Brown, pp.113–115.
6 Brown. p.114.

Chapter 21
1 Calthrop, Lieutenant John Boucicault de Suffield. Interrogation by MI5 1.5.45 – 4.5.45. KV-439 (1) and (2).
2 KV-2-439 – in October 1945, MI5 found his 'story unconvincing' and recommended he be prosecuted for collaborating with the enemy.
3 Calthrop, Lieutenant John Boucicault de Suffield. Interrogation by MI5 1.5.45 – 4.5.45. KV-439 (1) and (2).
4 Brown, John Henry Owen. MI5 statement about Lt John Calthrop. KV-2-439 (1).
5 Calthrop, Lieutenant John Boucicault de Suffield. Interrogation by MI5 1.5.45 – 4.5.45. KV-439 (1) and (2).
6 KV-2-439 (1).
7 KV-2-259 (2).

Chapter 22
1 https://blog.nationalarchives.gov.uk/escape-from-colditz/#comment-169434
https://ccnmtl.columbia.edu/services/dropoff/schilling/mil_org/milorgan_99.html

NOTES

2   Howat, Mabel. Imperial War Museum. Documents: 16229 box no 08/111/1
3   Chancellor, Henry, *Colditz: The Definitive History*, p.193.
4   KV-2-2828 MI5 report on the BFC establishing that Alexander Heimpel was the Abwehr officer who had the Gestapo brief.
5   K-2-439 (1) Brown's statement to MI5.
6   Rudi Reichoffen applied to join Waffen-SS. He was another stool pigeon sent to Colditz at the time. Platt, J. Ellison, Padre in Colditz (ed. Margaret Duggan), (Hodder & Stoughton, 1978), p.235.
7   AIR 40/1910. Official camp history of Oflag IVC. Morale low after failed escapes, p.17.
     WO 208/3288. Morale in 1943/44 took a dip because of failed attempts and tunnels being found. Also when the French and Dutch moved there was no competition for escaping.
8   Martin Schädlich's diary reveals for the first time why Sinclair's escape was foiled by the Germans. The last guard that Sinclair ordered to stand down had only just come on duty. For years the reason for the failed attempt has been variously blamed on the system ID checks, a changed colour code and Sinclair's German pass not being in order.
9   WO311/145 WO311/145/1. New NA file released under FOI shows the extent of the hunt for the Colditz guards implicated in the shooting of Sinclair, who said he had raised his hands when he was shot.
10   Green, Julius, *From Colditz in Code*, p.143.
11   Green, ibid.

Chapter 23
1   WO 32/11110 (M.371/5) Prime Minister's personal minute.
2   Chancellor, Henry, *Colditz*, p.280.
3   Platt, J. Ellison, *Padre in Colditz* (ed. Margaret Duggan), (Hodder & Stoughton, 1978), p.235.
4   Champ J. and Burgess C., *The Diggers of Colditz* (Kangaroo Press, 1998), p.183.
5   Champ J. ibid.

Chapter 24
1   *Platt, J.E.* p236
2   Eggers, p 142. In 1961, when Eggers came to write his memoirs he considered the matter so sensitive he gave Purdy an alias, Lt Grey. (So there was Brown, Green and Grey!).
3   IWM archives. Moran, Scarborough and Keats.
4   Official Camp History of Oflag IVC WO208/3282.
5   KV-2-259 (3), Maclean statement to MI5, p.7.
6   Platt, J.E., *Padre in Colditz*, p.240 and Reid, P.R., *Colditz: The Full Story*, p.226.
7   Green's statement to MI5. KV-2-259 (2) and (3).
8   MI5 statements of Purdy, Green, Brown, Merritt, Young and Todd. KV-2-259 (2).
9   Brown, p.127.
10   MI5 statements of Purdy, Green and Brown KV-2-259 (2).

11 KV-2-259 (3) and (4) Julius Green's witness statement to MI5. Green, Julius, *From Colditz in Code*, p.160.
12 KV-2-259 (3) Brown's MI5 statement recalling the Gestapo intelligence report read out by Heimpel. KV-2-259 (2) HO 45/25798 Green's statement recalling the conversation with Purdy.
13 KV-2-259 (2) Colonel Young's statement to MI5.
14 KV-2-259(4) Col Merritt's statement to MI5.
15 Imperial War Museum. Camp History of Oflag IVC. Documents 2412 Box no: Misc164 (2537)
16 KV-2-259, Statement of Lt Col William Tod of the Royal Scots Fusiliers, p.22.
17 Rudi Reichoffen.
18 CRIM 1/1738. Tod's witness statement at Purdy's trial.
19 http://irvinemclean.com/peerage/hopetoun.htm.
20 Davies-Scourfield, Gris, *In Presence of my Foes* (Wilton 65, 1991), pp.216–17. Memoirs of Gris Davies-Scourfield.

Chapter 25
1 Eggers, p.139.
2 Eggers, ibid.
3 Eggers, p.140.
4 https://www.northwichguardian.co.uk/news/18500274.war-hero-hartford-broke-free-colditz-castle/.
5 Moran, James Michael. Interview at Imperial War Museum https://www.iwm.org.uk/collections/item/object/80004773.

Chapter 26
1 MI5 file on German agent Lydia Oswald, KV-2-3386.
2 Brown, p.125.
3 Brown, p.126.
4 Brown, John, *In Durance Vile*, p.126.
5 Brown, p.127.
6 Brown's statements to MI5. KV-2-259(2) and evidence given at trial CRIM 1/1738.
7 Brown, John, *In Durance Vile*, p.128.

Chapter 27
1 Major Hughes of MI5 interview with Kenneth and Colin Wylie at the Atlantic Hotel, Hamburg 29 November 1945. KV-2-260.
2 Major Hughes ibid.
3 Davies, James. MI5 report on Purdy. KV-2-259.
4 Platt, J. Ellison, *Padre of Colditz*, p.245.
5 MI9 interception of Purdy's letters written from Colditz. KV-2-261 (2).
6 Correspondence between MI9 and MI5 about Purdy written in March–August 1944 KV-2-259 (1).
7 Court, John, *The Security Service 1908–1945: The Official History*, Public Record Office, p.306, 1999.
    Hutton, Robert, *Agent Jack*, p.253.

8   Martland, Peter, *Lord Haw-Haw*, p.106.
9   Reid, Patrick, *Colditz: The Full Story*, p.224.

Chapter 28
1   Eggers, Reinhold, *Colditz: The German Story*, p.142.
2   Purdy's letter secured by John Brown and admitted in evidence at his trial at the Old Bailey in 1945. KV-2-259 (3).
3   Eggers, pp.141 and 142.
4   Brown's statements to MI5 KV-2-259 and (2) CRIM 1/1738.
5   Lindemere's statement to MI5 September 1944. KV-2-259 (2).
6   Lindemere ibid.

Chapter 29
1   KV-259 (2) CRIM 1/1738.
2   KV-2-259 (3).
3   The forms were a record of the work each POW had performed while held as a prisoner. For example, many of the soldiers performed camp duties and services in the administration of the camp. Others were paid by the War Office for work that the Germans made them perform.
4   KV-2-259 (2) and *In Durance Vile*.
5   At the end of the war, Cecilienhof was seized by the Soviets and the palace was used by the Allied Powers as the venue for the famous Potsdam Conference.

Chapter 30
1   http://reader.library.cornell.edu/docviewer/digital?id=nur:01685#page /2/mode/1up.
2   https://www.jewishvirtuallibrary.org/the-british-free-corps and Adrian Weale, *Renegades*.
3   Weale, Adrian, p.114.
4   Eggers, p.144.
5   Reid, Patrick, *Colditz: the Full Story*, p.237.
6   KV-2-2828
7   Calthrop's statement to MI5 after his return to London. KV-2-439(2).
8   KV-2-439(2) Lt John Calthrop interview with MI5.

Chapter 31
1   KV-2-264 (2), p.25, Richard Paul Francis Maton's interrogation by MI5.
2   KV-2-264 (1) & (2).

Chapter 32
1   KV-2-259 (3), p.9.
2   Ibid.

Chapter 33
1   Court, John, *The Security Service 1908–1945: The Official History*, Public Record Office, p.306, 1999.
2   Memo written by Sinclair of SLB1 to Shelford of F Division, KV-2-259 (1), p.7.

3   CIA Freedom of Information Act release. Nazi War Crimes Disclosure Act.
    (FOIA) /ESDN (CREST):
    519bded9993294098d515617 https://www.cia.gov/readingroom/
    document/519bded9993294098d515617
4   Ibid
5   Ibid

Chapter 34
1   Brown, p.134.
2   Interview with Reg Beattie's son.

Chapter 35
1   Brown p.193
2   Brown, p.136
3   Brown, p.137

Chapter 36
1   K2-439 (2).
2   K2-439 (1).
3   Green, P165
4   After the Purdy spying mission, the Nazis were aware that Green was a Jew,
    albeit one protected by his British passport. If Green ever left Colditz, Eggers
    and Berger knew the Army dentist would make his report implicating all of
    them in atrocities carried out at the kaolin factory.
5   WO 32/11110.
6   3rd Battalion 273rd Infantry 69th Division.
7   Chancellor, Henry, *Colditz*, p.362.

Chapter 37
1   Brown, p.142.

Chapter 38
1   KV-2-259 (4), p.17.
2   Purdy's revised statement to MI5. CRIM 1/1738.
3   Gretel's letter and statement to MI5 October 1945. KV-2-260 and CRIM
    1/1738.
4   Purdy's second statement to MI5. CRIM 1/1738.
5   K-2-259 (1), p.9.

Chapter 39
1   James Davies statement in prosecution of Purdy. KV-2-259.
2   Lindemere's statement to MI5 KV-2-259(2) and later evidence prosecution
    CRIM 1/1738.
3   KV-2-259 (3) Lt David Jolly's statement to MI5 30.6.1945.
4   KV-2-259 (3), pp.12–16.
5   All members of the BFC were exempt from being tattooed with the SS blood
    mark.

NOTES

Chapter 40
1 Green page 17
2 Brown, John, *In Durance Vile*, pp 145–163
3 Ibid.
4 Ibid.
5 KV-2-60, p.69.

Chapter 41
1 KV-2-259 (1), p.39.
2 Treason Act 1945 (8 & 9 Geo.6 c.44).
3 KV-2-259 (2)
4 Eddy, J.P., *Justice of the Peace* (Cassell, 1963).
5 Eddy, J.P., *Justice of the Peace*, p.25.
6 CRIM 1/1738 The King v Walter Purdy.
7 KV-2-261.
8 CRIM 1/1738, Green's testimony, p.1.

Chapter 42
1 Many British captives continued to write secret messages in their letters home from enemy prisons during the Cold War. Codes are still taught to servicemen before they go on active service.
2 KV-2-259, Letter from Major Hughes to Col Derry marked secret, p.42.
3 KV 2/264.
4 Brown, John, *In Durance Vile*, p.147.
5 KV-2-259 (3).

Chapter 43
1 KV-2-259 (4), Purdy's statement, p.19.
2 CRIM 1/1738 KV-2-259 (4), Purdy's statement, p.19.
3 KV-2-259(2), p.33.
4 CRIM 1/1738, List of witnesses at Purdy trial.
5 Ormerod, David, *Smith and Hogan's Criminal Law*, p.404.
Support for this view is to be found in Lord Mansfield's judgement in R. v. Stratton (1779) 21 8t.Tr. 1229, in the course of which he declared (on p.1223) : '... if a man is forced to commit acts of high treason, if it appears really forced and such a human nature could not be expected to reset, and the jury are of that opinion, the man is not then guilty of high treason.'
6 K-2-259(3), p.21.
7 K-2-259(2), p.12.
8 Ibid.
9 Tod, Lt Col William 'Willie'. Second statement in the Purdy case taken on 1 July 1945. KV-2-259 (3).
10 KV-261 (1), *The Standard* dated 21 December 1945, p.20.
11 KV-261 (1), *Daily Herald* dated 21 December 1945, p.20.
12 KV-2-261 (1), Newspaper reports of the trial, 22 December 1945.
13 Author's interview with Alan Green, son of Julius Green.

Chapter 44
1 HO336/8.
2 CRIM 1/585/141 Purdy's criminal appeal papers.
3 KV-2-59, p.21.
4 Farndale, Nigel, *Haw-Haw*, p.315.
5 War crimes file into the shooting of Michael Sinclair. WO311/145.

Epilogue
1 HO336/8.
2 FO 371/109708.
3 Reid, P. R., *Colditz: The Full Story*, p.300.
4 Zentrale Stelle Ludwigsburg Az. VI 302 AR 1212/68.
5 Landesarchiv Baden-Württemberg, Dept. Staatsarchiv Ludwigsburg, EL 48/ 2 I Bü 2551.
6 Bundesarchiv Außenstelle Ludwigsburg.
7 Bundesarchiv Außenstelle Ludwigsburg, Stalag III-D, p.81.
8 Bundesarchiv Außenstelle Ludwigsburg, June 1976, p.122.
9 KV-2-260 p69
10 Howat, Mabel. Imperial War Museum. Documents: 16229 box no 08/111/1
11 Brown, John, *In Durance Vile*, Foreword, May 1980, Otago Medical School, New Zealand.

Index

INDEX

Biography

Robert Verkaik is an author and award-winning journalist. He was the Home Affairs Editor at the *Independent* and the Security Editor at the *Mail on Sunday*. He is the author of *Defiant, the untold story of the Battle of Britain*, *Posh Boys* and *Jihadi John, the making of a terrorist*.

He is a non-practising barrister and lives in Surrey.